In Search of Happiness

In Search of Happiness

Discovering the soul
through past lives

Swati R Shiv

JAICO PUBLISHING HOUSE
Ahmedabad Bangalore Bhopal Bhubaneswar Chennai
Delhi Hyderabad Kolkata Lucknow Mumbai

DISCLAIMER NOTE

Past-life therapy is not concerned with establishing truths in the external world; it is only concerned with healing negative emotions of the person, which cause problems in his mind. All the past lives, which Dev, the patient saw, have been reported as he spoke about them. We have no evidence to prove whether what he saw was true or not. The subconscious mind records events at the emotional level and it is possible that the images, which came out were not real in the physical, tangible sense but were used by the subconscious mind to explain the feelings he underwent during those lives.

Secondly, the techniques of past-life therapy explained here are traditional and lengthy. The idea of giving the details is to remove the fear of past-life regression or hypnosis from people's minds so that they can be used for healing the self, much more widely than they are being used now. It is no doubt useful to go to a therapist than try solving all your problems yourself. However, when a therapist is not accessible, there are no side-effects in trusting your own intuition and trying to connect to the spiritual realms.

Thirdly, some popular religions do not believe in past lives, and we are not arguing with them. Past lives do not exist in the literal sense because the soul is energy and energy can't be static in design.

Published by Jaico Publishing House
A-2 Jash Chambers, 7-A Sir Phirozshah Mehta Road
Fort, Mumbai - 400 001
jaicopub@jaicobooks.com
www.jaicobooks.com

© Swaati R. Shiv

IN SEARCH OF HAPPINESS
ISBN 978-81-8495-630-6

First Jaico Impression: 2014

No part of this book may be reproduced or utilized in
any form or by any means, electronic or
mechanical including photocopying, recording or by any
information storage and retrieval system,
without permission in writing from the publishers.

To my son Sparsh, whose autism motivated me to understand energies underlying apparent realities;
and
to my spirit guide, ShaishNaag, the celestial teacher of love, oneness, aggression, equanimity and balance.

CONTENTS

Preface	ix
PART 1: THE BACKGROUND	1
PART 2: A PAST LIFE CASE HISTORY – THE LOST SOLDIER	19
Chapter 1: Introduction	21
Chapter 2: Feeling Betrayed	26
Chapter 3: The Past-Life Connection	39
Chapter 4: A Life of Victory	54
Chapter 5: The Conflict in His Mind	62
Chapter 6: Towards a Life of Crime	67
Chapter 7: The Soul is Disappointed	76
Chapter 8: The Life of a Pirate	85
Chapter 9: One Life of Peace	93
Chapter 10: Karmic Balancing	97
Chapter 11: Love Heals	106
Chapter 12: Life Between Lives	121
Chapter 13: Sent Out from Heaven	135
Chapter 14: Salvation	145
Chapter 15: The Fanatic General	163
Chapter 16: The Mind of a Killer	182
Chapter 17: The Ninth Life: A Mafia Don	195
Chapter 18: The Warning	205

Chapter 19: Satan's Pull - Anger, Temptation And…	212
Chapter 20: "That is What Kings and Soldiers do…"	222
Chapter 21: The Racing Heart	232
Chapter 22: Conversation with a Spirit	241
Chapter 23: An Emotional Hunger (Inner Child healing)	253
Chapter 24: Future Visions	267
Chapter 25: Understanding a Soul's Life-Plan	275
Chapter 26: Moving On	282
Afterword	298
Acknowledgements	299

PREFACE

JUST SURVIVE OR BE ALIVE?

THERE HAS BEEN AN eternal debate between the negative and positive energies that combine on Earth to create life in physical form. The debate has over a period of time, turned into a battle of positive and negative energies. The book is being written to defeat the forces of darkness, which seek to crush the spirit of being alive and happy by resisting change in the existing monotonous structures. The war between the dark forces of light, is all about energies and words, that come devoid of weapons. It is instead, fought by the manipulation of energies through use of words and the eventual transfer of dark feelings from one being to another, that are subtly underlined with negativity.

The energies of darkness resist change and growth in thinking. They are manifested in a zeal to succeed mechanically and vehemently protect the way of life that already exists. Hence, they crush anything that seeks to rebel from what *is*. So the seed of change is crushed before it can bring about change. Dark forces take life as work and work as a chore to be performed. Light workers are the souls who work for creating faith and optimism in human life. They are alive, playful and forever seeking, self-healing and feeling happiness. They find expression in creative activities like writing, dancing, singing, painting, making love, etc.

The critical factor is that they make work a joyful expression of being alive, rather than a sacrifice or a duty. The energies of darkness seek to maintain the existing surface structures, no matter what. Instead of changing core, erroneous foundations, they spread darkness, gloom, emptiness, vacuum and fear. They doubt every leap of faith and instead of trying to break-free from negative clutches, they wait for death as a panacea from the pain of being alive. They take life's suffering as unavoidable destiny and death as liberation from pain.

The energies of Light seek to accept suffering but as a part of evolution. They learn to let go of material or traditional comforts to stay free and aligned with God. Detachment helps in being optimistic through difficulties in the present. Challenges are overcome with zeal to be non-negative; they give courage to dream and to create anew. The words and not the actions of a person indicate where s/he is vibrating as a soul at different moments of time. If the words depress your spirit, zeal and expression, then the person is speaking from a dark vibration at that point of time, even if s/he may be someone you can trust at other times in life.

Happiness for the soul comes from learning to be immune to dark vibrations such that they don't succeed in making us negative. It is important to not let seeds of doubts passed through casual words of the dark forces, crush our dreams from manifesting. Victory helps our soul be happy because we come on Earth to express the brightness of our spirit, so as to evolve to a higher level of consciousness.

Let us believe in hope over doubt, faith over disillusionment, love over revenge, exaltation over fall, and happiness over compromise.

PART 1
THE BACKGROUND

**Seeking the Soul Tree:
Your Past Life is the Window to
Your Present.**

EVOLUTION OF THE SOUL

It is presumed that we are happier than our ancestors. We seem to have evolved to a better quality of life because the last few centuries have witnessed tremendous advances in technology. However, this has not ensured that we face fewer internal conflicts, depressions or anxieties than earlier times.

Our focus on material advancement has made our pursuit of happiness rather lopsided. For example, buying a car might make us feel good, but that happiness can only be short-lived. This is because material goods do not change the negative energy structure underlying our problems. Therefore, the material object of comfort only serves to shift the focus of our problems momentarily. However, as long as our inner focus remains negative, the pain comes back in another form. For instance, after buying the car we may start worrying about its instalments, its maintenance, traffic congestions, etc.

The evolution of the soul means the ability to change the energy structure, underlying our problems through creating long-term happiness in life along with material advancement. We evolve as souls when we raise our human consciousness above the evolutionary needs of our earliest ancestors. Becoming happier helps us move closer in frequency to the Creator's highly positive frequencies. So, by moving closer to God's way of life, by believing in abundance, love and trust, we evolve as human souls; distinct from other animal souls that are primarily focused on survival.

> *As souls, we incarnate on Earth to understand how human experiences help us gain or lose positive energy. When we gain positive energy, we become happier and when we lose positive energy, we become sorrowful.*

As will be elaborated in the book, each soul plans a specific life purpose for the span of a life-time, and it gains positive energy or becomes happier as it moves closer to realizing that life purpose. Though the needs of human survival can be unanimous for all beings, happiness for each soul is specific and cannot be generally defined. Each soul comes with a unique life-plan and life purpose. Each person's happiness coincides with the path of pursuing his/her life purpose, and not by simply pursuing a traditional definition of success in Earthly terms. An awareness of our life purpose and how it has to be followed, to create more positive energy, is necessary to attain soul evolution. Developing awareness of our life purpose helps us understand what feelings we are seeking to attain in terms of happiness on Earth.

BASIC CONCEPTS OF SOUL EVOLUTION

All the metaphysical concepts outlined here have been established through reports given by several people who have undergone past-life and inter-life sessions with different regression therapists. People have reported similar encounters in their inter-life sessions, even without any prior knowledge about what to expect. The concepts, as explained, also incorporate notes from various books and workshops on hypnotherapy, past-life therapy, life between life therapy, spirit release therapy, neuro-linguistic programming, reiki, pranik healing, theta healing, etc. Even then, these conceptual descriptions are by no means exhaustive, as there is much scope for research and exploration.

THE SOUL

The soul is a tiny unit of life-force energy, which radiates light through the body and moves at a certain speed known as *vibrational frequency*. *This tiny unit of life-force energy enters the body and expands its light to become the soul of the body.* The speed at which the soul vibrates is termed as the soul's vibrational frequency or soul frequency. Vibrational speed or soul frequency varies depending on the level of soul advancement. It is the latter which varies depending on the level of soul advancement. Thus, the more positive the soul frequency, the more power it has to create. The more advanced souls have a higher soul frequency while the Creator, the most advanced soul, has a very high-positive frequency. Thus, the more positive the soul frequency, the more power it has to create.

Metaphorically, if we view the soul as the filament of the bulb, then the body would be the glass wall of the bulb through which the filament radiates light. The body is thus, the vehicle of the soul. The more powerful the filament is, the more light would radiate. Thus, the more positive the soul frequency, the more power it has to create.

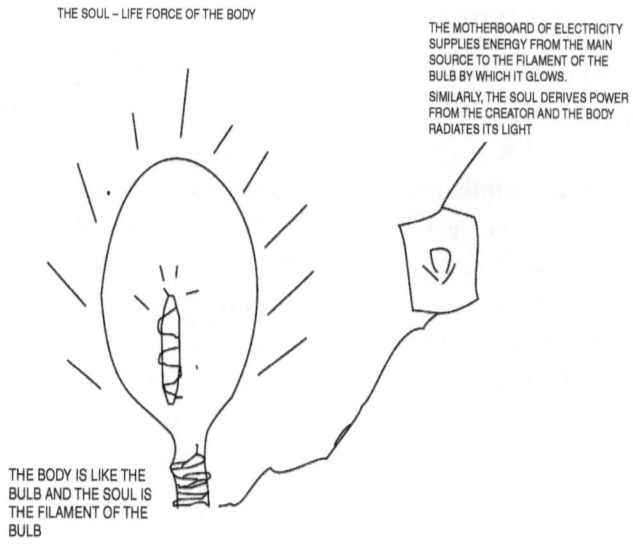

The Soul gets its power from a bigger source of light that can be called the ONENESS or the Creator, much like the filament of the bulb, which gets its power from the main electricity line. Just as a bulb is useless without its filament, the body is useless without the soul. It is the soul that gives life-force, as well as an identity to the body. *For example, if you say, 'My body is beautiful or my body is fat,' then, the 'my' is the soul – the life-force energy within you.*

THE GENERAL PURPOSE OF SOUL EVOLUTION

The Soul, by itself, is a Co-Creator of the universe. It is made of the same quality of energy as that of the Creator. It radiates the power of the Creator, just as a ray of sunlight spreads radiance of the Sun. All creation in the universe can be called manifestation of one collective consciousness, called the ONENESS or the Creator's consciousness.

> *If we imagine the Creator to be a big body of light, then the soul in a physical human body would be a tiny cell of light, that is a part of the whole, and yet distinct.*

Each soul takes birth to find its own identity, while remaining a part of the whole, and seeks to understand its contribution in the overall process of creation. Since the soul is a tiny part of the Creator, it participates in a course of soul evolution whereby, it learns lessons on creation in various dimensions of the universe. Earth is one of the learning schools for the evolving soul.

> *Earth is a physical dimension of the universe, where positive and negative energies interact to manifest physical forms. The soul learns the art of creation on the physical plane by learning to transcend negative energies into positive during its life on Earth. The learning occurs while overcoming obstacles which come in the process of creating desirable life experiences.*

Difficulties come as soul tests. If we stay worried and anxious because of difficulties, we destroy our happiness and fail in our soul tests. We are meant to overcome difficulties and increase the positive intensity of the soul. Through its many life experiences, the soul understands how negative energies can be overruled and how our efforts to attain success or love can lead to happiness in our lives instead of melancholy.

THE PURPOSE OF A LIFE ON EARTH

In each life on Earth, we as souls, plan to achieve a specific purpose. The purpose of life involves focusing energies on creating a particular kind of physical reality that would help us attain happiness in that life. Different souls have different life purposes and they are born with a skill set necessary to attain that purpose. For example, one person may have a desire to be a dancer while another may desire to be an engineer. In the process of the pursuit of these desires, the soul moves towards attaining its life purpose. There may also be other purposes alongside the primary one. Some general reasons for incarnation, which have been found in research are:

KARMIC BALANCING

> *This includes healing interpersonal relationships, developing mental capacities like intelligence, knowledge, understanding, insight, wisdom, while also increasing emotional capacity, self-reliance and creating. Karmic balancing entails evolving new ways of life through inventions in science, art and social sciences and understanding one's connection to the Divine source through prayers, meditation and being in silence.*

All these purposes are usually intertwined, and one serves the other. For example, while developing a greater understanding of relationships as a soul, you may also be repaying your karmic debt from past lives towards people you have abused. This individual purpose is also connected to a purpose for the world, that is, for Earth, as a whole. The soul also has to ensure that the planet's energies also become more positive through the work it does.

Through successfully making choices that help us feel happy and positive from within, while also manifesting our external desires, we can evolve to achieving our life purpose. The path towards achieving the life purpose is difficult but is accompanied with much emotional satisfaction. Since the soul is a unit of life-force energy, it understands its reality in energy terms and not in physical or tangible terms. From our soul's perspective, the praise, money, respect, success or power we seek to gain, through our efforts on Earth, are emotional experiences.

The individual life purpose, therefore, is a unique emotional experience that the soul seeks to accomplish during that specific journey on Earth. For an individual, incarnating soul, this purpose is the main reason for our births.

Negative energies, which come in the form of negative emotions such as fear or doubt, are obstacles in achieving happiness. These aim to divert the soul away from the life purpose into a meaningless pursuit of success or power, which cannot lead to any feelings of emotional peace or happiness for the soul.

THE LIFE-PLAN

To attain the individual life purpose, we make a life-plan at the soul-level before incarnating on Earth. All steps taken towards this plan are designed to lead us to attain the level of emotional training required to achieve the life purpose. The steps are coded at an energy level and they keep motivating us to pursue certain instincts over others. The life-plan does not come with permanent and detailed plans; it merely provides a general outline of the developments and challenges as well as our important confrontations, once we incarnate on Earth. All the points in the life-plan are connected, as in a map. Each stage can be understood as a follow-up of the previous one, though it may not be sequentially linked. All the difficulties and diseases we face, once on Earth, arise as part of the experiences we plan for ourselves, as souls. The plan is structured so that the soul encounters difficulties and it strives to overcome them and achieve its unique purpose of life. The soul also aims to reach a higher degree of emotional resilience as it transforms negative energy into positive.

By pursuing intuitive desires that propel us towards what we perceive as a potential route to happiness, we evolve as souls and raise our energy frequency to positive. So, we are on the right path if we realize love, success and happiness while pursuing our life-plan. However, there can be a dichotomy between the experience the soul desires and the path we choose to attain that desire. For example, if the soul drives us towards attaining success or fame, it seeks to evolve to a higher positive frequency by the fame it attains. However, if in the process of becoming famous or successful, the soul loses its essence of being, then it ends up feeling bereaved and devolves, instead of evolving. This means, the person is not on the right path; the life-plan is not meant for devolution to a negative state of being. Hence, each problem, doubt or fear encountered, while moving towards happiness is meant to be used for soul evolution by becoming emotionally more powerful than the negative forces.

> *The life-plan is made from the perspective of eternal life, since the soul lives eternally. A single life experience is planned as one step in the learning ladder of the soul. Each life-time aims to empower the soul and help it evolve to a higher level of consciousness/happiness.*

However, once on Earth, we forget our chosen life-plan as we intend to learn through experiences and difficulties. We try to practically go through each experience and make our choices. Over a period of time or over lives, we, as souls, understand, which choices help us feel happier and successful and which do not.

> *Thus, our circumstances are determined by our life-plan but how we think during those circumstances, is our choice. Each difficulty is meant to lead us to feeling more positive than we did before encountering it. Making the wrong choices, however, drowns us in a vicious circle of negative thinking.*

THE THEME OF LIFE

After having decided on the purpose of life, a theme is developed around the specific negative energies, which the soul will encounter and overcome in that particular life. For example, if overcoming the energy of rejection is the main life purpose, then the soul would face a pattern where emotions arising out of rejection would keep coming in his/her life. This might happen through different encounters with various people including parents, friends, teachers, lovers, colleagues, etc. Because of external rejection and past circumstances, the soul would develop an internal rejection of its own positive qualities.

The soul lesson involves loving and accepting itself in spite of facing rejection. That way the negative energy of rejection would get over-ruled, as the soul would learn to remain positive within; this in spite of being continuously and negatively attacked on the surface.

In this process of evolving, the soul would have to learn other soul lessons of emotional maturity like immunity to criticism, stoicism, perseverance, patience, self-love, faith in a higher good or God, as well as compassion and mind discipline. This would enable the soul to achieve its life purpose without letting negativity depress its spirits.

Each negative emotion represents a particular kind of energy of a negative frequency or speed of vibration. For instance, rejection, frustration and selfishness have different frequency levels. However, the soul may not be able to master the chosen set of negative emotions during its life. If it fails to convert the targeted negative energy into positive, the same theme will carry itself over to the next life. This will continue till the soul attains its desired level of advancement. Death is no block to the process of soul evolution, since the soul lives eternally. This will be illustrated in detail through the case history covered in the book. There are cyclical patterns in our lives that resurface in different life circumstances and in varying gradations, until the soul overcomes the negative energy at all levels.

During regression therapy, understanding a life pattern or finding the theme of life is a requirement. It helps us to decode the soul lessons behind repeated negative experiences of similar nature.

THE LESSONS OF LIFE

By understanding how to handle negative emotions, we as souls, can increase the quantum of positive energy that can be directed towards the creation of desirable life experiences. Learning soul lessons is necessary to achieve our primary purpose of life and realize the happiness we dream of. During the course of learning these lessons, we evolve towards a positive frequency and thus move closer to the Creator.

If we fail to learn our soul lessons, we become more sorrowful and less powerful during our life-time. The pattern of devolution continues with each subsequent life. This happens until the soul chooses to learn its lessons and evolve to a higher consciousness. Just focusing on external success in Earthly terms does not help in learning soul lessons because soul evolution entails a movement towards becoming more peaceful and happy from within. Happiness is not a result of external success on Earth. Though, if there is soul advancement, our soul would feel successful both internally as well as externally with its positive vibration.

Soul lessons are complex emotional equations, which need to be understood from the soul's eternal perspective to neutralize the negative energy accompanying the positive learning.

For instance, if the soul's lesson is learning compassion, then it has to be compassionate in circumstances where it may rather be selfish. To understand compassion, the soul would have to overcome the negative emotion of wanting to be selfish without feeling disavowed. If the soul is unable to defeat the negative energy of selfishness, it would not be able to feel successful from within, loved or happy; whereas another person, whose lesson is not compassion, may achieve happiness in the same circumstances without being compassionate. To be non-selfish, the soul may need to sacrifice its financial or work priorities, without feeling negative.

Soul lessons are usually integrated with one another. For example, overcoming rejection could be one of the emotions the soul has chosen; overcoming impatience and overcoming selfishness could be the second and third set of emotions chosen. Following these, a pattern would be created in the life-plan, where overcoming one pattern of negative emotions necessitates overcoming the other patterns.

> *For example, if you are a billionaire, you may need to develop patience and compassion to deal with a difficult work-force. Hence, by overcoming impatience and selfishness, you can overcome the feeling of being rejected by your work-force, which will then accept you as a person with positivity only because you have accepted them with the same.*

THE EARTH SCHOOL

Earth is considered a school from the soul's perspective. Souls come to Earth to have a practical experience of the physical dimension in all its aspects, including encountering negative energies. The intensity of negativity felt on Earth cannot be experienced on the celestial plane, that is a high-frequency dimension. On the celestial plane, there is no concept of time or space because, the soul can be in any place in an instant, depending on its speed of thought. Simultaneously, it can be everywhere at the same time, because at a pure energy level, there is no division of space. There is no need to wait for a thought to be converted into a physical, tangible experience, since feelings are as real as touching. Consequently, the soul has no concept of physical difficulties until it incarnates on Earth. On Earth, difficulties are artificially created through time and space limitations, so that our soul may evolve its consciousness while overcoming them. From the perspective of the soul, the training on Earth is necessary to learn how to mobilize energies accurately for the purpose of more complex creations in the universe. At higher levels of evolution, we merge with our higher selves and move on to creating planets and galaxies and life forms in them.

Whenever we focus on positive manifestations, negative thoughts come as distractions and prevent the positive from manifesting.

Positive creation can manifest when one trains the mind to accurately concentrate on solely experiencing the positive and surpassing the negative belief systems or seemingly insurmountable circumstances. In this process, our soul has to work on changing its belief systems that form several layers in the mind. If we cannot let go of old patterns of thinking, our soul feels suppressed at the emotional level. The beliefs that draw our attention to the negative, usually need evolution as they are carried over from several lifetimes. We consciously participate in this process of evolution by undergoing regression therapies, reading self-help books. We also allow ourselves to let go of rigidly held beliefs, which cause us endless sorrow.

Everything on Earth manifests physically. Hence, if the soul refuses to learn its lessons, the negative feelings accumulate and ultimately lead to physical problems.

That is why, when we feel good emotionally, it has a positive impact on our physical body as well. Also, the planet Earth gains in positive energy as our levels of individual happiness rises. When we are happy, we radiate positivity, and help other people be optimistic through their difficulties. But, when we are negative, we pull down the energies of others as well, just by our overbearing, pessimistic personality.

Being on Earth is a lesson in Oneness, from the soul's perspective. When several people feel negative, sad or doomed, the planet's energies get infected. As a result, people who would otherwise not feel sad, do so simply by catching on energies from mass consciousness. Since energies are connected, devolution or evolution of one soul affects all and evolution of all, affects the individual soul.

THE HIGHER SELF

The soul energy within a human being is a part of a bigger soul group called 'The Higher Self.' The Higher Self is a more powerful quantum of energy of the Creator than the individual body. When the soul takes birth in a body, its life force energy comes from this bigger whole, namely, the Higher Self. Like a ray radiates from the

Sun, the spirit radiates from its Higher Self. The Higher Self exists in a high spiritual dimension in the realm of pure positive frequencies. It is a bigger unit of ONENESS and is always in communion with the Creator. The Higher Self's energy is an important part of a personality; it is the true identity of the soul.

The soul gets its directions on how to evolve from its Higher Self. When we evolve, the life force brightens in light. Its vibrational frequency becomes more positive and more powerful.

Practically, this means that the Higher Self decides what our priorities and ambitions in life would be, and the challenges we would have to overcome while pursuing our goals on Earth. The Higher Self keeps guiding the soul through its life-time on Earth by using the subconscious mind as a control mechanism of the body. When we are drawn towards certain professions without any rational reason, or fall in love with certain people and not others, it is the Higher Self moving our energies to achieve its goals of evolution. The Higher Self also has complete knowledge of the person's past lives and makes life-plans that take into account, lessons of evolution left over from past lives that need to be mastered in the present life.

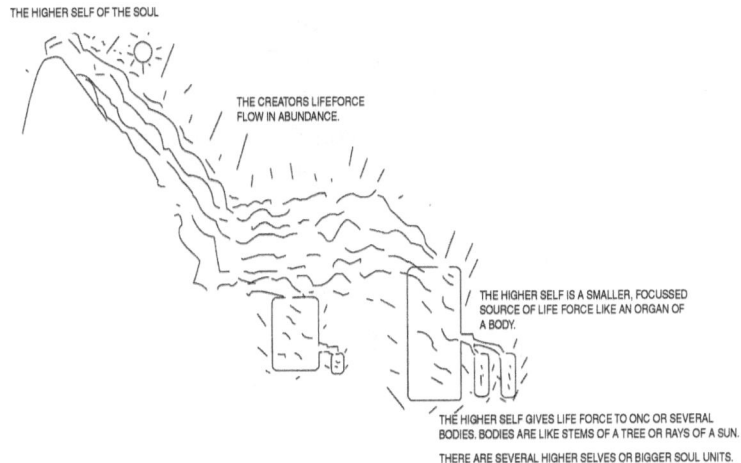

Just as, at birth, a soul comes from its Higher Self into a body, upon death, the soul rejoins its Higher Self back in the Light. However, if the person dies in pain, it cannot join its Higher Self back in the celestial plane, as it is supposed to. This happens when the soul dies feeling negative and it cannot raise its energy frequency again to match the high positive frequency of the Higher Self. It remains stuck as a spirit or soul fragment on Earth and keeps feeling negative over and over again. Then, the Higher Self intervenes to bring the stuck soul-fragment back home. Each new life-plan which the Higher Self makes for a reincarnating soul, aims to integrate lost soul fragments to help its overall soul consciousness evolve to a higher positive frequency. The Higher Power does push us instinctively towards a certain direction, but it cannot prevent us from falling in the well if we choose to jump. Thus, when we blame God or our Higher Self for things going wrong in our lives, we are not completely justified.

That is because we are essentially energies and can only be directed. We cannot be forced to move in some direction over others, just as flowing water cannot be forced to flow as ordered.

Water flows automatically wherever obstacles are cleared and a path created for its free flow. Similarly, our soul energy flows whenever there is an energy pull. Our soul energy is directed by our circumstances towards making choices that make us happy. However, the realization of what constitutes happiness comes over a period of time, as we understand 'cause and effect' equations from the soul's perspective.

THE SPIRIT GUIDES

Life on Earth is expected to be difficult from the soul's perspective: since the intention of life is to transcend negative energies into positive. Sometimes, challenges planned can be tormenting to an individual soul who feels alienated from its real home on the celestial plane. Hence, we have friends in heaven who enter into contract with us to help in executing our life-plan on Earth. These friends are called our Spirit Guides.

The duration of a contract to help may last a life-time or it may be made specifically for shorter phases. A Spirit Guide may guide us through life or during a specific period of tribulation. In a physical dimension they may come to us as friends, teachers or other people. If in the non-physical dimension, then the spirit guides communicate telepathically by sending thoughts to our minds through intuition, insight and dreams. Following the guidance might be challenging from conventional social wisdom, but helps us evolve to a more liberated, less negative way of thinking.

Once born on Earth, we do not remember our spirit guides nor do we recall who we truly are, or have been as souls, in our past lives. If our spirit guides incarnate with us as our friends, teachers or soul mates, we usually develop an instant, irrational liking for them. Irrespective of whether we can decipher their presence or not, these spirit guides exist. They are distinguished by the fact that they act like university professors, ready to help, but not to spoon-feed. They offer guidance but the responsibility for learning the intended life-lessons rests with the student.

Unlike ghosts from the dark sides, spirit guides do not threaten, bribe or force. They work more by using love as a driving force than magic or ritual. It is upon us to widen our limited vision, so that we are able to recognize those who become our spirit guides in the course of life.

INTERPRETATION OF A SPIRITUAL GUIDANCE FROM THE BHAGAVAD GITA

It is important to note that the guidance given, completely depends on interpretation for its accuracy. The guidance is similar to that given by the Gods in religious scriptures. These are often misinterpreted, leading to spread of darkness rather than light.

> *For example, in the Bhagvad Gita, Lord Krishna says: 'Take action. Don't worry about the fruit.' Most people take this line to mean that God is asking us to take action and not expect fruit from it, probably like in selfless service. However, that is not how it is meant if each word is carefully interpreted. The words are, Don't worry, not Don't Expect.*

These words of Lord Krishna are actually telling us not to have negative expectations and not to worry because worry in itself is a negative emotion. Negative energies and negative thoughts block the flow of positive energies. It is natural for a seed to bear fruit, that is, it is natural that our effort should bear a reward. The only way it cannot happen is when we worry about it and expect the negative. We keep digging the ground to check whether the seed is growing, instead of letting the seed grow. A negative thought amounts to a negative action from the soul's perspective of reality. It may take time for a thought to get converted into reality but all consistent thoughts do get converted into our reality, whether we intend them to or not. So thinking positive is the only way one can bring in positive realities in life.

> *Hence, Lord Krishna says that instead of worrying we can consistently take action to speed up the manifestation of our desires. Taking action to manifest positive expectations is as important as not worrying about its outcome.*

Secondly, it is important to bear in mind that the rewards may not necessarily mean material rewards; they can come in the form of positive energy and happiness.

> *It can be noted that selfless service is not selfless from the soul's perspective, since it aids in soul evolution.*

Selfless service can help the soul gain respect or repay one's earlier karma. Either way, it would help the soul in gaining positive energy and raising its vibrational frequency. If our efforts yield more negativity in our lives than positivity, it is like sowing seeds in the wrong way and eating bitter fruit. Every effort we undertake should naturally help us feel positive in some way. Regardless of the fact that rewards may not come in the form of material gain. Else, we might be better off not making that effort.

PRACTICAL GUIDANCE FOR EVERYDAY LIFE – CHOOSING HEALING OVER SUFFERING

Chronic difficulties can be healed for good, if we can connect to our subconscious mind and ask the soul what it seeks to learn by manifesting diseases, physical and emotional disorders, addictions, or misfortunes. Contrary to popular belief, suffering does not directly help in repaying for past sins or in soul evolution; in fact, it helps indirectly, only as much as punishment helps. It helps in understanding where we went wrong but it does not help in correcting the wrong. This experience of punishment arises naturally due to our focus on the negative aspects of life; it is a transitory phase between the wrong and the right way of doing or thinking. It is not meant to be a permanent way of life as is conveniently assumed by erring souls. For correcting the wrong, we have to create happiness in our lives and in the lives of others, in place of suffering.

> *If we go on suffering and cursing God or our luck, our suffering cannot go away.*

Suffering is energy of a negative frequency; it would let go of us, only when we choose to raise our soul frequency to a positive energy cycle of thinking/vibrating. Positive thoughts may necessitate giving up on comfort, reputation or success as conventionally defined. If we focus on short-term goals and remain in the same cycle of negative thinking, we may end up suffering more than feeling positive or peaceful. We suffer often because we resist change in the cycle. For example, we remain unhealthy and suffer if we resist exercise; or we stay married to a negative person and suffer because we resist divorce; we suffer a bad job because we fear loss of stability, etc.

However, if we let go of our ego-centred attachments to evolve above suffering, we allow ourselves to accept who we are and tell the world without inhibitions, that we made the wrong choices in the past. Often, fame or money is lost while rising above suffering as changing soul cycles is a process of spiritual ascension wherein we let go of superficial needs for material gratification. By focusing less on what other people think and more on our inner satisfaction, we can become much happier, wiser, and healthier as well as evolved souls, in the long run.

PART 2

A PAST-LIFE CASE HISTORY – THE LOST SOLDIER

Soul-Trekking through the Past: Break the Barriers between You and Your Life Purpose to move towards the Light.

CHAPTER 1

INTRODUCTION

DEV CAME FOR HIS first session in June, 2006. As Dev walked into my office, I noticed a look of amusement on his face. Dressed in casual jeans and a red T-shirt, he seemed to be in his early twenties.

Most of my clients are not as young. In my experience, very few young people have been open to subjecting themselves to alternate therapies, particularly hypnotherapy. So, he was an interesting change for me.

The first impression he gave was of a fair, tall, broad-shouldered young man with a slim physique, looking dazed, probably because of his glasses. He had a sharp nose, long thin lips, long cheekbones, and his heavy eyebrows met in the centre, which gave a piercing expression to his face. His features were more like those of a Greek or an Afghan, rarely seen among Indians.. His smile was relaxed and surprisingly friendly, as he greeted me. It was quite unlike the speculative look with which people normally greet a hypnotherapist. As I observed more of the boy, my curiosity was aroused.

Although he seemed to have a confident personality, he did seem to be clueless about why he was here.. Usually, clients take initiative in talking about their problems, but Dev seemed far from that. One of the first things he told me was that he is twenty-one, following which, he sat relaxed in his chair and kept looking down. Whenever I spoke, he suddenly looked up directly in my eyes, seemingly eager to open up, yet kept quiet. Either he was too shy or too scared to open up. Other than answering my questions to the point, he hardly divulged any information on his own except telling me his age, as if he was proud of it. I wondered how to approach him regarding his problem without mentioning the diagnosis his mother had told me about.

It must be mentioned here that Dev's mother visited me often for treatment for asthma. During the sessions, she would speak about him as she felt he was one of the main causes of her mental trauma. She had told me that her son was diagnosed with *schizophrenia* but was not informed of the disorder. All that they told him, was that he was suffering from depression and hence had to take medications to feel better emotionally. She reported that Dev had been under heavy medications since the last three years. Dev's parents were keen to see him become an engineer, even though he wasn't. The conflict started when they admitted him to an engineering college by paying a huge donation. Dev hadn't liked it and wanted to come back. His parents tried to coax him to stay there, but gave up after he threatened suicide. Within four months, Dev was back home to resentful parents who blamed him for ruining a good career.

His parents tried to exert pressure on Dev through friends and family so that he would return to pursue his engineering degree. This, however, made him more rebellious. First counselling and then psychiatric testing was tried. Dev was diagnosed with neurosis and borderline schizophrenia. He was put on medication for depression, schizophrenia and violent behaviour. Dev's mother could not cope up with his abusive and violent behaviour and she felt as if there was no hope left for him. The two main reasons being that firstly, she felt he had ruined his career for life by dropping engineering and secondly, she believed that he was severely schizophrenic. She equated schizophrenia with madness and hence thought that they were doomed to live with a mad man for life. This thought-pattern reflected in her contemptuous attitude towards him and this worsened his behaviour with her. His mother also suspected that there may be a spirit or ghost inside him as he used to complain of hearing voices some time back. She had agreed to bring him for hypnotherapy to check on that aspect. Interestingly, it was Dev who had insisted that he come for hypnotherapy sessions when he came to know that his mother was visiting me for her treatment. This was again surprising because a typical schizophrenia patient avoids visiting any kind of doctor. Even as I met him, he looked too relaxed and confident to be typically schizophrenic.

GENERAL AWARENESS: THE SUBCONSCIOUS PERSPECTIVE

Being a hypnotherapist, I could not make any judgments based on medical diagnosis. This is because in energy healing, the treatment is formulated to heal the causative energy underlying the apparent physical problem. It is understood that each problem, whether physical or mental, is created due to suppressed negative emotions residing in the subconscious mind. The experiences, which cause the negative emotions to rise are usually, a part of a life-plan made before taking birth. The purpose of incarnation in the physical body is to deal with the mental and physical problem such that the soul lesson is learnt and the soul feels evolved in the process. The problem stops troubling the person only after the person changes emotional focus from negative to positive.

FUNCTIONING OF THE SUBCONSCIOUS MIND

The subconscious mind makes up for about 90 percent of human mental capacity. The conscious mind, which is the mind we are aware of, makes up for only about 10 percent of our mind. The subconscious mind controls the autonomic nervous system and the functioning of the internal organs of the body. For example, it keeps our blood circulating, our heart pumping, our limbs working etc. It is also a storehouse of all our memories, programs and habits. There is a co-relation between the soul, the conscious mind and the subconscious mind.

> *If we compare our body with a car, then the soul is the owner of the car, the conscious mind is its driver and the subconscious mind is its engine.*

The soul decides the priorities in a person's life, that is it decides, which way the car would go. Instructional data is passed down in an energy form, from the conscious mind to the subconscious mind by way of the emotions or feelings, entailed in the thought. Hypnotherapy works on the premise that all disorders – mental and physical in the body are created due to negative instructions being passed down from the conscious mind to the subconscious mind. By focusing on negative emotions in some aspects of life, the conscious mind sends instructional data to the subconscious mind. This leads to manifestation of the negative in the organs, meant to handle those situations, thus leading to physiological and psychological disorders, due to a constant flow of negative hormones to the organs concerned, leading to their malfunction, over a period of time.

Each person is different and his/her circumstances are different. Hence, the kinds of difficulties s/he faces at an emotional level cannot be generalized. Nor can the method of tackling those difficulties be universalized. The therapist needs to tackle the healing of suppressed negative emotions with a specified healing pattern depending on the extent of negativity, one is caught in. If the person feels dejected because he/she is consistently stuck in some area of life, then that thought would lead to incessant pain in his/her legs, hips, hands and so on; in other words, affliction in any organ responsible for movement.

Asthma is an example of an ailment that can trigger in the present life of the person, whenever the person feels emotionally suffocated or bullied in the present life. Recovering from asthma would firstly involve healing the trauma of death in the previous life. This would empower the person to deal with similar situations in the present life. Secondly, it would require helping the person change his/her thinking pattern to positive. This is enabled by understanding why the soul is in a situation where it feels negative; and how it needs to change its belief system to be able to detach from it physically or emotionally.

If a problem does not appear to have any rational cause in the present life, then, it needs to be diagnosed by accessing the past lives of the person. A past-life problem can be triggered by an incident in the present life which echoes the trauma of the past life. Whether the problem comes from a past life or the present would again depend on the individual context of the person. For example, when we attempt to find the root cause of asthma during past-life regression therapy, we often discover that those were the people who died from poisoning, drowning or suffocation in their past lives. If the problem is only due to death by breathlessness in a past life, then the person can recover from asthma after a session of therapy. Catharsis occurs when the person realizes that the same situation does not exist in the present life. However, catharsis or healing during regression is unlikely if soul lessons are unfinished. The problem continues in the present life if the person feels emotionally trapped in a similar situation as he/she did while dying in the past life.

I had to find out what suppressed negative emotions were stored in Dev's mind. I could not go by the label of schizophrenia because it spoke nothing of the person or the difficulties he might be facing.

CONCLUSION OF THE SESSION

Emotional management therapy attempts to make a link between the soul, the conscious mind and the subconscious mind. The technique I was using to access Dev's subconscious is a step by step, logical process of understanding how the subconscious mind works, so that he could train it to think positively with self-awareness. Dev's subconscious mind was creating problems in his energy balance because he was focused on the negative. As we were to eventually discover, he was focused on the negative because he was not following what his soul desired him to.

CHAPTER 2

FEELING BETRAYED

THE FIRST SESSION

DEV WAS SITTING QUIETLY in a chair which was diagonally opposite mine. Between us was a table on which were kept crystals to be used for aura-cleansing during therapy. His left hand was on the table. He was silently sitting with his head down. Since he was not divulging any details about his problems, I decided to ask him directly, his reasons for coming to me.

"Okay, let us start with what brings you here?"

"I have depression," he looked up, and nodded.

"Tell me how exactly you feel."

"I feel BAD," he replied, looking down again.

"What do you mean by 'bad'?"

"I can't focus. I feel disturbed all the time," he shrugged.

As I continued to probe deeper, he told me in a low tone that he felt that the main reason for his feeling depressed was anger with his parents.

"They betrayed me," he said.

"Both parents?"

"Dad is okay but I don't like his way of dealing with things," he reflected.

"And your mother?"

"I hate her," he said furiously.

"Why?"

"She betrayed me," he replied in a low tone, as if he was controlling several layers of anger in that tone. As he spoke, his jaw went hard, his fists tightly clenched and his eyes became red with suppressed anger.

The intensity of anger which was being reflected by his body language appeared strange. I also noticed his peculiar choice of words. Several young people feel angry with their parents, but betrayal is not common.

The word conveyed strong emotional baggage. I noted that Dev had used the word twice, with respect to his parents. In my practice, we always work with any unusual words the client uses, as words are the key to what is going about in his subconscious mind.

"What makes you feel so?"

"I wanted to join the army ever since I was a kid," he paused, reflecting. "My mother always spoke as if she understood. But, when the time came for me to choose a career, they insisted that I pursue science."

"Why science?"

"They wanted me to pursue engineering..." he reflected and continued, "I never liked those coaching classes."

"What didn't you like about them?"

"It was the attitude...the whole thing...I didn't like it at all. This was not what I wanted to do. I wanted to go in the army."

"Why did you want to go in the army?"

"I don't know...I feel as if I belong there," he said, confused.

"Okay. What do you want to achieve by going there?"

"I want to fight for my motherland. If I can't join the army, I feel I have nothing to live for," he spoke in despair.

"But, you continued with the sciences any way. You did go to the engineering classes and passed in your higher secondary exams."

"Yeah!" He grimaced ruefully.

"How was your result in 12th?"

"I did not do as well as I expected."

"That could be because you also had to study for engineering exams simultaneously."

"I could not concentrate as well as I could earlier," he replied in a tone which sounded as coming from someone who felt he had failed in his life.

"And then you went to the engineering college."

"They said it would be good for me," he replied angrily.

"What made you come back from there?"

"I did not feel any passion there…They kept saying I should go back…But, I told them I would not go," he shrugged.

I could not find any rational reason, which could explain why he felt so agitated about being coerced into a career he did not like. Several parents, especially, in India choose professions for their children, the belief being that children do not know what is good for them. Some children rebel, but, rarely so strongly.

Dev spoke in a tone which said that he felt that his parents had cast a fatal blow upon him by sending him to a course, which he did not want to go into.

"I hate my mother. I would have gone in the army, but for her," he claimed, several times throughout his therapy.

"How did she stop you? You could have gone after you came back from engineering?"

"I did not give the NDA entrance exams. Otherwise, by now I would have been a soldier…I made a mistake. I should have gone…I was betrayed…" he mused again.

"Why do you use the word betrayed?"

"I trusted her…" he replied. "They promised me that they would let me go into the army if I finished graduation."

"Okay, so you joined graduation?"

"Yeah…I joined correspondence in commerce," he nodded.

"Okay…What are you doing now?"

"I have taken the final exams …" he shrugged.

"Are you still planning to join the army?"

"Yeah… I have given the INA entrance exams … But, it is too late now. I missed out on four years of service," he again said despondently.

"But, if you get through, you can still go."

"I won't get that kind of promotion now. I could have gone then…I feel bad," he said again.

"What do you do the whole day?"

"Nothing…I wish I could kill all the enemies," he replied grimly, with his fists clenched.

The intensity of anger he displayed led me to suspect that there was a past-life issue involved. It had been triggered by a particular incident in his present life, but I needed more information to be sure.

DERIVING INVOLVEMENT OF A PAST LIFE

"How old were you when you started feeling this turmoil in your mind?"

"Seventeen," he replied.

"What was specific at seventeen which had never happened before?"

"I felt restless. I could not concentrate," he replied reflecting.

"And before that you had never felt this way?"

"No," he answered determined.

"Anything else?"

"I started having heart palpitations often, for which I consulted a doctor," he said.

"What did the doctors say?"

"They could not find any physical problem," he replied, doubt reflecting in his tone. "But, it continued. Then they said it could be a mental problem. So I agreed to meet a psychiatrist."

"Did that help?"

"Not really…He gave me antidepressants but the palpitations still continued," he explained perturbed.

"Do you still have that problem?"

"It comes and goes," he nodded.

"Does anything specific happen when it comes?"

"No," he shook his head.

"I mean, emotionally? Are you particularly anxious or tense about something?"

"No, nothing," he denied again.

"Okay and this never happened before you were seventeen?"

"No," he stated.

That was a pretty specific answer. I noted down the age and continued to probe deeper. Problems occurring out of the blue at a certain age are usually due to a subconscious past-life connection to that age. From his answers to my questions, it seemed that his inability to join the army had made him feel unsuccessful. However, from a therapeutic perspective, it was the feeling of being labelled a failure which bothered him the most, not the army, per se.

That clearly pointed to an unresolved past-life issue being triggered off. If some particular emotion hurts intensely without the external circumstances justifying the hurt, then there is a past life involved. Intensely, Dev felt like a failure and his external circumstances did not justify the extent of his hurt. Also, his strong desire to go in the army indicated a past-life issue. We usually have a strong drive to follow professions that we have pursued in past lives but did not live long enough to practice them. In such cases, there is a feeling that the soul-purpose has been left unfinished. However, if our circumstances prevent us from following that profession, then, it means that our Higher Self or the wiser soul within us, no longer desires that profession. The wiser soul has a different life-plan to achieve its desired purpose. However, the abandoned profession would continue to appear very compelling. Understanding and healing such a strong urge usually requires therapeutic intervention by going into the past life involved.

A CRAVING FOR POWER

"Okay, tell me about other aspects of your life, your friends, interests, hobbies."

"I had a girlfriend," his tone was calmer as he spoke of her.

"Where is she now?"

"She died of AIDS. She was a cocaine addict," he replied.

"Oh...You must be sad about that."

"Nah...now, I've accepted it. I only feel bad I could not rescue her...I didn't have enough resources...I tried to tell her parents but they did not believe me..." he reflected, grimly.

"When did it happen?"

"One year, four months ago..." he said in a low tone.

"How? What happened?"

"She injected herself with a needle... That killed her," he explained, looking away.

I could make out from his tone that he missed her. His inability to rescue her and her parents' indifference towards his attempts to help her aggravated his feelings of worthlessness.

Everything in his life seemed to point to a theme, anger against injustice, feeling betrayed by family. There was a life plan at the soul level which we were yet to decipher.

"Do you have other friends?"

"I have friends...sometimes I fight for them," he nodded.

"What do you mean?"

"They call me when they need help...I'm good at fighting," he said, nodding to himself.

"So, you fight to help them."

"Yes," he stated in a proud tone, "they make money from it sometimes."

"You fight for money?"

I was suspicious about how much about what he said was true. His mother had told me that he often made up stories, as part of his schizophrenia.

"Nah...I don't keep the money...I am thinking of learning fire arms like pistols," he continued.

"Why?"

"To join the mafia," he replied candidly.

"But what about the army? Have you dropped that idea?"

"No, that is also there...If I don't get into the army... There is good money in this business," he contemplated. "But, something stops me."

"What do you mean…something?"

"I feel sick later…I feel bad," his lips twitched as he said it.

"That is understandable…when someone else suffers, you can't feel happy."

"Yes… it doesn't help," he shrugged. "I could still do it … My friends keep calling me," he told me again in a self-approving tone. "They say…there is no one like you…but…," he shrugged, with a thoughtful denial on his face. "It is as if… when I hurt someone else, a part of me hurts as well."

That was the beginning of him understanding his spiritual self.

Dev's craving for a life of crime and violence was perhaps because of the quick money and success that he thought, he would get. That he thought, was the only way to avoid feeling worthless. Also, he had immense anger piled within and the violence helped him release it temporarily.

"If you feel you are only good at fighting, army is a better option than joining the mafia. At least, it is ethical."

"Yes…these guys…they invite fights… And then they run away…I have to fight for them," he nodded.

"So, they are using you?"

"Not really…they are friends," he replied.

"But you said you want to fight for justice… do they fight for justice?"

"No…they don't," he replied thoughtfully. "I want to join the army," he added passionately.

"Have you thought of any other profession if you don't get through in the army?"

"Yes…I thought of of joining the police force," he answered.

"That is fine, too," I said feeling relieved.

As we kept talking, he spoke more about the army.

"It's a passion I cannot describe in words," he said in an emotional tone, his left hand close to his heart.

"Why do you feel so so drawn to the army?"

"I want to free the country from its enemies. I want to fight for justice," he continued, strangely passionate.

"Why?"

"I don't know. I have to do it…It has been there as long as I remember. I want to understand why," he continued thoughtfully. "Do you know why it is there?"

"I am not sure yet…We could find out."

I would like to do that," he spoke with hope in his voice.

"It appears there is a past life involved. I'll have to take you into hypnosis to find out."

"Do past lives exist? You believe in them?" he asked me incredulously.

"Yes… I do believe that past lives exist…There is not one past life, but several. In hypnosis, it comes up as a story. Some people believe it is a past life while some don't. However, seeing it explains the root cause of the problem, that is, how you see it in your subconscious mind."

"Okay, if you say so… you're the therapist, you should know," he replied.

"I will take you into hypnosis now."

He nodded, looking curious.

"You will not fall asleep. It is a semi-trance state but you will be in control…I would give you a lot of confusing instructions so that the conscious mind gives up on reasoning…When the conscious mind is confused, it passes on the control to the subconscious mind and we can access information from the subconscious…Then we can find the reasons for your problems."

"Okay," he nodded understandingly.

"Past-life therapy also helps us understand that each life has a purpose and a lesson attached to it. A person's problems can stop causing pain, only if he understands his life purpose and does whatever is required to achieve the goals."

"That makes sense," he replied nodding.

I was relieved to hear that he was willing to pursue a treatment, which made sense to him. When people just follow the treatment blindly, they expect hypnotherapy to work like magic, and take no responsibility to consciously change their negative thinking patterns. That works against the healing process.

"I'll have to give you a trial session of hypnosis first. In the first session, you can't go into a past life, since you may not trust what you see. So you may block the images from coming up. Once you start trusting the process, you will get clear images."

"Okay, let's do it," he replied, almost eager.

THE PROCESS OF CUTTING THE EMOTIONAL ENERGY CHORD BETWEEN TWO SOULS

The process of cutting the emotional energy chord is used when a person is sensitive to another person but the attachment is negative. This leads to lowering the person's self-esteem and blocks his/her positive growth in some way. Cutting the chord is very useful when a person feels emotionally ditched by another person; if a loved one has died; if there has been a traumatic divorce; when a parent is overbearing and the adult child feels suffocated; or when the boss or a peer is abusive, and so on.

It is equally effective between two living people, as with one dead and one living person, since energy/emotional attachments can exist between souls irrespective of whether they are living or dead. When we deal with two living people, it is merely the reduction of the emotional suffering due to excessive control that is diminished; the person does not go away from our life physically. In case of one dead and one living person, we try to send the spirit of attachment to the Light or heaven so that it no longer sucks energies of life from the person's body.

"In today's session I will remove foreign energies from your body."

"What does that mean?" he asked, reverting with a doubtful tone.

"Usually, all of us have energies from other people in our body…When we feel too negative, it could be that we are carrying other people's emotions with us…I would like to remove any such energies in you."

"I don't think there are any foreign energies in me," he stated assertively.

"You do think of your girlfriend often and feel bad."

"But, she's dead," he replied clarifying.

"Yeah…She's dead in body but her energies may still be with you…Through those energies, she can exercise control on you."

"But, how can we remove that?" he asked.

"There will be an energy chord between her and you…In trance you will see it…you will need to cut the cord."

"I am not sure I want her to go away completely," he said with resistance.

"She will not go away. She will still be there in heaven. Only her control on you will go away. She will be freer and you will be freer… Now, that her body is not there, keeping her energies on Earth will not help her or you… Have you entered other relationships since she died?"

"No," he replied, "I don't want to."

"Why? It has been one year and four months. Sharing your problems with someone might help."

"There is nobody like her…" he replied shaking his head.

"Maybe, you do need to let go and move on…"

He was looking down at his hands as usual with a contemplative look on his face.

"You can rebuild the chord any time. It's an emotional attachment. The energy can be recreated anytime. It is your choice. We are only removing any negative pull if it is there."

"Okay, let's do it then," he looked up and nodded his head in affirmation.

Now that I had permission from his conscious mind, I took him into hypnosis.

Once he was in a semi-trance, I guided him through a visualization process.

"Now, see yourself in a beautiful garden…the air feels fresh there. Can you see yourself there?"

"Yes," he replied.

"Keep walking down the garden and you'll come across a rail track. When you see it, say yes."

"Yes," he replied after a pause.

"Walk along the rail track till you see a dark tunnel."

"Yes," he replied again after a pause.

"Now, stand in front of the tunnel. It is very dark inside…but at the other end you see a dim light. When you are at the entrance of the tunnel, say yes."

"Yes," he replied.

"You can't see anything, except the dim light at the other end… As you watch the dim light, call your girlfriend to come at the other end…A figure appears…As you focus, you know it is your girlfriend…When you see her at the other end of the tunnel, say yes."

"Yes," he replied, a little surprised as he saw her there.

"Now, as you focus, you will see a cord between you and her… it can be made of any material: light, glass, rope, steel, anything… Do you see it?"

"Yes," he replied almost instantaneously.

"What is it made of?"

"Light," he replied.

"Which colour is the light?"

"Red," he replied.

"Ok, is she saying anything to you?"

"No," he replied.

"Is there anything you want to say to her?"

"No," he stated again in a firm voice.

"Ok, then cut the cord from near your body. You can pray to a God that you might believe in or an angel or a friend to cut the cord for you…You can use any instrument to cut the cord like scissors, a laser beam…Anything which first comes to your mind…Once the chord is cut, she will be gone."

"Ok, it's done," he replied in a more assertive voice.

"Has she gone?"

"Yes," he replied

"Now, put some blue colour on your body, the part where the chord was …there may be a little hurt there. With the colour blue, it will be healed."

"Yes," he replied.

"Is it healed?"

"Yes… it is better," he replied.

"Now, see yourself after one week, completely healed and feeling light and free."

"Yes," he replied.

"Where do you see yourself?"

"In my house."

"How do you feel?"

"Okay," he replied.

"Okay, now come away from the tunnel back into the garden."

"Yes," he replied.

"Now, come out of the garden."

"Yes," he replied.

"Now, I'll wake you up… Once you wake up, you will be back in this room, feeling refreshed and relaxed… Let all this be integrated in your mind when you sleep tonight."

"Yes," he replied.

He woke up, looking relaxed and refreshed.

"How do you feel?"

"Good," he nodded a little amazed still, at what he had witnessed.

"You were surprised to see her there?"

"Yes, she was there," he nodded, surprised that her presence had felt so real.

"Yes…you would be more willing to let go now and she would also feel free to move on."

"Yes," he nodded.

"Now, that you had a good experience, you should be able to see your past life clearly in the next session."

"Okay," he nodded.

"Other than your desire to be a soldier that you want to understand, your life seems to be mostly on track...You have completed your graduation. Your parents did want you to be an engineer and you could not be, but that is a matter of opinion. It is nothing to be sad about. You have yet to start a career. There is no reason why you won't be successful."

"Yeah..." he smiled, looking relieved.

After this session, Dev felt less sad about his deceased girlfriend. Also, his depression reduced as he started seeing his reality from a different perspective. He continued to meet his girlfriend in his mind, till about two more months. After that, we had another similar session. Subsequently, he could move on.

THE SOUL'S PERSPECTIVE

The idea behind past-life therapy is to help the person understand the perspective of the soul. Once the person realizes how his difficult circumstances are actually aiding him in achieving the purpose, the awareness makes him emotionally stronger. He feels less of a failure in achieving his desired goals.

CONCLUSION OF THE SESSION

Dev's case was a good example of the emotional conflicts we all face in our lives. Our conflicts may not always be as extreme but at some level they do persistently keep troubling us. A focus on that, which is absent, makes our focus shift away from what we have accomplished. If we have had an experience of trauma, failure or suffering, maybe, that is just what the soul desired, in order to evolve. We need to remember that each life is a new experience for the soul. A struggle for happiness is likely to be a part of this experience. Dev needed to understand why he was suffering from his soul's perspective, to find what his soul desired him to do.

CHAPTER 3

THE PAST-LIFE CONNECTION

DEV CAME EXACTLY ON time for the next session.

"I don't think I have a past life," he stated.

"We can try to find it."

He thought for a minute and agreed.

"Okay, let's do it then," he nodded.

There was anticipation on his face, as he looked up. Since this was his first past-life session and he was sceptical, I didn't expect him to find his experience very exciting, but hoped it would help him understand his soul needs.

I briefly explained to him the process of past-life regression thus:

"In Past-life therapy, you go in a meditative trance trance, where you remain alert throughout but focused on the problem that pre-occupies your mind. You are not in my control, but in your own control. As I give you instructions to get into a trance, you would need to co-operate and willingly imagine. Remaining conscious while being in trance is important. If a person goes off to sleep he doesn't remember anything and that does not help him in getting healed.

The first past-life session is a disappointment for many people as they cannot believe that what they are seeing is real. They feel it is their imagination. Since, they are not completely asleep, their conscious mind interferes. They keep questioning their own mind about whether what they see is real or not that prevents information from coming in. The past life starts feeling real only after a few sessions, when the person starts trusting the process."

"Okay," Dev nodded eager to begin.

"Okay, then, I would start with your aura cleansing and start giving you instructions. The instructions would be simple but confusing. Accept the first fleeting impressions, without wondering whether they are right or wrong. This is not an exam. Don't worry about going wrong. We will interpret the images later. If there is any discomfort or problem, stop me…In between the sessions, once you relax, I will ask you to lie down on the couch. Then, I will take you into your past life."

"Okay," he nodded.

DEV'S FIRST PAST-LIFE SESSION

Initially, Dev could not see anything but as he focused, images started opening up from his subconscious mind. I could make out that he was seeing something from the changes in his facial expressions, but he did not say anything. Probably, he could barely make out the pictures he saw or he could not believe that what he was seeing was a real memory.

I coaxed him to speak up, "What do you see?"

"It's hazy," he replied.

"As I touch you on your forehead, you'll be able to focus. NOW! FOCUS."

"There's a soldier. He is being attacked by a lion," he said and stopped.

"Okay…What happens next? FOCUS."

"He is on the ground, bleeding, not moving. The lion is clawing at his heart," he replied.

"Then, what happens?"

"Nothing, he's not moving. He's dead," he replied in a flat tone.

He had reached the death scene of a past life where he saw himself as a soldier, falling after a fight with a lion.

The subconscious mind reaches the scene which is most significant for the present life. Then, the client has to be directed to other scenes before the death scene to get more information about that life, which reveals why the death scene is so relevant for the client's present life..

"Move backwards in time before the soldier falls. Step into your body. Feel your feet. Do you feel your feet? Where are you now?"

"Yes! It's me! I am a soldier. I am fighting with a spear," he spoke. He sounded surprised. Then, he stopped speaking.

"Fighting who?"

"A lion," he replied.

I continued to ask him questions to get more information. As the mind focuses only on what is asked, the past life emerges as different slides of a film.

"What are you wearing?"

"I'm dressed like a soldier," he shrugged. Then, he stopped speaking again. Since the soul cannot see with eyes, it can only decipher impressions of the reality existing in the external world. Answers are given to the point asked and then the mind goes blank again. Relevant questions need to be repeatedly asked.

"Where are you? What is the year that comes to your mind?"

"Around 2-3 thousand years back," he paused as if surprised at the answer himself.

"What is the colour of your skin?"

"It is light," he replied in a slow, flat tone, his eye-balls moving under closed eyes as he was noticing the colour of his skin on his body.

"Light, meaning?"

"Like European," he replied focusing more.

"Which country? Give me the first name coming to your mind."

"Greece," he replied.

"Ok…How is your hair? Long or short? Which colour?"

"Long, wavy… golden brown," he replied.

"What is the colour of your eyes?"

"Light brown, translucent," he replied.

"Are you tall or short?"

"Same as now, tall...," he paused as he focused more, "...his hands are very strong."

Dev was now replying from an observer position, since he was addressing himself as HE instead of I.

I waited for some time as I watched his face. His expression was intent as he was getting the feel of that life.

"How old are you? Give me the first impression coming to your mind."

"Seventeen," he replied.

"Do you have weapons?"

"Yes. I have a spear."

"Who are you fighting, other than the lion? Do you see any person there, other than you?"

"No, no one else," he replied looking around

"Okay...as I touch you on the forehead, be with another person from that life...Now!" I touched him on the forehead. "Where are you now?"

"I am with the king ...It is before the fight. I am in chains," he replied, focusing.

"Do you recognize the king?"

"He is my father. He has ordered the fight," he replied.

"Why has he ordered the fight?"

"I slept with my stepmother," he replied instantly, as if he didn't need to focus to find that information. It was there, right away. That meant it was very important.

"Why did you do that?" I asked him to get more information. We needed to find how exactly that life was affecting his present life.

"We are in love," he replied.

"Move backwards in time, to a scene where you are with her."

"We are near a river. She is beautiful." He spoke almost with a sigh, in a low husky tone of appreciation.

"What are you doing?"

"We are walking by the river, talking," he replied.

"Talking what? Focus."

"She is generally talking about her husband," he replied.

"What is she saying about him?"

"She doesn't like him," he replied.

"Are you in love?"

"No, not yet," he answered.

"Ok, move to the scene when you become lovers as I touch you on the forehead and count 1, 2 and 3. NOW," I moved him forward to that scene.

"Yes! We are by the river again. She is standing by me. She wants to run away with me," he replied.

"Why?"

"She loves me. I have to rescue her from the king, my father. She is not happy with him. She is crying. He abuses her often. She is scared of him," he replied.

"Why did she marry him?"

"She was forced by her father," he replied.

"Look into her eyes. Do you recognize her feel? Have you known her in your present life?"

A person from a past life may still be there in the present life as a lover, spouse, father, mother, brother, friend or acquaintance. One can make that out under hypnosis by trusting the first impressions one gets about that person. The features are different but the energy feels familiar.

I was wondering whether this was his old girlfriend who had died of drugs in his present life.

"No," he answered.

"Ok! What do you plan to do now?"

"I am planning to build an army to defeat the king," he replied.

"Do you have resources to do that?"

He paused, focused and spoke.

"Yes! I am very powerful. I am the commander of the king's army. I have won many battles for him. I have some allies of my own I can call upon," he replied confidently. I took him to another significant event of that life where he sees himself as a soldier.

"I am eight years old. I am learning to fight with a spear," he said.

"Where are your parents?"

"My mother is dead," he replied.

"See yourself with her before she died. How is she with you?"

"She is nice. She loves me," he replied and nodded to himself appreciatively.

"Do you recognize her in your present life?"

"No," he replied.

"Are there any brothers and sisters?'

"One stepsister," he replied.

"How is your relationship with her?"

"I am close to her. She is the only friend I have," he nodded, as if affirming that fact to him.

"How is she with you?"

"Not good. She plays with me but she also cheats on me sometimes."

"How does she do that?"

"By complaining to my father, talking about my mistakes to others, making fun of me," he replied.

"But, you feel close to her?"

"Yes," he replied almost defiantly.

"Do you recognize her from your present life?"

"Yes, it's my mother," he whispered.

"Ok, move to the next significant scene of that life. What is the first impression you get?"

"I am standing in front of an army," he replied.

"Why?"

"I am the general. We are preparing for battle. I am saying something," he said.

"What are you talking about? Focus."

"It is something in that language. I can't make out," he said.

"What do you feel it means?'

"KILL UNTO DEATH!" he screamed.

"Ok, then what happens? Move to the next scene."

"We go to fight. It's a neighbouring kingdom. They have come to attack us," he said.

"Move to the next significant scene."

"We have won the battle."

"What weapons do you fight with?"

"Swords, spears, bows and arrows," he replied.

"What are they made of?"

"Wood with metal at the head of the arrow," he replied noticing the weapons.

"Ok, move to the next significant scene. What happens?"

"I am chasing a king on horseback," he continued.

"Which king?"

"The enemy king…he's a barbarian king," he replied. "I am saying something to him."

"What?"

After a pause he said, "it sounds something like, *I will chase you till the end of the globe.*"

"Then, what happens?"

"I get him. We are coming back victorious," he replies with satisfaction in his tone.

"Okay…what happens next?"

There was a sudden shift of tone in his voice. "I am caught by the king's soldiers. I am in jail."

"Why? What happened?"

"The king came to know about me and her," he spoke slowly.

"How?"

"I am betrayed by someone I trusted," he replied.

"Do you see who?"

"I am being brought in chains in front of the king," he said. There was anger on his face. His teeth were almost clenched as he spoke.

"There is a woman standing there. She has reported me to the king." He paused as he focused harder, frowning.

"Do you recognize her?"

"It's my stepsister," he said hoarsely. "She has betrayed me to the king, my father." This was significant for his therapy as *Betrayal was the most important feeling which consumed him in his present life.*

"Why?"

"She did not like our relationship," he said.

"How did she know about it? Who told her?"

"She overheard my plans for making an army. She went and reported to the king," he replied.

"What did she get by reporting?"

"Money. She betrayed me for money," he spoke with anger and hatred.

"Move to the next significant scene."

"I am standing with the king. I am going to fight the lion. We are talking something," he replied.

"What?"

"If I survive, I become the king. That is the deal," he replied. From the way he spoke, he seemed confident that he would win.

"Then?"

"I am fighting the lion. It has got me. I am on the ground. My heart is bleeding," he replied.

"How do you feel?"

"I failed to rescue her. I could not kill the lion." He spoke with remorse and disbelief in his voice.

He could not believe that he, who had been indestructible all his life, had been killed by a mere lion.

Thus, he died feeling like a failure, defeated because of being betrayed.

"Ok, move above the body and stay with the spirit."

We always ask the client to move above the body and be with the spirit, at the point of death. That helps in removing the fear of death. Also, it makes one understand the emotions the soul dies with, as they are usually the same negative sentiments, which we repeatedly encountered in the present life.

"What are you feeling now?"

Suddenly, the expression of disbelief on his face was replaced by that of anger.

"I have to get justice. I have to take revenge from the king and that woman who betrayed me. If only I could get a second chance, I would kill the lion," he spoke vehemently. Dev had died, in his past life, with a feeling of failure, betrayal, hatred, anger and an obsessive need to get revenge. I tried to heal the negative feelings before sending the spirit to the Light. "Ok, now, realize that was a long time ago. There is no point in keeping the hatred in your mind. Can you forgive the king and the stepmother for what they did?"

He did not reply. He wasn't sure.

"Could you try to forgive them?"

"Ok," he nodded sceptically. He had complied with my request, for the sake of therapy, but anger did remain within him.

"Good...Be with the spirit. Call them in your mind; call your father, the king."

"Yes," he replied.

"Is he there?"

"Yes, he is there," he nodded, looking surprised that he had come.

"What does he look like?"

"He's...Big, fat, and ugly," he replied.

"Ok, forgive him. Say that you forgive him."

"Yes," he nodded.

"Is he saying anything in reply? Any words coming to your mind?"

"No," he shook his head.

"Ok, then send all his energies back to him, take your energies back from him and see him disappearing to wherever he came from."

"Yes," he nodded after doing as told.

"Now call your stepsister."

"Yes," he nodded.

"Tell her you forgive her."

"Yes," he nodded.

"Have you forgiven her?"

"Yes," he replied.

"Now, send the energies back to her, take your energies back and send her to wherever she came from."

"Yes, she's gone," he said.

"Ok, now completely disconnect him from that life. Realize that it was a different life with a different script and this is a different life with a different script. You don't need to carry emotions from that life to this life. Tell your mind to disconnect and let go. Let the soldier's spirit go to the Light and you come back here."

"Yes," he replied.

"Ok, now, I'll wake you up. As you get up, let all this be integrated into your subconscious mind."

I disconnected him from that life and brought him back in control of his conscious mind.

"I am going to wake you up from 1-5. As you get up you will feel relaxed and refreshed.

And whenever I say *Deep sleep* for the purpose of hypnosis, you will go quickly, calmly and deeply to this state or even deeper. Your mind will be very relaxed and the body calm.

Now, let all this be integrated in your subconscious mind when you sleep tonight. 1, 2, 3, 4, 5. Eyes open, wide awake."

On waking up, usually, the person remembers almost everything that he sees during the session as he is in a semi-conscious state.

When Dev woke up, he could not believe what he saw was his past life, "I wasn't sure it was real. What do you think?" I told him, "I think it was. I saw your facial expressions and tones changing as you narrated different events. You were emotionally involved in the experience."

"Does it work that way?" He asked me, still doubtful.

"All clients feel that way after their first past-life session. Those impressions will keep coming back to you now since we have removed the life from the subconscious records and brought it up to your conscious memory. Once we interpret the life in the next session, you will realize how it is affecting your present life."

He was happy that he had seen himself as a soldier. As he left, he was still speculating on whether it was real or not, but I knew that slowly it would sink in.

DIAGNOSIS – INFERENCES FOR DEV'S PRESENT LIFE

Almost all of Dev's emotional problems in his present life could be specifically traced back to this past life. These are discussed, one by one, below:

EMOTIONAL CONNECTION: ANGER OVER BETRAYAL

The Greek soldier felt deeply betrayed by his father, the king and his sister. He wanted to take revenge upon them. Dev constantly felt he had been betrayed by his parents in his present life, who were his father and sister in his past life. The reason he gave at the conscious level – that they spoilt his career in his present life by not letting him join the army on time, could not explain or justify the extreme hatred with which he spoke about them. The fact that he was subconsciously being governed by the personality of the Greek soldier, explained it. The spirit of the Greek soldier was alive in Dev.

AGE CONNECTION

The Greek soldier in his past life had been around seventeen when he died. All the problems in Dev's present life had started when he turned seventeen. Diagnosed with borderline schizophrenia, Dev felt like a failure as he had fared badly in exams and had dropped out of engineering. It was around this time that he had started undergoing severe palpitations in his heart. It must be mentioned that the Greek soldier had been wounded in the heart when he died at seventeen. Whenever Dev encountered dejection and loss, all the suppressed, revengeful anger of the Greek soldier resurfaced. The feeling of failure was a trigger for his subconscious mind, to raise the same emotions in their worst form, as he had felt at the time of death of the Greek soldier. In other words, this feeling of failure specifically triggered the soul of the Greek soldier to come up and overtake his mind.

This life also explained his gang fights. Dev could not refuse anyone who needed his help, as if he wanted to compensate for not being able to rescue the woman he loved; so even though he knew it was wrong, he just had to fight. Also, he used to lose control while hitting. He was careful not to kill anybody but he hit until the person almost died. Hitting is a way of releasing suppressed emotions/energy. The need to hit could be traced back to the suppressed rage, the Greek soldier felt at not being able to defeat the lions.

EXTERNAL EVIDENCE: DEV'S MOTHER SAW THE SAME LIFE IN HER REGRESSION

It is rare that two people see the same life during their individual therapies but it happened here. This was probably because both of them found that life traumatic. Dev's mother was undergoing therapy for asthma. She wanted to understand why she was suffering so much in this life. In her past-life regression, she saw herself as a beautiful dancer, happy, wealthy and the object of desire for many men, She eventually saw herself betraying her brother to the king with whom she was in love. She recognized the brother as Dev and the king as her husband, Dev's present-day father.

She said that her brother had been very close to her but she could not let him go against the king. However, when she saw her brother being killed so brutally, she felt guilty and remorseful. After the fight, she saw herself throwing away the money which was given as reward to her. Next, she saw the mob outside the arena, throw stones at her. She went mad and wandered aimlessly in the streets. Then, she abused the king who eventually got her imprisoned, where she died. She was remorseful and miserable at the point of death. During her session, when we spoke to her spirit just after she died in that life, it said, "I am bad. I killed my brother. I hate myself. I have to pay for it."

THE SOUL'S PERSPECTIVE

Dev's mother's soul blamed itself for the sin it almost unknowingly committed and carried it over to her subsequent lives. She had been choosing the role of a victim and suffering to punish herself for betraying her brother. However, she made the same mistake life after life, by betraying him in different forms. Thus, the karma could never get repaid and the soul kept repeating the same theme. For example, in another regression of hers, we saw that she was his mother in a later life and again, prevented him from marrying the girl he loved. She died suffering with asthma in that life as well. Doing sessions with members from the same family was interesting, as their stories were confirmed in each other's sessions. Three characters from a past life, who hated each other at the point of death, had come together again under the same roof as one family. It was no wonder that there was so much tension and distrust amongst them in their present life. Their souls wanted to evolve above the negativity. Hence, they were coming back together life after life.

CONCLUSION OF THE SESSION

As Dev left after his second session, he was happy he had understood his need to be a soldier. However, his problem of feeling like a failure because of betrayal by his parents, remained. It made him aggressive as he was always on the defensive with them. The first thing we needed to do, now, for him to be able to succeed in his present life, was to remove this feeling of being a failure from his subconscious mind. For that, we needed to get a glimpse of a life in which he had lived victoriously.

GENERAL AWARENESS: THE IRRATIONAL HUMAN MIND?

Dev's emotions appeared irrational from the perspective of his present life but seemed perfectly justified when viewed from the perspective of the Greek soldier. The problem was that he was carrying over emotions from his past life to his present life. This is a common problem, which all of us face but do very little about. The transfer of emotions from a past life to the present is the same as the transfer of emotions from childhood to adulthood in the same life.

Memories have an energy component attached to them, that is the feeling entailed in the memory. This energy component stays alive even if the memory is forgotten. Whenever the person encounters a similar kind of emotional setback, this suppressed energy component gets awakened, as memories of like frequencies attract each other. If one keeps getting hurt in the same place repeatedly, the pain increases more with each new hurt. The same holds for physical and emotional hurts as well.

Most of our emotional reactions, which appear irrational to us are a result of mental energy circuits from past lives or childhood. Such a chain of reactions takes nano-seconds to form, and the person reacts from the subconscious level, without even being aware of the first link in the chain consciously.

For example, each time Dev was rebuked by his parents, a chain reaction was getting triggered in his subconscious mind as follows:

I HAVE FAILED (in others expectations) leading to – I AM DEFEATED (a recall of the memory of feeling defeated at an energy motion level) – leading to – I WAS BETRAYED (a recall of the feeling of being betrayed) – leading to – I AM ANGRY (internal anger reaction) – leading to – I WANT REVENGE (a recall of the need for revenge) – leading to – I WILL KILL MY ENEMIES – leading to – AGGRESSIVE OUTBURST (indulging in violence).

This energy chain governed his actions, without any conscious planning by him to misbehave. Our irrational negative reactions occur because subconsciously we want to save ourselves from getting hurt again, unlike when we were not emotionally prepared for what happened. As a result, we choose a fight or flight reaction to a situation that can be otherwise handled tactfully. Either we react too strongly from the beginning so that we do not get as hurt as we did in the past, or we are very timid and suppress ourselves more than necessary. In both cases, we lose out on our emotional balance and cannot achieve what we seek, to evolve spiritually or mentally.

CHAPTER 4

A LIFE OF VICTORY

AS DEV SAT DOWN for his next session, he looked smug. He was eager to discuss his first past life again and probably, reassure himself that what he saw was true.

"I did not believe in past lives before I saw my own. Even now, I am not sure that it was a past life. Could it be my imagination?" He asked me once more, looking directly into my eyes for an honest answer.

"Instead of worrying about whether it was real or imaginary, focus on whether it helped you understand your need to be a soldier or not. Do you understand yourself better now than earlier, when you had not seen this life?"

"Yes, it makes more sense than the other things," he said, reflecting.

By other things he meant the explanations given to him by his parents, psychiatrists and astrologers.

"Whether anyone believes it or not, it makes sense to me," he continued, reflecting again on the life he had seen, "I feel bad that I failed to rescue her… If only I got a second chance…I could kill the lion."

"That life is over now…That girl and the lion were a part of that life…But, you would get a chance to rescue several people, when you join the army."

"Yeah, maybe…If I get through in the army!" He said ruefully.

Dev appeared to be very concerned that he would fail to get through the army entrance exams. The depression in his voice indicated that the fear came from a subconscious level.

"You died as a failure in the life you saw. The feeling you die with, deeply affects your present life. To heal that memory, we have to look for a life where you have been successful and continued to be so even at the time of your death. This will replace that old negative memory of failure."

"Nah," he shook his head, and sat in thought for a minute. Then, he asked with sincere hope in his voice. "Can we not find a way to kill the lion now?"

"You are asking whether we can change the past. It depends on your belief. If you can make yourself believe you can do it, then maybe you can. We can re-script that life under hypnosis by re-scripting the memory and you can relive that life in your mind and kill the lion this time."

"But, would that change the reality?" he asked, curiously.

"Reality is how you perceive it. The memory is in your mind's control. You can change it."

"Nah... I want to change the reality," he reinstated.

"How does that reality matter to you in your present life? In today's world, how will killing a lion help you? The lion is symbolic for the mind. It represents a big challenge. You have to defeat something which seems as big to feel successful in your present life...That is why it is important to look for another life where you died with a sense of achievement."

"How do you know such a life exists?" he asked me, doubtfully.

"The soul plans different experiences. It wants to experience life in different ways to understand all its aspects. If the soul has planned an experience of failure, it must have planned an experience where it was successful as well."

Dev looked down, deep in thought; he was still wondering how he could have failed to kill the lion. His twenty-one year old mind was harnessing the drama he had seen in his past life.

"We have to try," I told him, cutting through his thoughts. "We can't leave it at this. This memory is foremost in your mind. We have to replace it with memories of a more positive life, so that you start feeling successful and stop attracting negative energies."

"Ok, let's try it then," he nodded in agreement and removed all reservations from his conscious mind and fully co-operated during the session.

We started the induction process of getting him to relax and go into a semi-trance state. Dev went into the hypnotic semi-trance state faster this time.

DEV'S SECOND PAST LIFE

This time Dev saw a life where he was a Roman soldier in medieval Europe. He was highly ambitious and successful and led many wars as a victorious general. He saw himself being applauded by his king and people cheering him on the streets as he returned from the wars. He won one war after another and kept pursuing conquests as if in a zeal to prove he was indestructible. The feeling of victory sunk in Dev as the soul imbibed the energy of victories. However, again he had died a violent death, upon being betrayed and stabbed by another soldier after the war was over. It was revealed that the soldier was sent by his own king as the general had become too powerful.

Yet, the soul felt victorious at the moment of death as he had died feeling triumphant, managing to kill his assassin before he fell. However, it was indicated by his subconscious mind that there was an undercurrent of having failed as a soul. This was emphasized by the Greek soldier's appearance in this regression, as a reminder, that in this life too, the soldier had not achieved his life's purpose. Further probing revealed that the Roman soldier had failed because he had served an unjust and oppressive king. He had the opportunity to end the oppressive reign of the king by replacing the king himself, but uncertainty and fear had stopped him from taking this course of action. As a result, he was betrayed by the very king he had served and died unhappy and dissatisfied. This was revealed through the appearance of a light or his higher soul, who reminded Dev that he has failed as the Roman soldier as well. Dev was aghast at seeing the Greek soldier again and wanted to get rid of the image once and for all. Again, he asked me if he could kill the lion. "Can we go back and fight the lion again?" he asked me, while in the semi-trance state.

"Okay, I will take you backwards in time where you are the Greek soldier and you can fight the lion again."

USE OF RESCRIPTING A PAST LIFE

Rescripting a past life is a healing technique which aims at overcoming a habit of negative thinking by changing the subconscious memory of a negative event from a past life. It involves going back before the most traumatic event of that life and changing the course of life such that the event does not occur. So, the memory of feeling helpless at the moment of death is erased. Otherwise, it involves entering the negative event and changing its outcome to positive. Rescripting creates an internal energy shift towards positive, as the feeling of being helpless is replaced with feeling powerful as a soul.

The person is taken back to the point where he felt helpless and led to re-enact the incident in his mind. While reliving the memory, the person can change the entire sequence of the memory or his own reactions in it, such that he feels positive, powerful or less negative at the end of it.

If the process of re-scripting works, it helps the person manifest positive feelings in his present, far more realistically than otherwise. That is because an old belief that the positive cannot manifest, is broken at an energy level. The person starts feeling better subconsciously, since he/she no longer expects the negative to manifest again, as an unavoidable consequence of life thereby making effective choices in life. As a result of re-scripting a past life memory, usually the person's present life takes a dramatic turn towards the positive in exactly the same way, emotionally, as it was re-scripted in the mind.

If Dev could kill the lion in his mind, that memory of being defeated by the lion would be replaced in his mind, if not in reality.

RESCRIPTING THE LIFE OF THE GREEK SOLDIER

"As I count 3, 2, 1, you are back in that life. You can run away with your lover before the fight or you can change the deal with the king or you can fight the lion again. You can choose. Give me the first answer that comes in your mind, as it comes from your soul."

"No, I want to kill the lion," he replied with determination.

"Ok, see yourself fighting the lion and winning, as I touch you on the forehead…NOW!"

I touched him with a slight, sharp tap on the third eye on his forehead. That sudden tap breaks the existing thought flow and acts as a trigger for the mind to move to another moment in time. I waited as I saw expressions changing on his face as he was fighting the lion.

After a few moments, a look of dismay came on his face again.

"What happened?"

"I could not kill the lion," he replied in a low tone. I could make out from his face that he was seeing the Greek soldier with his heart bleeding, fallen on the ground. If rescripting had not worked, it meant that his Higher Self probably, did not want him to believe that he was indestructible.

"Ask your Higher Self if there are any other ways you can rescript that life so that it doesn't give you a feeling of failure. Give me the first answer which comes in your mind."

"No, you can't rescript that life," he replied on behalf of the Higher Self. Whenever he used *YOU*, it was an indication that the voice was coming from outside his own mind.

That was it.

"Ok, then disconnect from that life. Come back to the life of the Roman soldier as the spirit."

All his feelings of victory, after seeing the life of the Roman soldier, diminished upon seeing the bleeding Greek soldier.

"What are your thoughts now as the spirit?"

"…The Greek soldier also lost because of his fear of failure. He could have escaped from the gallows. However, he kept hoping and waiting for the right moment. Because of his fear of failure, he did not even try to escape," he continued. "The same fear continued with the Roman soldier. He knew the king as unjust but he kept fighting wars for him because he could not rebel against him; that fear of failure prevented him from becoming the king."

I tried once more to heal his feeling of being a failure through the Energy Shower technique. Taking the energy shower is like taking a bath to infuse energy in our minds; it helps in cleansing and revitalizing the soul. Using this technique, the person can remove negative energy that envelopes his body by seeing dark smoke leaving the body and positive energy filling in its place. It also helps in aura cleansing and in breaking adamant clusters of negative energy.

"Ok, we will try to remove the feeling of being a failure once more from your mind…Join your Higher Self, the light you saw above your head…Be in the Light."

"Now, let the feeling of failure come off you as balls of dark smoke leave your body. See your body surrounded by grey energy and see the shades of grey falling off you. See the negative energy leaving your body and getting released in the light…Along with it, release all your feelings of failing, in the light…And as the dark energy leaves your body, you feel lighter and lighter as you are filled with the pure healing energy of light. Your mind and body relax and heal."

"Ok," he nodded his head and joined the light above his head.

"Let me know when you feel lighter. Let it just wash off you and see yourself glowing in Light as you are filled with its positive energy."

I waited for him to heal himself in the Light.

"I can't do that completely," he said after a few seconds.

"Why not?"

"I don't know," he shrugged and replied.

"Ask your Higher Self."

"No. You have to keep that feeling so that you are not defeated in this life," Dev replied on behalf of the Higher Self. I could not interfere with what his Higher Self wanted as it could be related to the purpose of his present life. So, I disconnected him from that life and woke him up.

RELEVANCE FOR DEV'S PRESENT LIFE

When he woke up, Dev had a smile on his face. He looked thrilled. "I have always been a soldier," he declared.

"Yes, that is why the desire is so strong probably."

His face glowed as he remembered his victories. He did not even once mention the failure of the Greek soldier or his being a failure in his present life, after this session, until I brought it up.

THE SOUL'S PERSPECTIVE

The Roman soldier had been successful in Earthly terms but he had failed from the perspective of the soul. He had been acknowledged and appreciated on Earth probably because of which he got carried away and forgot his soul mission. Due to a repeated lapse in judgment by the Greek and the Roman soldier, the soul-purpose had been left unaccomplished. The Higher Self intervened to warn Dev not to repeat the pattern in his present life. Since there was an unfinished soul-purpose, Dev's subconscious ambition in this life was to fight for justice and help those who were weak and oppressed. However, at a conscious level, Dev misinterpreted it as a desire to go in the army.

However, by joining the army, it was possible that Dev would repeat the mistake made earlier by the Roman soldier. Upto this point, Dev displayed traits of the Roman soldier by imitating the latter's thoughts. Much like the Roman soldier, Dev too fought out of blind loyalty for friends who were at fault. It was likely that he would carry forward the same thought pattern to the profession he chose. As a soldier in the army, he would again have to fight defined enemies of the country, irrespective of whether his efforts led to justice being accomplished or not. Dev needed to understand the perspective of his soul to get the peace of mind he desired.

CONCLUSION OF THE SESSION

The first step was to make Dev understand that he had to use his abilities to fight for a just cause and for that, he had to use his own mind. There was a conflict between the mind of his soul and mind of his consciousness, that we had to resolve.

CHAPTER 5

THE CONFLICT IN HIS MIND

THE CONFLICT IN HIS MIND

DEV'S SOUL AND CONSCIOUS mind were in consensus that he should join a profession where he could fight for justice. However, there was a conflict between what the soul desired him to achieve and what he chose to achieve. The conflict arose because the conscious mind interpreted this need to fight for justice as a need to join the army, whereas the soul did not. For the soul, fighting for justice was not synonymous with joining the army. A life in the army had not led Dev to achieve justice for the weak in his previous lives. Convincing Dev that the soul's perspective mattered wasn't easy.

"In the army, you might not be helping the weak and the oppressed." I suggested.

"How can you say that? I am protecting the people of my country from the enemies," Dev asked.

"Who are the enemies? How do you define that word?"

"As a soldier, I am not supposed to examine who is the enemy. I just fight when I am asked to. I will die for my country," he replied defensively.

"How will you know that the war you fought helped people get justice? How will your martyrdom ensure justice for people?"

Again he replied, "That is not my problem. I can't question the army because if I do, I will lose my job."

"But your soul *wants* it to be your problem. The soul wants *you* to question...How can you choose a profession where you can't ask questions? What if you support the wrong cause because it is part of your job?"

"What is wrong in killing a terrorist or an enemy?" Dev was assuming being a soldier meant fighting for justice.

"The enemy soldier is also fighting for his country and a terrorist is fighting for a cause. So it is just a matter of perspective."

"Come on! You are stretching it too far!" he protested.

"Your Higher Self probably wants you to realize that, wars are fought more for greed than need. However, at the soul level, greed is not justified because there is enough for all. What is the need for a war? A war presumes that it is all right for one man to prosper at the expense of another man."

"That is true...... But one can reach the top to ensure justice," he stated.

"Do you need to be a soldier to reach the top? Would you be able to ensure help for the weak and oppressed people by being a soldier?"

"No, that is not a soldier's job. The government has to do that. I will defend my country when it is threatened by outsiders." he repeated with pride.

Dev was unwilling to let go of his beliefs. I reminded him of the Roman soldier.

"Why don't you try to consider other professions where you would have more discretion and power? This would be better than blindly following orders.

In the Army, you may not agree with the decisions you are expected to obey. You can't use your own mind. Needing to be a soldier to get power to fight for justice made sense in the medieval ages, not anymore." He pondered over it as though he had never thought of it earlier. He was confused and getting tired now. I thought I'll end the session soon and let him think. He by then, took the discussion in a new direction.

"Look, this is just a job; I have been thinking of pursuing MBA. However, I want action and adventure; I want thrill," he argued, trying to explain again, using different reasons this time.

"I thought your aim was to fight for justice. Now you say that you want action and adventure?"

"Yeah! I was also thinking I'll join the army, learn mountaineering, adventure sports, use big guns, have all the fun," he explained.

"There are other ways of fighting for justice, where you can have the thrill and guns and more discretion. How about I.P.S? Have you thought of that?"

"Yes, but police service is not as exciting. I want action. The army has more action," he clarified.

"But, if you only choose action, you may never get the peace you want."

"Yeah! True!" he nodded in despair. He finally noticed that there was a conflict in his mind.

"Let us at least look at the prospect of a profession where you can do justice, not just follow orders blindly. If you protect injustice in the name of following orders, your soul-purpose is not served. There is no point in wasting another life doing things which do not give you what you desire."

"Yeah! That actually makes sense. Look, if I don't get through the army entrance exams, I was planning to give the police entrance exams next year. That is a tough exam. I need a year to prepare for that. I thought I could do MBA on the side," he explained.

"Is there no other profession where you can find adventure and thrill?"

"There are but they don't pay. I thought of scuba diving but the training is expensive and my parents were not willing to fund that. Besides, it has no action. I want to play with guns," he replied.

"Police service seems to be the best option then. You will get some action, guns and you will have some discretion as to where and when to use them and not to. As a soldier you will be largely helpless in choosing situations where you can render justice. You will just be obeying orders. You have such an independent mind. You may not like that."

"Yeah! That is there. Now, I have seen two lives as a soldier. So, at least, I understand why there was such a strong need inside me. Maybe I can join the police," he replied considering the prospect seriously.

"Yes, and we can look at other lives where you have not been a soldier, yet been successful."

"You think I have more lives?"

"There is no harm in trying to find out. If you can feel successful doing something else, it will give you the peace you are looking for."

"We can try. But, I don't think I have had any life where I wasn't a soldier," he replied assertively.

"How can you be sure? We can look for a life of non-violence where you felt successful. Meanwhile, start reprogramming your mind with positive affirmations. You will receive the energies you send out to the universe."

I wrote some new affirmations after consulting him on how he wanted things to be in his life. Dev stated again that he wanted to be a soldier. Right now, only that thought made him happy. I let that be, for the time being, as it was the feeling of happiness which was crucial for his recovery right now. As the session ended, he seemed pleased with himself, though he was reflecting on our discussion as he left. His mind was being torn apart at the thought of what he may be getting into by becoming a soldier.

THE SOUL'S PERSPECTIVE

Dev had to realize that the purpose of the soul could not be achieved by following blindly what others considered success. He had to make a conscious effort to take responsibility for his actions and its consequences, on himself and others. For satisfying his soul's craving, it was necessary that he balanced his work in the world with the work the soul wanted him to do. So, it was safer if he could find other ways to fight for justice where he would also be individually responsible for ensuring justice.

CONCLUSION OF THE SESSION

Our next attempt was to find a life of non-violence where he felt successful, so that he could have more career choices other than the police or the army.

GENERAL AWARENESS: ARE WE MENTALLY JAILED UNDER DINOSAURIC INSTITUTIONS?

Dev's second past-life session brought up another common problem which is one of the main causes of negative energy in the world. It is our need to follow institutionalization without questioning or allowing change in the set norms. We have structured our life around a wall of institutions like schooling, marriage, armies, and health services, which set the norms of how we should live our lives.

These norms are largely focused on achieving external measures of success, as defined by conventional doctrines, irrespective of whether these measures satisfy our core soul needs or not. These institutions block soul evolution because of their resistance to change. They don't accept new thought necessary for expanding horizons of the human mind towards a happier world. Because these institutions exist and we feel compelled to follow them, we feel like victims of negative circumstances.

As evolving souls, we feel jailed at energy levels due to repeatedly feeling mentally suppressed, even though we are not physically jailed.

These institutions can be called the DINOSAURS of society, because they are big in terms of the influence they exert and slow in terms of their ability to change. At an individual level, we need to know, just as Dev had to, that we *do* have the power to bring about a change in the system. Our thoughts impact the process of creation in the universe.

CHAPTER 6

TOWARDS A LIFE OF CRIME

JOINING THE MAFIA

I WAS LOOKING FORWARD to explore a life of non-violence in our next session. However, Dev walked in with his eyes blood-shot, lips pursed in anger and fists clenched hard. Intuitively, I felt that there was so much of unchannelized energy within him that it could cause harm unless redirected constructively. I reset my mind, forgot about the session of non-violence, and started talking about what could have led to the current development.

"What happened?"

"I have decided that I will join the mafia. Nothing can change my decision now," he said with a grim, determined expression.

This was shocking indeed. What if his criminal instincts could not be controlled? If he had decided, what could I do to stop him now? How much was I responsible for it as a therapist?

However, if he was sitting here in a therapy session to inform me of his decision, then there was scope for changing it. I quietened my nerves and reacted to him nonchalantly. While I made general conversation with him, my mind raced to find the trigger which had caused this thought process to take over his mind.

"But until yesterday you were looking for peace of mind?"

"Yeah! All that is there…But big cars, hot babes, money…who doesn't want all that? That will give me happiness," he replied.

"Will it? Are you sure? What will you live for?"

"Power. I will have power; I will be the king," he elaborated.

Further probing revealed that he had met friends who were

offering him big money to be part of a drug Mafia. He seemed very excited about it while I was perplexed at his naiveté.

He was discussing his career choice of joining the mafia with me as if he thought I would approve of his decision. It just did not occur in his mind that he was talking about committing a crime. This indifference to crime was another indication about why he may have been diagnosed as a schizophrenic. Dev was indicating a lop-sided thought pattern repeatedly. There were two extremes to his personality. One wanted power to establish justice for the weak while the other just wanted power even if it destroyed the very fabric of humanity. It did not matter whether what he was telling me was imagined or real. From a therapeutic perspective, this was harmful for his mind. There was a pressing need to bring in positive thoughts in his mind.

I put forth my arguments again in a different way. "What about peace of mind which you were looking for? Will selling drugs give you peace? Your girlfriend died of drugs. You want more people getting addicted to drugs?"

"No, I don't," he took a deep breath and sighed.

"I hate drugs; they killed my girlfriend."

"Yet, a part of you keeps pulling you to join the mafia?"

"Yes, I don't know why," he mused.

"How do you feel exactly?"

"I feel good but I can't explain the feeling accurately in words. That feeling of power gives me a high…I beat up that guy who was supplying drugs to her. I duped him saying that I wanted to buy drugs. He came alone. Then, I caught him…I almost killed him that day," he spoke with pride.

"How did it feel after the fight?"

"Not that good," he replied truthfully. "That guy was bleeding badly from his neck. It was almost twisted. It was a bad sight." There was a slight remorse in his voice as he spoke.

"So, you don't feel good after the fight. You feel guilty?"

"No," he replied immediately on the defensive. "I go for a drink;

then I am fine," he spoke proudly now, reflecting on his strengths. It gave him a sense of self-worth.

"Would power, money, cars and girls satisfy your need to fight for justice?"

"No, they won't," he said, reflecting on my question. "But, everybody works for those things alone."

He was influenced by consumerism, by the superficial belief endorsed by popular culture that a profession or job is for material satisfaction and not for the fulfilment of our life's purpose. So I asked him, "will other people's definition of happiness get you happiness? Will destruction get you happiness?"

"No," he replied, slowly thinking about it.

"When you die and reflect back, would you feel happy? Would being a mafia don mean anything to you at the point of death? That you destroyed so many lives with drugs?"

"No, I don't want that," he instantly reflected.

Now he was off-guard. "I'm not sure. It is an attractive option I have but something is stopping me."

Finally, he said he was not sure. He was open to changing his mind. Now, we could start working with hypnosis to get answers from his subconscious mind. I needed him to talk to that part inside his mind which was driving him to join the mafia.

"Ok, so one part of you wants to go in a line of violence and crime and the other wants peace. Is that right?"

"Yes, that is right," he replied slowly, taking his time to grasp the intensity of my question.

"So, shall we do a Parts Integration? You will have to go in a light trance state. We can check what your subconscious mind is looking for by driving you in different directions. Then, we can work to integrate the two parts to resolve the conflict in your mind."

"Ok... if that helps," he agreed.

CONFLICTING PARTS OF A PERSONALITY

"Okay...when there are two conflicting parts of a personality, we can resolve the conflict between the two parts through Parts Integration. A conflict exists because your personality is divided into two parts that reside in your subconscious. You can call each part and question it until we get answers that tell us of the soul's decision and its reasons for those decisions.

Usually, the result of this exercise is a mutual consensus between both these parts as each realizes that the purpose of the soul is the same for both. Then a common method for achieving the purpose, which is acceptable to both, is reached. Once both the parts get integrated, inner personalities stop pulling the person in opposite directions.

So, can we do this? Does it sound okay to you?"

His willingness was essential for the process to succeed.

"Ok, let's do it," he nodded. He looked confused but was willing to give it a try.

THE PROCESS OF PARTS INTEGRATION

"We will call both the parts on separate palms of both hands. You have to keep your hands stretched out in mid-air, from the elbow, with palms stretched outwards. Through the session, you have to balance them that way. That will keep your conscious mind focused on balancing the hands. Your conscious mind will be hypnotized in that state. So, it will not interfere when we ask questions to your subconscious mind."

I helped him hold his hands bent and stretched straight from the elbow, till they felt relaxed while being suspended.

"You can take a deep breath and close your eyes if you feel comfortable or you can keep your eyes open too."

He closed his eyes. His hands were relaxed and he was sitting straight on the chair.

"Ok, now call the personality which wants you to indulge in violence. Is it there?"

"Yes," he replied, instantly.

"What does it look, feel and sound like? Anybody you know?"

"Yes, It looks like that guy who had killed the lions," he replied.

"Ok, the Greek soldier. Now, call the personality which doesn't like violence. Is it there?"

"Yes," he replied again, almost instantly.

"Who does it look, feel and sound like?"

"Like me," he replied.

I started asking questions from the personality which liked violence. Dev was in a light hypnotic trance. The answers were coming directly from his subconscious mind.

"What is the intention behind liking violence?"

The personality of the Greek soldier answered, "I like violence because it gives me action and power."

"Why do you need action and power?"

"Because I feel powerless," he replied. The answers were specific and brief but they touched the core of the issue.

"Why do you feel powerless?"

"Because I died as a failure," he replied.

Dev, in his conscious state, never understood why he had a need for violence. His subconscious mind knew immediately. He needed violence to feel powerful; otherwise he felt powerless.

"What was the intention behind dying a failure? Why did you plan death as a failure?"

"So that I would work hard to accomplish anything which gives me power," he replied

"What do you mean by anything? What specifically would give you power?"

"Reaching the top," he replied.

"What do you mean by reaching the top? Can you give examples?"

"Like in rock climbing, mountaineering, adventure sports, fighting for justice," he replied.

Being a mafia don was nowhere in his list. So, I asked him specifically about violence, bringing him back to the issue we had started with.

"What about violence? Would violence get you to the top?"

"Violence only brings destruction," he replied.

"How?" I asked him, relieved and amused by this sudden change of thought pattern. While I had been haggling with his conscious mind for almost an hour, it was his own subconscious mind that convinced him in a few minutes.

"It brings suffering for the self and others," he replied. "It harms us, it hurts," he continued.

"Violence harms others. But, how is it suffering for the self?" I asked him. The focus of our discussion is always the person himself, not any other. When a person changes his thinking from the roots, it is always in the interests of the self, not any other.

"Makes me feel guilty... It makes me feel bad," he replied.

"How does it do that? Can you be more specific?"

"Blood makes me feel bad," he replied.

"How?"

"I can relate to it. It makes me feel as if a part of me is bleeding. I feel repulsed, looking at it," he replied.

The subconscious mind answered from the soul level, where, all beings are part of ONE whole consciousness. For the soul, it feels the same whether it hurts another's body or one's own. Without a physical barrier of the body, it is not possible to clearly demarcate the movement of energy. Thus, at an energy transmission level, when you use anger to hurt another person, it hurts your own energies as much.

"So, do you want to reach the top by pursuing violence to harm other individuals?"

"No," he replied.

"How will you get action and power then?"

"I can get action by getting into adventure sports, serving the country," he said.

Finally he had gone round a full circle. He had wanted to join the army before deciding on becoming a mafia don and now he again desired to join the army.

We confirmed the Greek soldier's decision with the part standing on his other hand that was Dev himself.

"Ok, now let's talk to the other part on your other hand. What is its intention behind not liking violence?"

"Violence causes destruction. I want to create a life which is just for all," he replied.

"How do you want to do that?"

"By doing something productive," he replied.

"How? Can you be more specific?"

"Do something productive to serve my country like joining the army or the police," he replied.

"Would that be productive for you as well?"

"Yes. It would help me and the world," he replied.

"So, now both your parts have decided that they do not want to use unjust violence to get action and power. Both want to serve the country by doing something productive, rather than causing destruction. So, let both your hands join as one. Join your fists together and bring them close to your chest...Let the energy from both hands merge and become one colour...Now, let that energy enter your heart. Open the palms and hold them on your chest, facing inwards. Feel the energies from both hands integrating and going inside you...You may see two colours merging as you take the energies inside."

"Ok," he joined both his hands and put them on his chest. Then, he took a deep breath and inhaled.

"Which colours did you see merging?"

"Red and blue," he replied.

"Ok... Red is the energy of anger and blue is the energy of peace." He had seen the colours he needed to see merging.

"You can relax your hands and open your eyes now. Your conscious mind is back in control as soon as you open your eyes."

"Ok," he replied and opened his eyes. He looked relaxed.

"How do you feel now?"

"Good," he nodded, after opening his eyes.

"Do you still want to join the mafia?"

"I don't know...I'll think about it," he replied, not wanting to change his decision immediately.

"But, you do remember that you almost killed the drug dealer who was supplying drugs to your girlfriend. What if someone else's boyfriend wants to do the same with you?"

"No... I don't want that," he said shaking his head. "Ok, that is it. I have decided. I won't join them," he stated firmly.

"Are you sure? You won't change your mind if they call you again."

"Yes. I am...I only decide once. I'll tell them. I can't sell drugs and without drugs there is no money in it. If she had not died of drugs, I might have joined them...but, not now," he replied, with firm determination.

He looked relaxed now after the session.

"Thanks," he said and smiled with relief. "What next?"

"Next time we have to look for a life of non-violence."

"Err...I am not sure I have a life like that," he stated again.

"We'll try."

"Okay," he agreed as he left.

The anger was gone from his body. His eyes had been red when he had come in. As he left, they were calm.

THE SOUL'S PERSPECTIVE

As was evident from this session, Dev's soul was far clearer than Dev was in his conscious state on what is productive and what is destructive. The soul, speaking from Dev's subconscious mind, stated clearly that it wanted power to get justice for the weak and oppressed and not for misusing violence. It believed that violence caused destruction. Contradictorily, in his conscious state of mind, Dev considered power and violence as complementary. As a result, he was always in conflict with his subconscious mind. For the first time, in this session, Dev experienced his own ideology as distinct from others. He realized with surprise that he as a soul, had values and beliefs which were not the same as those of his parents or friends.

CONCLUSION OF THE SESSION

It took us some time before we realized that the trigger to use his strengths destructively to gain power, came from within Dev's house and not from outside. He was particularly decisive about pursuing crime as a profession, each time he felt defeated in the house in an argument with his mother. Disapproval by his mother invariably led to the arousal of the Greek soldier's energy within Dev. In Dev's subconscious mind, where the Greek soldier ruled, defeat was equated with failure and failure was equated with death. So, whenever Dev felt defeated, he felt emotionally killed and wanted to hurt back with vengeance, to feel alive again.

Dev realized that he was subconsciously being driven to do something which his wiser self basically did not want to do. It brought him to the decision that he must control the Greek soldier's impulses. He learnt to appreciate his own distinct ideology, as against other people's definition of power or success which had made him focus more on feeling revengeful than positive.

In subsequent sessions, Dev's Higher Self showed more lives which again contradicted his present belief systems about his soul's perspective on success and power. He started realizing that our soul has a profound ideology which is not based on human heritage or tradition, but on reason and understanding for the need of energy balance.

CHAPTER 7

THE SOUL IS DISAPPOINTED

WHEN DEV CAME FOR the next session he was in a calm mood. I reminded him that we had to do a past-life regression to find a life of non-violence. He was again sceptical but agreed to proceed.

UNWANTED DEVIATIONS FROM THE PLANNED SESSION

The Greek Soldier Comes Again

Dev started seeing images within a few minutes of starting induction. His face, in a semi-trance state, suddenly became alert. His eyes, though closed, became focused as on seeing something. He gave a slight jerk of his head to the right and took a deep yawn almost simultaneously. In the next instant, his shoulders straightened and he nodded to himself as if waking himself up to an alternate reality under closed eyelids. It was almost as he was telling himself – 'Ok! Get ready.'

These gestures became a kind of switching on trance pattern for Dev from this session onwards. It seemed as if his own energy would lie down and another dormant energy within him took over. His facial expressions changed from focus to bewilderment. "Are you seeing something? What is it?" He looked confused as if he couldn't make out why he was seeing what he was seeing. Then, he spoke. "It is the Greek soldier. He is standing in a kind of fog. Everything's red around him."

I wondered why he had appeared when we hadn't even started the past life regression yet. This personality in his subconscious mind seemed to be taking decisions on its own. It was too powerful to lie low.

"Why is he there? Is he saying something?"

"No, his heart is bleeding a lot. He is just standing there in the red fog. He looks angry," Dev replied, looking dismayed. His lips twitched in revulsion as he spoke of the bleeding heart. His closed eyes rolled sideways seemingly wanting to look away from the scene in his mind.

"Ok, he is saying something," Dev said after a pause.

"What is he saying?"

"PAINT THE SKY RED!" Dev said loudly.

"What else is he saying?"

"He is saying he is there to remind me of his failure so that I don't fail again in this life," Dev replied.

"Ok," I nodded, "We are going to look for a life of non-violence now. Does he have anything more to say?"

Dev was quiet for some time as he waited for him to speak.

"No," he said after a minute, "he is gone now." Then, he took a sigh of relief and started concentrating on his breathing again.

We continued the induction process. As part of taking him deeper into trance, I next asked him to visualize a light entering from the top of his head.

"See a beautiful colour entering from the top of your head and as it enters it relaxes you. Which colour do you see?"

"Blue!" he replied

"What kind of blue?"

"It's a nice blue," he nodded his head smiling at the colour he saw.

I guided him to let the light travel inside each part of his body. Halfway through the process, as he was focusing on the light travelling to his body parts, he started seeing images again.

THE SECOND DEVIATION: APPEARANCE OF AN OLD MAN

"I see something," he said, indicating me to stop speaking.

"Ok," I stopped, surprised at what had come up now, "What do you see?"

"I am old. I am walking down the steps of a building," he said, confused at what he saw.

"Where are you?" I was wondering if he had already reached a past life without me giving the command to his subconscious mind as yet. This was the second diversion in this session, when his subconscious mind had acted spontaneously, that is, shown him a picture without us asking for it.

"It is Greece. It is an old building. There is a small window. I can see the sea from it," he said.

"What are you doing there?"

"I have a book in my hand," he said.

This was confusing. Dev was not an avid reader. Why should he be seeing himself with a book in his hand in a past life?

"I look very peaceful," he added.

That was a positive sign.

"That is good. Which year is it?"

"I can't make out," he said, while his eyes were trying to focus.

"Is it a past life?"

"I don't know," he replied, looking even more confused now.

"What are you wearing?"

"Regular clothes – trousers and a T-shirt, like I wear now and glasses," he replied.

"Which book? Can you make that out?"

"No. It's gone now," Dev said suddenly.

"Where has it gone? As I touch you on the forehead be in that life again."

"No, I cannot see it," he replied. He looked relaxed and started concentrating on his breathing again.

It was surprising that the picture came and vanished suddenly. It could be a future scene because his clothes had been contemporary. Nevertheless, it was an important picture because he had seen himself looking peaceful.

I told him to continue with the visualization to relax him further and then moved him onto a past life. However, we did not see the Old man again until a few sessions later.

DEV'S THIRD AND FOURTH PAST LIVES: A BRITISH AIR FORCE PILOT AND A NAZI SOLDIER

Though I gave a command to Dev's subconscious mind to show us a life of non-violence where he had lived with a feeling of success, we did not exactly see the lives I expected. Either he did not have complete lives of non-violence or his subconscious mind did not register the 'non' and just showed us lives of violence. However, the lives he *did* see, helped him understand the futility of violence. Apparently, his Higher Self had a plan because of which it was showing him the lives which he saw.

Dev's third past life was that of a British air force pilot who fought and died during the world war. He had won medals for his bravery and died in glory. This life, though ending in glory and not betrayal, was not the life we wanted to see. So I asked Dev to try and see another life which was peaceful and devoid of violence. Instead, he saw something that was bewildering. He was a Nazi soldier fighting in the Second World War and had died in a suicide mission, thus achieving martyrdom.

A PARALLEL LIFE OF THE SOUL

Dev fought in the Second World War, from both sides, the Allies and the Axis. The likely explanation was that he was seeing a parallel life. While he was fighting as a soldier in Germany, he was living a parallel life in Britain, that is, he was in another body at the same time, as an air force pilot. In case of parallel lives, the same soul splits into two parts or even more. The soul is made up of energy. When it splits, the quality of energy remains the same in each soul. It is like when a torch beam passes through a hard wooden chair, it splits into two parts but the quality of light remains the same; though the power of each split beam may be lesser than that of the ONE whole beam of light.

Hence, the same soul energy can incarnate in several bodies at the same time if that suits its purpose of evolution. Practically, parallel lives means that two persons would have a similar energy frequency, and hence would have similar temperaments, similar body build, similar fears etc., but would be facing individual challenges from a different set of circumstances. Dev's soul had chosen an experience from both sides of the war. It was as if the same person was fighting himself. Dev as the German soldier was fighting Dev, the British soldier.

Though, since one was in the air force and the other in the army, it was unlikely that they met each other. Metaphorically, however, it was a brother fighting a brother since both were part of the same soul energy. Was the Higher Self trying to tell us that there must be several souls like him in the war, kin fighting each other, at the soul level or that we are all part of one whole consciousness, and when we kill another, we harm our own energy in some way?

THE SOUL FEELS DEFEATED

At the end of recounting his fourth life, Dev's face was shining with pride at his glorious deeds on the battlefield. The next moment however, he saw the Greek soldier in the lion fight again. The look of success on his face vanished.

"The Greek soldier is there fighting the lion," he said in an exhausted tone, sounding tired of being reminded of his failure.

I wondered why he was being reminded of failure now.

"What is he saying?"

"Nothing. He is defeated. The lion has got him. It is clearer than ever before," he replied in a low tone.

"Is he saying anything? Join your Higher Self. Ask why has he appeared again when you died successfully?"

"The voice is saying: *But, the country didn't win the war,*" he replied.

Germany had lost the war. To the Nazi soldier, the mission had been as big as the lion fight, and he had died winning it.

According to Dev's Higher Self, however, the enemy had won again. The image of the defeated Greek soldier indicated that his effort had again been futile. The soul had sacrificed another life for a cause which did not fulfil its purpose of life.

THE HIGHER SOUL'S PERSPECTIVE

On waking up, Dev realized that he had seen parallel lives. "I must've fought for both sides. The planes and the weapons were both of the same time period," he reflected. "Which country was I fighting for then?" It dawned on us that his Higher Self was showing him the futility of the concept of being loyal to a country, as the same soul was fighting on both sides of the war. His Higher Self had been indicating repeatedly that it wanted him to fight for justice of the weak and oppressed, but Dev always misunderstood the soul's craving as a need to fight for one country. Hence, in this session, his Higher Self showed him parallel lives to make him realize what it actually meant. There were weak and oppressed souls dying on both sides of the war.

> *Dev had chosen a life of violence and achieved success from his own perspective, but his soul was disappointed. It wasn't because he had chosen a life of violence; it was because the violence was not justified.*

CONCLUSION OF THE SESSION

Dev's soul was disappointed because he was unable to undo social conditioning and develop his own judgment on the method of fighting, which would ensure social justice. Dev was disappointed at the level of his conscious mind because his sacrifice of life was not recognized at the soul level. Taking away another soul's free will by killing it in war or by murder, creates negative karma for the killer. This is irrespective of whether the killer is legally authorized to kill in Earth terms as a soldier, or not. At the soul level, taking another life is justified only when it is needed for survival (as animals kill for food), or in self-defence from a tyrant; not for any other reason.

Dev, as the Nazi soldier, killed as part of a job wherein he fought for power and glorification of his country – needs that are not considered justified from the soul's perspective. His sacrifice of life did not help his soul evolve in any way. Rarely is effort towards destruction, productive from the soul's perspective. From the perspective of the soul, there is no difference in killing as a criminal and killing as a soldier, as in both cases, the person kills for material considerations. Dev's next two lives as a criminal were shown to him in this session itself to prove this point to him.

GENERAL AWARENESS: NEED FOR MASS DECONDITIONING

Dev was unable to meet the needs of his soul because he got swayed away from his life purpose due to external pressures to earn and succeed in life as soon as possible. He never cared to question the beliefs and values he was conditioned into. Feelings like peace and happiness were of no consequence to him as he rode high on success and power.

Our social development is such that the need to be superior is drilled into us from our childhood. Competition in all areas like getting the highest grades, winning only by defeating others, etc., only reinforce division and separation as the milestones to success. Happiness is a positive energy that can be created by spreading positive energies of love, sharing and compassion. This is most often side-lined in the race for mechanical success. We rarely ask ourselves questions like: what use is success if it does not lead to happiness? Or, can we be in harmony with ourselves if we make others feel inferior in our zeal to succeed?

INDIVIDUAL THINKING MAKES UP MASS THINKING

We teach our children to solve problems without using violence but we justify violence at the collective level. Defence constitutes one of the many significant parts of a nation's backbone. Children grow up inherently believing that violence is an unavoidable tool of action, as it is used by grown-ups. In fact, mass violence cannot even be expected to diminish until it is made redundant as a means of coercion at individual levels.

WARS HAVE HAMPERED SOUL EVOLUTION

Wars, which are so heavily discussed in our history books, films and folk tales, have hampered soul evolution because of several reasons:

- War used force to suppress people's rational thinking. Therefore, they discouraged logical deduction of thought in human beings. Misuse of strength encouraged shorter and quicker routes in dealing with problems that did not lead to long-term solutions. Wars have failed to show us that situations demand an expansion of human consciousness which goes way beyond the need to compete.

- Because of wars, powers at different levels got transferred to physical strength rather than the intellect. Developing the body became more important than developing the mind.

- Soul evolution became secondary to external display of power or success. Values like inner satisfaction and developing innate soul-qualities were sacrificed; material display of happiness became dependent on display of power by flaunting wealth or beauty rather than evolution towards a higher level of internal light, peace and happiness.

- Wars led to taking away free will of humans and created negative Karma for the oppressors and victims (who became subsequent oppressors) on a large-scale, the effects of which had to be borne by several future life-times.

MENTAL ANGUISH OF A SOLDIER

A soldier kills to earn bread for his family or to protect civilians from outsiders. Yet, it is the soldier's soul who pays the karmic debt for killing. Giving monetary awards or medals is hardly any justification for expecting the soldier to take the burden of killing upon his consciousness. Does his family, or his country, or his fellow beings need him to sacrifice his consciousness to feel better themselves? Finally, it is the soldier who loses out, not the people who declare wars.

CHAPTER 8

THE LIFE OF A PIRATE

DEV'S FIFTH PAST LIFE: A PIRATE

DEV HAD SEEN TWO lives as a soldier. However, I was still wondering why his subconscious mind was not showing us a life where he had lived peacefully and died feeling successful. I asked him whether we could try once more to look for a life of peace and success. He agreed. At the second attempt, the life that Dev saw was that of a pirate. He was initially thrilled at the idea of seeing himself as a pirate – pillaging, looting ships, accumulating wealth and evading law.

Before he had become an outlaw, he had been a poor child, neglected by his family. Then he had accidentally killed a merchant in anger, when the merchant's carriage had thrown mud on him while passing by. Later, his life as an outlaw had ended when he was captured and hanged publicly for his crimes. He had died in disgrace and despair. As soon as he has finished narrating his death, I asked him to join his higher soul and ask about the meaning of this life.

"What was the main purpose of that life-time? What was the lesson learnt?"

"Violence doesn't help…" he replied.

"Be with the spirit. How does the spirit feel?"

"Awful. He wants to make up for this life by serving his country," he replied.

"Ok…Ask the spirit to join the Light above him. Is he there?"

"Yes," he replied.

"Ok, now, ask the spirit what was the life-plan for that lifetime? What was your purpose?"

"You were to become a big merchant," he replied. He was addressing himself as YOU, meaning someone else was speaking to him from the Light, probably his Higher Self.

"How could you have done that? Ask?"

"If only you had forgiven the merchant and let him go, he would have felt apologetic. He would have come back and adopted you. He would have named you as successor. You would have become a successful merchant," replied the voice, elaborating on the original life-plan.

"Ok, be with the Light... Imagine a shower coming from top and all the negative energy washing away like smoke...when you feel lighter, tell me."

"Yes," he replied.

"Now, go and join your Higher Self in the Light."

"Yes," he replied in a tone of resignation.

"Has the pirate gone?"

"Yes."

"Then, be back in your present life...violence doesn't help. Let this learning be integrated in your mind when you sleep tonight."

I counted him up, "1, 2, 3...20, Eyes Open. Wide awake."

He was feeling better as he opened his eyes.

But he looked remorseful still. "It was horrible, the way that pirate was killing those people," he said with a shudder.

"Yes, it was," I agreed and reminded him, "have you decided not to be a criminal in this life?"

"Yeah, never," he said shaking his head with relief.

It was interesting to note that Dev admitted that he felt bad killing. This was the first session in which he said he felt bad while doing the work he did to earn his livelihood.

THE PIRATE LIFE – THIRD SESSION: GOING INSIDE THE BRAIN

As Dev was feeling better emotionally, he stopped his anti-depressants within twenty days of past-life therapy. He also wanted to stop the medication he was taking for schizophrenia as it had a side effect of making him sleep too much. Because of sleepiness, he could not concentrate on his studies and fared poorly in his exams, which he did not like. So, he stopped the medicine for a while. For three weeks after stopping the medicine, he was feeling better emotionally and calmer physically. Then, one day one day he was very low when he came for the session. He said he was disturbed because his brain felt funny. There were severe vibrations on the back of his head. His doctor admonished him for not taking his schizophrenic medication for this problem.

"When did they start?"

"This morning, I was listening to music and suddenly this noise began in my head," he replied, looking worried.

When a body part suddenly develops a problem, we can go to that body part under hypnosis. We use a visualization process. The problems are identified with the first metaphoric images associated with the pain in the subconscious mind. Also, we see the colours and energies of the body part before the problem began and how it changed after the problem. We can also talk to the cells which are affected by treating them as individual persons with a voice and memory.

We decided to delve into his brain through hypnosis to find out the root cause of these vibrations.

We needed to call his spirit guide for this process.

I took him into trance. He went in quickly. I counted him down a stairs of twenty to take him deeper in his subconscious. At the bottom of the stairs, I told him:

"Go to the door you see at the end of the corridor."

"Ok, I am there," he replied after a pause as he looked for the door.

"Open the door. You will find yourself in bright light. This is the light of your own being. When you are there, tell me."

"Yes!" he drawled.

"Ok, now see a helicopter come there with your spirit guide as the pilot. He will take you to the body part which is affected. Is it there?"

"Yes!" he was more excited now.

"Which colour is it?"

"Green," he replied, amused at the idea of a helicopter ride.

"How is your spirit guide?"

"He's...a cool guy," he nodded and looked pleased to see him.

"Ok. Tell him to take you to that part of your body which is causing disturbance. As I count 1, 2, 3, at 3, you'll be there, 1, 2, 3...NOW!"

"Yes, we are there." He nodded affirmatively.

"Where are you?"

"It's inside the brain," he replied.

"What is happening there? Give me the first impression coming to your mind."

"An earthquake," he said spontaneously.

"Ask a cell to come forward from the affected area. Ask when this started? Accept the first words coming to your mind." *(Cells have a memory of previous lives stored in their DNA coding, which can be accessed to find the root cause of a disease.)*

"Yes..." He paused, as he heard the cell. "It says, 'This morning when you were listening to music."

"Ok, now ask what is the connection of that music to these disturbing vibrations in your brain. Go back to the root cause of these vibrations. 3, 2, 1, NOW!"

"Ok, it's the pirate..." he drawled, understandingly. "He is looting people and killing them."

"So, what is the connection?"

"He *makes them play music before killing them,*" he explained.

"Ok, how is he feeling as a soul as he kills these people?"

"Bad," he replied with genuine remorse in his voice.

"Ok, is there any other reason for these vibrations in your brain?"

"No," he replied.

"Ok, move forward in time when the pirate dies. How is he feeling?"

"Bad! He is saying he's sorry," he replied.

"Be with the spirit. How does the spirit feel?"

"Bad. He wants to make up for this life by serving his country,"

"Ok...Ask the spirit to join the Light above him. Is he there?"

"Yes," he replied.

"Now, ask the spirit, in the Light, why music is causing those vibrations."

"Certain actions connect you to the other lives," replied Dev. He was addressing himself as YOU, meaning someone else was speaking to him, through him.

"Who said that?"

"A voice came from above," he replied.

"What actions?"

"*Violence, alcohol, music,*" he replied.

"Ok, now, thank the voice and disconnect from that life. Tell your subconscious mind that this is a different life and a different time. The same disturbances need not be created when you hear that music as you are no longer killing people. You have decided not to be a criminal in this life. Hence, the lesson is over. You realized that killing people makes you feel bad. Now, that you have learnt your lesson, you need not suffer from it anymore. The same mental anguish need not be created."

"Ok," he nodded.

"Be back in the present and go to the cell and ask it what you can do *now* to heal your brain. Is there anything you need to do in your present life, apart from disconnecting from that past life?"

"STOP," he replied on behalf of the cell.

"Stop what?"

"Stop listening to that music," he thought for a while and replied.

I wasn't sure that came from his subconscious mind. But, I let it be since he was in trance.

(Much later he told me that he used to listen to a genre of music with a hard drum beat and he used to think of beating up people from other communities, while listening to that drum beat, as it used to make him quite hysterical. His soul wanted him to stop thinking these thoughts. The vibrations were created so that his focus would shift away from indulging in those violent thoughts, as the soul realized that feelings get converted into reality on the physical plane. The cells were telling him to stop having those thoughts but he wasn't yet ready to accept that in his conscious mind. Hence, he misinterpreted the cells' message to stop as – *stop listening to music.*)

"Ok, then do that. Now go back before you had these vibrations this morning. See the affected area as calm, as if the earthquake is over."

"Yes, I am there," he replied.

"Imagine you have a camera. Take a picture of the calm brain."

"Yes," he replied, immediately following instructions, without resistance.

"Now, come back to the present and paste this calm picture on your brain. Now, see your brain as calm as in this picture at present."

"Yes," he replied.

"How does that feel now?"

"It is better," he nodded.

"Ok, then with this picture of a calm brain in your mind, sit in the helicopter again and come back to the door you had used to enter your body."

"Yes, I am there," he replied.

"Thank your spirit guide, and come out of the door."

"Yes."

"Now, as I count you up from 1-20, be back in control of your conscious mind. Your brain is calm now."

"Yes, it is," he replied.

I counted him up, "1, 2, 3…20–Eyes Open, Wide awake."

He was feeling better as he opened his eyes.

IMPACT OF THE PIRATE'S LIFE ON THE PRESENT LIFE

Other than the fact that Dev could not listen to music for relaxing, an irrational fear, which was associated with this life, was that

Dev was literally scared of pulling a pillow over his head. We discovered this fear when, to release his anger, I had suggested that he could put a pillow over his face and scream. That would help release the need to indulge in actual violence. However, Dev said he couldn't do that... "I can't put a pillow on my face. If I keep a pillow I can't see...someone would come and kill me."

This feeling was from the pirate life, where a cloth was put over his head before beheading him. In fact, even the anger that his body wasn't buried with respect, remained with him.

"What did you do with the bodies of the people you killed as a pirate?"

"I threw them in the ocean," he answered off-handedly.

"Then, what did you expect the people watching, to do with your body?"

"Okay...Okay," he had shrugged.

"You hadn't connected the two acts by yourself? It didn't strike you, did it? It is easier to blame others."

"No...Ok, I know violence doesn't help...I will block those urges and shift my mind to other things," he agreed.

I left it at that. I did not want to push it into healing, as Dev had to learn how to shift his energies to focus on the positive by himself.

THE SOUL'S PERSPECTIVE

The soul had planned to become a big merchant in the life planning stage. However, the life plan went astray when he took one wrong step. Instead of throwing the stone at the merchant, had he forgiven him, the merchant would have adopted him. At the planning stage, the soul had not expected the boy to get so angry that he would kill the merchant. The life plan was not made taking into account the extreme negative feelings which come up on Earth. This happens because the soul lives in a no-negativity zone. It cannot comprehend the extent to which a negative feeling can consume a person once he is on Earth.

Though Dev became a pirate and killed people by choice, his soul never accepted this profession. This life explained Dev's need for becoming a soldier in his next two lives. The lives of the German and the British soldiers were planned after this life. In these lives, he made up for the life of the pirate by sacrificing his life for his country by joining the national army. However, as the leadership was corrupt, he again failed to do justice to his soul. He could not help the weak and oppressed; he could not achieve justice even when he fought against the law as a criminal or with the law as a soldier.

CONCLUSION OF THE SESSION

In this session, we had again failed to find a life of peace. Before giving up on the idea, I made one last attempt to help Dev find a life of peace and success.

GENERAL AWARENESS: IMPACT OF BEING A MURDERER IN A PAST LIFE

Traumatic experiences or mis-deeds of past lives impact us severely at a mental/emotional level in future lives, until we can free ourselves from the clutches of the negative energy of abuse. A soul, who has been a murderer in a past life, may choose several methods to repay his karma and free himself of the feeling that he is BAD. I have found that people suffer from either or all of the following problems, if they have died feeling BAD about themselves in previous lives.

I had a client who would get extremely hurt if anyone called him a murderer or mad, even as a joke. Upon hearing the word, he would feel like he was having a nervous breakdown. His body would tremble, his blood pressure would rise and his mind would go into extreme panic. He could not complete his studies satisfactorily and had problems at work because of his extreme and anxious temperament. It was found after several regressions that he had a past life as a serial killer. To prevent past life energies from getting carried over, forgiveness, detachment, belief in a higher consciousness, perseverance and patience, are crucial soul lessons to be learnt. This has to happen from both positions: the victim as well as the oppressor.

CHAPTER 9

ONE LIFE OF PEACE

WE HAD NOT YET seen a life of peace maybe because Dev did not want to see it yet, or was not ready to face that aspect of himself. However, we decided to explore again.

DEV'S SIXTH PAST LIFE: ONE LIFE OF PEACE

Dev was in a trance.

I again gave the command to Dev's subconscious mind. "Look for a life of success where you had died feeling blissful and successful."

He started seeing images instantly.

"I see an old man. He is sick."

"Ok, be in the body. How do you feel?"

"At peace. I am lying on a bed ... very weak," he said.

"Is there anybody with you? Look around."

"My son is there," he replied.

"Ok, what happens next?"

"It is over. I am above the body," he replied.

He had reached the last scene of that life. I took him to an earlier event in that life to get more details about that life.

"What do you see?"

"A ... jungle ...it's hazy," he replied.

"Are you there in the jungle?"

"Yes, it is a soldier," he said, still in the observer's position.

Just as I was wondering whether we had truly reached a life of peace, he clarified. "No, an archer. He has a bow and arrow."

"What is he doing?"

"He is shooting someone with the bow and arrow," he spoke in a low, flat tone as if he could not relate to the archer much.

"What does the archer do for a living?"

"He works for the king…His aim is very good," he nodded his head as he replied.

"Is there anything else significant in that scene?"

"No," he replied in a flat tone.

"Ok, then move to the next significant event of your life."

"I am killing a king," he replied focusing again.

"Which king? Why?"

"I don't know… maybe the enemy king. There are two kings standing side by side. I shoot one with my bow; he dies," Dev was sounding indifferent.

"Why did you kill him?"

"I am awarded a piece of land," he explained.

"Then, what do you do with it?"

"I leave the life of the soldier and settle down as a farmer," he continued in a low tone.

"Do you like being a farmer?"

"Yes. That guy never liked being an archer," he replied on behalf of the farmer, again from an observer's position.

We had seen one profession where he had lived peacefully, for at least half of a lifetime. I mused on the prospects of this life for his present life. Dev had been thinking about opening a strawberry plantation in this life, at his mother's suggestion. He had not been sure if he wanted to do that, though. Now, that he had seen a past life as a farmer, he may want to give that profession more thought.

"Ok, move to the next significant event of that life."

"It's the same scene again. I am on the bed. My son is there," he drawled.

"Is your wife there? Did you get married in that life?"

"Yes, I did. I had a good family. She died a few years back," he replied.

"Do you feel successful as a farmer?"

"Yeah!" he replied, but spoke half-heartedly.

"Ok, be above your body with the spirit. What are the thoughts in your mind?"

"There is a blue light above me," he replied.

"Is it saying something? What are the words that come to your mind?"

"It says, *you betrayed your own king. The enemy king awarded you the land,*" he replied.

The Greek soldier appeared again…

"What is he saying now?" I asked feeling sorry for him.

There was not one life where he was not reminded of failure at the time of death.

"*He has come to remind you how it feels to die after breaking a promise so that you don't do it again,*" he spoke in an affirmative voice and addressed himself as *YOU*. The energy being in the blue light appeared to be speaking through him. It was most probably his Higher Self again.

Once again, Dev's past-life spirit was not at peace at the time of death. We had seen a life where he lived peacefully, but it had been founded on betrayal. Hence, he did not feel at peace within. I decided to give up on finding a life where the soul had felt at peace and finally woke Dev up.

He had seen four lives in this one session. He was smiling as he got up. He was happy on seeing four more lives of adventure and violence. He had pursued professions that he speculated about often in his present life. He had seen no life of peace, but he did not regret it. In fact, he was looking very confident of himself when he woke up.

THE SOUL'S PERSPECTIVE

In all these four lives, Dev chose the path which could not lead to the achievement of his soul's purpose. His rational mind led him to fight for causes that spread more injustice, than justice. The fact that the Greek soldier appeared at the end of these lives, clearly indicated that from a spiritual perspective he had failed to succeed.

CONCLUSION OF THE SESSION

Dev realized in this session that he had to stop hitting people indiscriminately. He saw that it made him feel remorseful at the soul level. Hence, to find peace within him, he reduced interaction with his friends and stopped getting involved in gang fights. He also saw that his main skill was as a soldier. He said he did not like the life of the farmer much. So, he decided he had to go in the army or the police. However, Dev's Higher Self continued to give us messages and show us more lives of violence. After four months of therapy which hereafter became more intense, we finally did see a life of peace., That, however came much later; after Dev and I had gone through several sessions of soul searching.

CHAPTER 10

KARMIC BALANCING

DEV WAS FEELING BETTER. However, I noted with much despair, that he had lived many lives of suffering. Dev was trying to repay karma for some sin he had committed but was unable to evolve above the suffering. Dev was repeatedly dying the death of a victim of circumstances. This was the core pattern, which needed to be broken for his focus to shift to positivity on a long-term basis. The karmic cycle could be broken if Dev as the Greek soldier, understood that he had suffered because he had made someone else suffer in a previous life. Then he could take steps to create positive energy to replace the negative karma he had created.

Past-life therapy does not help in repaying karma, per se, but it can help in finding the root cause of the karmic debt. Realizing this, the person can move on to get out of his karmic loop through a process of self-realization of the cause and effect of his actions. To help Dev break this pattern of feeling I had to help him find the life prior to the Greek soldier's life, wherein he had betrayed somebody. When I told him so, he looked at me disbelievingly. "Do you really think so? No, I can't have betrayed anybody. I am not that kind of person."

"Now, you are not. But, maybe earlier you were… Usually, when we consider something despicable, we are sure to have done it ourselves in an earlier life, and regretted it at the time of death."

"Nah…," he shook his head. "How can I have a life so old? The Greek soldier's life was already two or three thousand years old. I don't think I have lived longer than that."

"For the soul, there is no time. The soul is eternal. There has to be a life before this one because your lives are revealing a pattern. A soul lives the life of a victim if he has lived the life of an abuser and wants to make up for that sin."

"How is it possible?" he persisted, still unwilling to try looking for another life.

The only way of making him question his own beliefs was to make him talk to his own subconscious. When he realized that deep within, he did not agree with what he proclaimed on the outside, his stand mellowed. Within five minutes of getting into the hypnotic trance, he looked disturbed. His eyes moved as if to try to focus on a picture. Then, his expression changed to exasperation.

DEV'S SEVENTH PAST LIFE: THE ORIGINAL SIN

It was the Greek soldier again, indicating that he was aware of what we were trying to find out. "Ok, then ask him to go. Continue to focus on your breathing. We are looking for a life where you betrayed somebody or which is the root cause of you having been betrayed repeatedly."

Lives where the soul has itself made mistakes, do not come up easily, as the victimized soul does not want to see itself in the role of the abuser. After some time, Dev started seeing pictures. There was a bewildered look on his face, as if he couldn't believe that such a life existed.

"Do you see anything?"

He was quiet for another second before replying, "Yeah, we are fighting with tribes. It is really old."

"Where are you?"

"It's a jungle," he paused

"Are you using weapons?"

"Yeah. There's a spear made of wood with an iron at the end, a shield, stone clubs…they're crude," he said noticing them carefully, as weapons were his passion.

"Who is there with you?"

"Our king and some soldiers," he replied.

"What are you?"

"I am one of the soldiers," he nodded his head with pride as he replied.

"Do you recognize anybody? Does anybody seem familiar; someone you have seen in this life?"

"The king...He could be my father but, I am not sure," he replied after focusing.

One can never be sure if the same person is there in the present life or not because the person seems to be different in the past life. We can only rely on our intuitive feeling to know.

"That's Okay...How does it feel fighting with those weapons?"

"Ok," he shrugged his shoulders and replied, his facial expression showing he wasn't very thrilled about using them. "They are simple weapons."

"Are you also a tribal?"

"No, we are a little better off...but it's a very old civilization, nothing much there," he said.

"Then, what happens next?"

"We have killed the tribals," he replied in a satisfied tone. What are you doing next?"

"I kill our king," he replied in a matter-of-fact tone.

"Why?"

"For wealth," he replied.

It was noticeable that there was no intonation as he spoke of killing his own king. It was as flat as could be. Usually, when a client sees himself doing something bad, there is sadness, guilt or disbelief in tone. But, Dev's tone was as cool as if this was just another part of life which he was seeing. Death, even his own, seemed to leave him untouched. He seemed to lack realization that he had sinned at a conscious level. However, at the soul level, he had created negative karma. The same soul who was his king in the Roman life became his father in the next life. That father betrayed and killed him just as Dev had betrayed and killed his King. I tried to find out more, to make him relive the incident vividly in his past life. I was trying to get the soul, the spirit within the body, to speak up as it had in earlier sessions, since it aroused his inner conscience.

"Who gave you money for it?"

"The king's father," he replied.

"Why?"

"He is a tyrant. His son is planning to take over his kingdom. He cannot defeat him using fair means. So, he uses this ploy," he replied, reflecting on what had transpired.

"So, the son would have ensured more justice for the people?"

"Yes," he nodded affirmatively.

"So, by killing him you took away that justice. Because you killed him, people continued to suffer under the tyrant king."

"Yes," he replied in a low tone.

"Ok, move to the next significant event of that life. Do you get the money?"

"No…The king's father gets me killed," he said.

So, he was betrayed by the tyrant.

"What are your thoughts at the time of death?"

"I am bad. I should not have betrayed my king," he said. There was remorse in his voice.

"What is the spirit feeling after it leaves the body?"

"Bad!" He replied.

"Ok, ask the spirit what was the purpose of that life?"

"I was to kill the evil king and establish justice. Instead, I got carried away," the spirit replied in a low voice, feeling remorse. Dev's facial expression was one of self-rebuke.

> Dev's purpose of life in all subsequent lives was to ensure justice for the weak and oppressed. That was his lesson also, which was being carried over from this life.

"Ok, ask the spirit to go and join the Higher Self and see it getting healed in the light. Ask the Higher Self whether the spirit can be forgiven?"

"No, you committed far more atrocities in later lives. You have to heal all those souls, whose purpose of life you took away. Only then will you be free," Dev replied on behalf of the Higher Self.

I disconnected him from that life and woke him up.

THE SOUL'S PERSPECTIVE

Dev's Higher Self had clearly told him, in the session, that the negative karma he created in this tribal life, could not be forgiven because he had accumulated much more negative karma subsequently.

METHODS OF KARMA REPAYMENT

Karma is a measure of energy exchange. It is the amount of positive energy created versus the amount of negative energy created in the thought process accompanying an activity. Irrespective of whether the act is outwardly positive or negative, if we feel negative during the activity, we release negative energy and when we feel good, we release positive energy. Negative energy remains as karmic debt until transcended into positive by the soul's choice of thought and action. According to the karmic law, there are two methods of karma repayment or karmic balancing –

The first method is that the soul chooses to suffer in the same way as it made another soul suffer previously. If it was an abuser in a past life, it chooses to be a victim in the present. This step is necessary to help the soul understand that it committed a mistake by hurting another soul, which it may not realize automatically. However, the soul, when victimized, can ignore/neutralize the hurt it receives. This can be done with positive thinking techniques like meditation, tolerance, patience, compassion, forgiveness etc. If the soul converts negative thinking into positive with effort and intention, the soul can break the karmic cycle.

It would then emit positive energy. This would help the soul to come out of the negative loop. Also, by facing the trauma of abuse, the soul would know inherently, that this method of pursuing power is humiliating to others; therefore, it is a wrong method to pursue.

For instance, Dev's soul lesson was to achieve justice for the weak by obtaining power himself. His means of obtaining power led him to committing a sin. He was betrayed in the next life so that he could understand how it feels to die a death of betrayal – so that he does not use this method of obtaining power again.

If he could have ignored the betrayal, he would have achieved his purpose of life differently, in his next life. However, Dev could not free himself from feeling revengeful. The negative energy was too intense and had a strong hold on him. The soul got caught in a karmic loop and the cycle of abuse and victimization continued. This was seen clearly in his past life regressions.

The focus of Dev's soul on Earth remained upon neutralizing the energy of betrayal rather than on achieving the purpose of life which was to achieve justice for the weak and oppressed.

As in Dev's case, suffering does not necessarily ensure karmic pay-back. Self-realization of cause and effect takes a long time to come. Meanwhile, suffering leads the soul to feel more negative in the short run, leading it to indulge in revengeful acts. With suffering chosen as the repayment method, the karmic cycle can continue endlessly, unless a higher level of realization comes into the soul with evolution.

In the second method of repayment of karma, the soul has to create as much positive energy for another soul as it had created negative energy by indulging in abuse.

For example, if the soul had enslaved other people, it may choose to become a missionary and help slaves or rescue them, in the next life.

This step of karmic repayment can get activated only when the soul evolves to a higher level of consciousness and can empathize with other souls. This second method of karma repayment, usually, involves a focus on healing other souls, that were harmed in the abuser's life. The soul still has to suffer in some way, since it has a negative karmic debt. But the form of abuse mellows, because of the life-plan. The problems are emotionally experienced at the level of feelings and not physically, like by being unfairly rebuked, bullied or scolded. For example, if a soul killed three people in a past life, it may be born in the same family in the next life. He may be repeatedly betrayed and abused by his parents or siblings so that the soul feels emotionally killed each time. The abuse continues until the negative karma is converted to an equal or higher quantum of positive energy through the soul choosing to focus on feeling good amidst trauma. The soul learns to neutralize the hurt and evolves to a higher positive frequency by choosing to ignore the abusers as devolved souls; help and forgive than take revenge. Once the negative karma is repaid, the soul moves away from the abusive environment by choosing to let go.

The emotional suffering in place of physical suffering ensures that extreme negative feelings like revenge remain under control while positive feelings like patience, tolerance and compassion develop. Hence, the focus can remain on helping other souls. The second step of karmic repayment was the method which Dev's Higher Self told him to use in this life to be free of the negative karma he had created. "You have to heal all those souls. When you heal all the souls whose purpose of life you took away, you will be free."

This second step is usually adopted by the souls in their life-plan when the first method fails. This had happened with Dev, and happens with most of us. We keep suffering because we are unable to forgive the abuser.

> *When we heal other souls, our thinking pattern which focuses on suffering, breaks its stronghold. This happens as we start searching for positivity thus focusing on evolutionary aspects of thinking.*

For example, if Dev could shift his mental focus from betrayal and revenge, to staying happy, *he could have perceived the betrayals as being mere obstacles in life and moved on to being positive.*

CONCLUSION OF THE SESSION

Dev wanted to heal himself. But, he wasn't ready to change his choices yet. He wanted to achieve his purpose without changing his belief patterns. As we continued talking, I realized that the personality of the Greek soldier still had a strong-hold on Dev's mind. Maybe a fragment of the Greek soldier's spirit was still stuck on the Earth plane because of which it kept reappearing. Usually, spirits go to the Light after the death of a person but when attachments are too strong, soul fragments remain on Earth. One way to help the Greek soldier's soul now was by healing his heart of the pain and disappointment he felt while dying.

Dev kept saying that he was disappointed because he could not rescue the girl he loved. If the girl forgave him and took him with her to the Light (celestial plane), then maybe, the Greek Soldier would also let go. In the next session, we decided to go back to that life and call the girl's spirit to heal him. If the intense negative emotion of being unable to rescue her was blinding his reasoning senses, then her spirit could help us.

GENERAL AWARENESS: KARMA FORMS THE SYLLABUS OF A LIFETIME

Diane Stein, the author of *'Essential Energy Balancing'* writes, 'Karma is pain carried over lifetimes. It is woven into our mind-grid when the soul plans birth in a human body. It forms the belief system the person is born with and which needs to be changed or evolved as part of soul evolution. Each incarnation gives the soul a chance to experience, grow and learn in a different physical body. Karmic patterns carry over several lifetimes, circumstances and situations, till the negative energy is transcended into positive.'

Thus, karma forms the syllabus of a lifetime. It decides the kind of negative emotions we, as souls, want to overcome in one lifetime. Just as a course syllabus entails the subjects and the problems, the student has to understand to move to a higher grade, our soul's life plan too entails the kind of emotional lessons of maturity it needs to imbibe, to understand happiness. A pattern of recurring problems is usually karmic, as they occur due to the soul testing itself. If the soul is unable to learn the lessons in that life, the test passes on to the next life.

When the soul is able to use a difficulty as a means of evolving to a higher level of consciousness, it succeeds in transcending its karmic debt into positive energy.

CHAPTER 11

LOVE HEALS

WE HAD DECIDED TO go back to the life of the Greek soldier in the last session because there was a possibility that his spirit had not gone to the Light. The spirit was stuck on Earth in anguish. It had been causing continuous mental turmoil to Dev, because of which he was unable to free himself from his aggressive tendencies.

SPIRIT RELEASE: THE CONCEPT

Spirit release is the process by which souls, who have not departed after death of the body, are helped to go back to heaven. Heaven is used here, as a term to describe a non-physical dimension of Light where spirits live in their energy bodies. In heaven or the celestial plane, positive frequencies are much higher than on Earth.

Earth supports more negative frequencies since it is a physical dimension. The physical form of matter is naturally denser than a non-physical form of matter just as solids are denser than air. Dense physical forms vibrate at a lower/more negative frequency than spirit forms since their atoms and molecules move at a lower speed of vibration. Therefore, spirit bodies are lighter and feel more positive than human bodies while their soul's vibrational frequency is higher. Whereas, the vibrational frequency of souls in human bodies is less visibly radiant.

The spirit which comes from heaven in a human body has to lower its frequency to be able to stay in the physical body. Only then can it match the lower speed of the physical matter. So, being in a physical body is, in a way, a more negative experience for the soul than being in a spirit body. After death of the body, to go back to being a free spirit, the soul has to raise its frequency again to match the vibrational frequency of the celestial plane.

To raise its frequency, the spirit has to let go of its negative emotional attachments on Earth and raise its frequency to positive. Only by letting go of its tightly held attachments and freeing its energy to match that of the higher realms, can it go back to the non-physical dimension of heaven. A negative spirit that cannot rise, stays focused on incomplete emotional attachments of Earth wherein its live body energy feels heavy and dense. If the spirit continues being very negative, it feels alive but is dysfunctional because its body is gone. So, it feels helplessly stuck in pain, which makes its soul vibration frequency very low and it reaches a dimension of hell-like existence with low and dense frequencies.

Yet, the choice to go to heaven or remain in hell is the spirit's own. However sinful the spirit may have been on Earth, if it can stop being negative, it does not need to remain on Earth or in hell after death. The spirit has to go back to become pure again as remaining here would only reinforce its negativity, not heal it.

At all moments of time, the spirit has a choice to free itself of its negativity and go to heaven after death. It can cleanse its dirty energy, go up to the celestial realm and come back rejuvenated to finish its remaining life purpose or repay existing karmic debts.

However, the process of detaching isn't easy. For some spirits, who have been very negative on Earth, this process of letting go can mean a complete loss of identity of the negative self. *For instance, if a spirit dies as a powerful king or saint or don, but feels negative at the point of death, it cannot go back to the celestial realm feeling negative.* That is because we cannot enter heaven with a negative mind-set as that perpetuates our low soul frequency. Hence, all belief patterns or values which make us worried, sad, mean or anxious have to be dissolved to enter heaven. *So, the spirit who dies negative, has to remove from its mind its false sense of ego, its sorrows, its anger with self and others, etc.*

Returning from Earth after a life, is like quitting a role played in a film and going back home; but some souls get so attached to the film and their role in it, that they cannot cut the chords on Earth voluntarily.

RETURNING AS SOUL ENERGY TO THE CELESTIAL REALM

At the point of death, the soul-energy gets out of the body and sees a light somewhere around it. The soul feels pulled by the light, as if somebody is calling it back. It responds to the call, revolves in a circular motion to raise its frequency, throws off all that negative energy which is dense and finally enters the gate of Light. When the spirit rejoins the light, it ends its present life-journey on Earth. The call from the celestial dimensions comes in an energy form, that is, it is felt, not heard. So, the soul energy can respond to it only when it feels free at the moment of death. It cannot respond to the energy call if it is too heavily stuck with its own thoughts.

Rejoining the Light after death doesn't always happen. If death is sudden, as in an accident, illness, war or murder, the person may not realize that he/she is dead and hence may not go into the Light. Also, if the person has several emotional attachments and responsibilities on Earth, which he does not feel ready to let go but has met an unexpected end, the soul may not want to leave for the Light when called. For example, if the death is unexpected, the person may have responsibilities of family, business etc., which he/she wants to wind up before leaving. Thus, it may not leave for the Light when called. Then in such cases, the soul may get fragmented and parts of its energy may remain on Earth.

When the spirit remains stuck on the Earth plane, it ceases to live or age. It just gets frozen at the time of death, with the same thought which it died with. This thought keeps repeating itself. For example, there is a past life where I died by getting burnt on a stake. I was a queen, deeply in love with my husband, who was a king. He later turned tyrannical after fighting too many wars and I committed suicide, and leaving small kids behind, who died subsequently due to family politics. That life plays itself on me very often when I keep feeling that I should not detach myself from my kids, as I would leave them in despair and they may die emotionally, if I prioritize my freedom.

As a result of my predominant thought pattern that I cannot leave my kids alone, added with the karmic repercussions of that life, I haven't been able to leave my kids and go out to earn money in spite of financial problems. Whenever I have tried working, one of my kids has fallen sick and I have felt selfish by choosing to work outside than from home. The paradox became worse because I have had two broken marriages, due to husbands who turned tyrannical. So, the same life has been repeating itself where I have felt like committing suicide but could not run away leaving the kids and repeatedly felt helpless emotionally. After healing myself several times, and coming to terms with what *is*, the spirit of my past life is more at peace. It now travels back and forth from light and waits to find a solution which ensures justice. When she goes into the Light, her energy is rejuvenated but when she rejoins the body, she is restless to work for the Light in speed and release.

> *The spirit wants to experience the energy of justice and peace on Earth. It wants to live the thought that it got and did justice to be able to free itself and go back to heaven. It is like completing a life purpose and then going back rather than going back upon death of the body. However, the spirit cannot achieve its life purpose without a body; it needs the co-operation of a body to complete its life purpose.*

The spirit that is fragmented gets attached to a body which thinks like it does, since soul frequencies have to match for spirit attachments to happen. That person may be the spirit's own future incarnation, who faces similar problems or any person who felt as negative as the spirit did at the moment of death or at any point of his/her life. The stuck spirit has no awareness of a future time-zone.

It does not record changes which keep happening on Earth. It only keeps reliving and regretting the negative circumstances it died in. The negative focus increases the pain of emotional traumas for the person the spirit is attached to, whenever similar situations recur at the energy level.

In the face of trauma, this spirit rises up. A mental program which is focused on a negative gets reactivated and starts causing extreme physical or mental problems.

> *For example, in Dev's case, he would have normally felt hurt by his parent's insensitive attitude but due to the spirit of the Greek soldier, he felt severely betrayed by them. The feeling of betrayal was an extreme situation of the emotion of not being understood.*

CONVINCING ANOTHER SPIRIT TO GO BACK

The stuck spirit usually is not released by itself, but it may get released when we do a past-life regression. However, many spirits die as part of their life-plan and have no real purpose left from the soul's perspective. They can be convinced to leave when made aware of their life-plan. *Like, I've had clients whose dead grandparents' spirits were attached to them out of love and anxiety and who left when convinced that it was time to let go.*

Also, spirits who are not aware that they are dead are ready to leave when they are made aware. Even if a life purpose is unfulfilled, the spirit can be convinced to join the light, asked to heal and come back and join a parallel body which has similar energies, if it still needs to remain on Earth. Usually, when the spirits go back, they realize that the karmic retribution has been achieved and there is no need to come back.

> *I had a client who had severe spondilitis. She came for a regression therapy, during which we went into the root cause of the back pain in her shoulder. In the session, she saw herself as a man about four hundred years back. He had a terrible temper and often beat his wife. One day he killed his wife in anger. This*

man was punished, by his community. He had to carry a log on his back on which he was to be hanged. He died while carrying the log in a forest. The spirit of the man however did not go into the Light as it was absorbed in thoughts of guilt and remorse. It did not realize it is dead or that life is over. It kept reliving the guilt time and again.

Hence, in spite of death of the body, the spirit kept carrying the log on its back and remained in the forest. That part of the soul energy remained frozen at that point of time, and rejoined another fragment of its own soul when the soul energy reincarnated as my client. At an energy level, the log represented the emotional burden the soul was carrying because it was unable to let go. During therapy, we had to convince the soul to let go of the negative energy of remorse so that it could forgive itself, release the log, accept the love of God and go in the light. As a woman, this client had been facing abuse from her husband since several years who had been the same soul as his wife in that life.

When the spirit realized, it had compensated for its crime and had learnt to respect the weaker sex, it went away as its soul-lesson was learnt. This woman had had shoulder pain since several years, which vanished after this session.

I suspected this to be the case with the spirit who was attached to Dev. The Greek soldier's spirit seemed to be hovering on Earth, seemingly frozen in that life. Whenever it appeared to Dev, it appeared in the attire it had died in as the Greek soldier. It also kept reliving the same feelings again and again. That is why Dev repeatedly saw him getting defeated by the lions. The spirit was apparently consumed with energies of failure, revenge and frustration. Because its intensity was so strong, it was activating these negative feelings in Dev repeatedly by making him focus on similar energies from the environment. Probably, the spirit was not even aware it had died.

LOVE HEALS

The process of energy healing requires that the soul of the person is willing to accept the positive energy of love from another person or soul. He should openly allow that energy to enter him for healing to take place. Dev was unwilling to trust anyone. He was focused on negative emotions. Hence, he had created mental walls, which prevented him from accepting love or healing energy. These negative feelings were originating from the Greek soldier's life, as he was unmotivated to being healed. This was because healing required positive energy, which meant letting go of vengeance that the soldier was unwilling to do. Hence, we had to find a way to convince the Greek soldier to let go.

HEALING THE HEART

The Greek Soldier's weak point was his bleeding heart, that was also the symbol of both his failure and defeat. He used the image of the bleeding heart to trigger similar feelings of mental anguish in Dev. The heart had been torn apart by lions when the Greek soldier died. Dev used to feel tormented each time he saw the bleeding heart. Also, he used to comment each time he regretted not having been able to rescue the girl he loved. Hence, the need for revenge was fuelled by the injustice done to the girl. If she could be called from the celestial plane, he could be motivated to let go of the need for revenge and allow healing to take place.

My plan was to go back into that life to the moment when the Greek soldier had died, call the spirit of the girl to heal him at the spot he died, and then ask him if he had joined the Light. If the answer was no, Dev had to tell him to go to the Light with the girl. I was hoping for co-operation from the Greek soldier because it would enable his spirit to stay with the spirit of the girl he loved. Once the Greek Soldier was healed, a large chunk of stuck negative energy in Dev's mind would get freed. That way Dev could gain control over his mind much faster.

DEV'S PAST LIFE AS THE GREEK SOLDIER REVISITED

We started the hypnosis session. As usual, Dev went into a trance. He saw the lion fight within five minutes of getting into trance.

"Ok, I see it!" he said. "It's clearer than it's ever been."

"What do you mean?"

"It is as if I am there," he nodded and focused, "there are more lions."

"How many are there?"

"Six," he replied, counting mentally.

"I kill the first one," he continued in an excited tone, his face looking jubilant. I wanted to ensure that the girl was around before the Greek soldier got killed. So, I directed Dev to focus on her.

"Do you see the girl around?"

"Yes, she is sitting next to the king," he replied.

"What is she doing?"

"She is smiling when I kill the first lion," Dev said.

"I can hear the crowds cheer," he spoke with wonder, since in his first session he had not heard any sounds. The sounds made that life all the more real to Dev.

"Then, I kill the second lion, then the third," he continued narrating.

"The fourth one gets me. I would've killed it but another one comes at my back. It is pulling me down. The one in the front attacks my heart. I have fallen down," he said.

"What happens next?"

"Nothing. It's over…Two lions attacked at the same time. I was unable to defeat both together," he said, shaking his head in disappointment.

"What about the girl?"

"She stabs herself," Dev said focusing on her again. "She… takes a knife from the king and stabs herself. First she stabs herself vertical, then across the stomach," Dev concluded.

So, the girl had committed suicide. I had to call her spirit fast to his side before she left for the celestial plane.

"Call her. Ask her to come to you."

"Yeah, she's there," he said, nodding his head.

"How does she look?"

"Beautiful," he said with a sigh, and continued focusing. "Her eyes."

"What is the colour of her eyes?"

"They are … green," he said tenderly.

"Okay…What is she wearing?"

"A gown … her hair are tied back as usual," he replied.

"As usual? Did she usually tie her hair?"

"…She ties it because I like it that way…"

"What colour is her hair?"

"Golden, brown," he replied.

"How old is she?"

"She is young," he replied.

"Tall or short?"

"She is… small built," he replied.

"How is her attitude generally? Is she shy or talkative?"

"She is docile and obedient…likes to talk with me only," he replied.

"Okay. Does she want to heal you? Ask her?"

"Yes," he replied.

"Ok … Then, tell her to give you energy. Ask her to send love to your heart."

"Ok, she is," he replied, nodding an agreement again.

"Tell her to use the energies of the universe to heal your heart. Ask her to put her hand on your heart and send energy. See it heal."

"Yes," he said, nodding his head to indicate it was happening.

"Tell her to put green colour and light pink. Green is the colour of the heart chakra and pink denotes love."

"Yes, she has," he said. I was surprised that she did it before my instruction. Her spirit knew what to do, which colours to use. A guiding force from the Light was helping our sessions.

"Is it healing?"

"A little," he nodded.

"Now, also ask her to hug you."

"But, how can she hug me? I am bleeding all over," he spoke, revulsion showing on his face.

"It doesn't matter. Let her hug you. That will send more energy to your heart."

"Okay, she is," he spoke after some time.

"Ok, keep receiving her energies for some time, till your heart is completely healed. Tell me when it is done."

He was quiet for some time. "Ok … She is going now."

I was surprised to hear she was leaving, when I had not instructed his mind to send her away. "Where is she going? Is your heart healed completely?"

"It is half healed," he replied.

"Then ask her to stay and heal it more."

"No," Dev refused in a firm tone, on behalf of the Greek soldier.

"Why not?"

"I can't accept it anymore. I have to take revenge. My honour is at stake," he replied.

That was funny. How can your honour be at stake, when you're dead? Did the Greek soldier know he was dead? I had yet to ask him.

"She's gone now," he said.

"Where has she gone?"

"She's gone into the Light," he said. I made out from his expression that he could see the Light.

"Then you follow her."

"No, I can't," he replied.

"Why?"

"I have to take revenge," he replied again with a touch of steel in his voice.

"Revenge against whom?"

There was no answer. I told Dev to ask as himself.

"Ask the Greek soldier whom he wants to take revenge from? What does he say?"

"*Revenge against God,*" Dev spoke again on behalf of the Greek soldier. Whenever he spoke on behalf of the Greek soldier, his voice and tone changed to that of the Greek soldier. The Greek soldier had a more confident tone and his vocabulary usage reflected the way a soldier from the medieval European period would speak. I was confused about what to do next. I asked guidance from my spirit guides, since they always help when asked. Some thoughts or visuals flash in the mind suddenly as if somebody is actually answering. The answer is more felt than heard. Now, the answer which flashed was that I had to let the spirit of the Greek soldier do whatever it wanted to right now. That was probably the only way to let out the negative feelings from his mind. The spirit wanted to take revenge from God.

So, I told him to call God and take his revenge. I was a little sceptical on whether it was appropriate to call God and whether God would be offended by the Greek soldier's anger but my spirit guides assured me that God could handle it.

"Ok, call God then, and you can take your revenge."

"Call God?" he questioned in a surprised tone as if he could not believe God could be called.

"Yes, send a request to the universe asking God to come. He will come."

He was quiet for a few seconds. I wondered what was happening. I was not certain myself whether God would come or not, but I trusted the insight, and acted on it.

"Ok, he's there. He looks different." Dev said. I was relieved.

"How different? How does he look? What is he wearing?"

"He is wearing some kind of a robe. He is big." Dev replied, a confused expression on his face, as if he did not understand what he saw. "He has armour around him."

That was strange. I, too, had never thought of a God with armour around him. "Which God is he? Ask."

"It is the Greek God of war," he replied in a slightly amazed tone. Neither Dev nor I had expected God to appear in the attire of a Greek God. But that he did, made it all the more real. "Maybe that is why he is wearing the armour."

"Yes," Dev nodded, looking unsure of how to deal with him.

"Tell him whatever is there on your mind."

"I don't want to say anything," he said. "I want revenge."

"Take revenge, then."

"How?" he asked me, "I want a fight."

"Ok, do that. Invite him to fight with you."

I waited for some time. Dev looked more confused.

"I can't hit him," he said.

"Why not?"

"He has got something around him. I can't reach him," Dev replied.

"Is it some kind of a shield?"

"Yes," he nodded, clarity dawning on him on what it was around him.

"What is its energy made of? You ask for the same weapons he has and then attack him."

"I can't," he said.

"Why not?"

"It's made of love," he said.

"So, you see armour made of love around you," I told him, hoping to trick him into accepting love.

"I can't," he said, "I can't do that. I have to take revenge."

"But to take revenge from God, you have to be like him."

"No, I don't want to take revenge from him," Dev said firmly, changing his mind.

That, he did not want to take revenge from God was a major revelation for Dev. Until now, anger against God was a major reason of turmoil in Dev's mind. Calling him the devil, his mother complained that he refused to follow religious rituals in his family. This reinforced his belief that he was bad. Dev often spoke against God in anger, blaming God for his sufferings. That these feelings in his current life were a carry-over from his life as the Greek soldier was surprising.

Now, during the session, for the first time he realized that God was not bad. God came to him with a shield of love around him. He realized it was pointless to fight with an energy made of love.

Dev never spoke with anger about God again, though he did continue to claim that he did not believe in God.

"Ok, then you can follow the girl and go to the Light," I told the spirit of the Greek soldier again, hoping to catch him unawares and send him into the Light.

"No, I can't. I have to take revenge," he replied.

You said you don't want revenge from God."

"I have to take revenge from the people who betrayed me," he said.

"Who are those?"

"My father and my sister," he said.

His father and his sister were his parents in his current life, as we had found out in the first session.

"Forgive them. Let go."

"No, I can't forgive them till the day I die," he said.

Now, this was a statement which showed that the Greek soldier's spirit did not realize he was dead. How could a dead person use the words – 'till the day I die?'

"Does the Greek soldier know he is dead? Ask him directly."

"He is silent," he replied.

"Tell him."

Dev nodded and told him.

"What does he say?"

"He looked up. He is confused. He's looking around," Dev replied, paused and continued, "Ok, he believes it now…He is going into the light."

Phew! The Greek soldier's spirit finally realized he was dead. He had been sitting in the same spot since the last 2000 years, without realizing he was dead.

"Ok, follow him. See that he joins the girl."
"Yes, he has," Dev replied.
"Keep track of him. See where he goes."
"Ok, he is gone now," Dev said after a few seconds.
"Where?"
"He is sitting there in the light talking to her," he said.
"Can you make out what they are talking about?"
"No, but they look happy," he replied after some focusing.
"What about his heart…Is it healed completely?"
"No…It will heal only after I achieve the purpose of his life. It is half-healed now," Dev replied.

I realized the seriousness of the situation when he said that. There were no short cuts to heal Dev. He would have to pursue the path the Greek soldier sought, to achieve his purpose of life. Dev could not get the peace of mind he desired until the bleeding heart healed completely. We still were not clear about what specifically was Dev to do to achieve the Greek soldier's purpose of life. Would it be fulfilled by joining the army or the police or did he need to do something else to heal himself from the anguished heart?

As his therapist, I did not want him to take his choices lightly anymore as the soul had already spent several lives trying to achieve the purpose of life of the Greek soldier. Now, it was high time that the Greek soldier's heart got healed and Dev felt at peace. So, next, I took him to the celestial plane. This session is called a Life between Life session as it is the place where the soul stays between two lives and where it makes the plan for its present life. We wanted to know what the life-plan was for this life. What was it specifically that Dev needed to work at for the Greek soldier's heart to be healed completely?

CONCLUSION OF THE SESSION

When Dev woke up, after his Life between Life session, I asked him how he felt when the girl came to heal him.

"Spooky," he replied.

"Why?"

"It was weird, almost real," he replied.

This was a turning point in Dev's therapy. After this session, Dev started believing more in the work we were doing, and hence, allowed his conscious mind-set to adapt to his subconscious requirements.

CHAPTER 12

LIFE BETWEEN LIVES

A BRIEF DESCRIPTION OF THE LIFE BETWEEN LIFE PLANE

Where do We Live When We Die?

THE IDEA THAT WE continue to live after we die or what we commonly know as an 'afterlife' is not easy to comprehend but the fact is that memories of past lives exist. Working on these memories has a therapeutically healing effect. This implies that there has to be a space where we live after we die on Earth, and before we are reborn again. This space is called *the life between life plane*. It has also been referred to as the celestial plane, heaven, the white Light, the Other Side etc. The life between life space is considered to be our real home, whereas Earth is like a school where we come to learn some lessons and go back.

It is only positive frequencies that can be experienced in the celestial plane as it is at a higher dimension. It is free of all negativities and problems that arise due to limitations of time and space on the physical dimension. Our spirits have bodies as on Earth but they are made of a lighter substance/energy. We, as celestial spirits, are connected with God all the time and we feel whole and loved, not alienated as on Earth, due to an illusion of separation. In the Life between Life space, we have memories of all our incarnations on Earth and on other planes of the universe. In fact, our spirit makes the life-plan for the next incarnation after reviewing the plan executed in the previous life. We take up those lessons in the next life that have been left unfinished in previous lives.

> *Life between Life sessions are needed to find out conceptual details about the life-plan with the aim of understanding the main purpose of life. They also help to find out which emotional lesson is planned to be learnt when a problem is being encountered.*

THE MAKING OF A LIFE-PLAN

The first step, while making the life-plan, for the soul is to decide the specific lessons it wants to learn during its incarnation on Earth. Then, the soul decides on how it is going to learn those lessons. The soul plans to learn several of its lessons through family relationships (family includes parents, caregivers, relatives and associations through marriage), as one cannot escape family ties. Family members may be our biggest critics and hence may also be our most valuable teachers.

Family members become teachers because from their behaviour we learn what to do and what not to do. For example, if a person has an impatient father, his/her lesson may be to not lose patience as s/he may have been exposed to its ill-effects from childhood. We usually, choose those souls as family members with whom we need karmic healing. Hence, there are frictions in families. Other than choosing our family for learning emotional lessons and for karmic healing, we may also choose a particular family because we feel we need that kind of upbringing financially or socially, to achieve our main purpose of life. Very often, our biggest challenge to move forward in life is to learn to undo beliefs and values, which make us lower our self-esteem. Several of these beliefs and values come from the kind of upbringing we have.

> *Dev had chosen his family keeping all the above considerations in mind. His family members were his biggest critics, and hence his biggest teachers of what to do and what not to do. He needed karmic healing with them. And, he also needed the kind of upbringing, values, conflicts and financial support they provided, to achieve his main purpose of life. The emotional patterns from*

the Greek soldier's life were repeated in Dev's present life. In his present life, as in the Greek soldier's life, he was in conflict with the views of his parents. It was a love-hate relationship from both sides.

His parents behaved almost the same way with him as they had in the life of the Greek soldier. In the life of the Greek soldier, the king, his father always expected him to perform and win him accolades. The Greek soldier had started fighting when he was nine years old, and won a war when he was fourteen. This shows that as a child he was under pressure to perform as an adult. When he did not obey the king, and posed a threat to his pride, he was thrown in the lions' den. The step-sister of the Greek soldier was always dishonest in her dealings with him and favoured the king at the cost of ditching him.

In his present life also, Dev's father showed love to him only when he performed. He expressed cynical disapproval whenever he lost even if it was at a school game. Hence, Dev was always under intense pressure to perform and felt that if he did not perform, nobody would love him. Dev's mother sympathized with him sometimes but spoke negatively about him to his father and other people. When he overheard, he felt ditched.

The emotional lessons had got carried over from that life to this life because he had been unable to learn them in that life. Two obvious lessons involved were forgiveness and self-love for Dev. Maybe, his parents had to learn the concept of unconditional love and acceptance in face of defiance, being non-judgmental etc.

Dev's case is a visible example of a life-plan and how lessons get carried over from past lives. The same happens with all of us. We face most conflicts in our relationships with our loved ones as most lessons are attached there.

THE CONCEPT OF DEATH

Death is also planned in the life-plan. We do not die unless we choose to. Subconsciously, we are always asked before death whether we want to leave and our body dies only if we silently agree to leave. The Death point is referred to as an exit-point in some books, an apt term because death implies essentially, an exit from the Earth plane for the soul.

A life-plan has four-five exit points planned, given the level of challenges we opt for. If we want to die early, we may plan to die through an accident, a heart attack, a disease, an ambush as in war etc. But, we may not take these exit points and die after living a complete life as of old age. The exit point is also a transit point. Along with exit points, difficulties are clubbed which may be so intense that they may make the soul want to leave the Earth plane instead of staying and solving the problem. If the soul stays on, it would have to change its vibrational frequency more towards positivity, inspite of repeatedly facing several problems.

However, if the soul learns its lessons, it can recover while feeling positive from the crisis during its life. This would happen in a way that leads to soul evolution more than success at a material level. Often, the soul loses on wealth or success in conventional terms as it rises to a higher level of energy consciousness.

However, if the soul chooses to die with the problem instead, that is equally acceptable. The soul may choose that it is not yet ready for the lesson and postpone it. It can learn the planned lesson by planning the same problem in the next life-time, like Dev was doing, life after life.

> *However, though death is a relief for the leaving soul and hence need not be feared, Death cannot be used as an escape from problems. Suicide is usually not an exit point.*

When a person refuses to grow emotionally, either by waiting for death, dying early or by committing suicide, it is time wasted for the soul as the soul has to relive the same life, all over again, with the same emotional problems for mastering its soul lessons. The life-plan is virtually repeated till the soul is able to achieve its purpose of life. *Dev had been repeating the same life-plan since two thousand years only because he chose to die early almost each time and still wanted to.*

THE COUNCIL

When a soul makes a life-plan on heaven, it takes help from his/her spirit guides. Once the plan is made, it has to be submitted to a Council in heaven. The Council is like an Editorial Board. According to reports given by diverse people who have journeyed to the LBL plane under hypnosis, the Council has about twelve evolved souls. They have the appearance of old wise men or women.

The Council checks on each soul plan and decides whether it is feasible or not. The feasibility needs to be assessed because the soul may make too difficult a plan in order to learn its soul lessons fast. For example, a person may plan emotional setback and financial separation from a lover; or a fatal heart attack may follow a business failure one after another/at short intervals in its life on Earth. His situation, therefore, may get so traumatic that the soul may decide to die rather than deal with the sadness and rise to a higher positive awareness. Had the heart attack and separation happened at spaced time intervals, the person may have had the zeal to fight back and recover to being optimistic again after each setback. Recovery would have led to learning of soul lessons of emotional maturity and making the body adapt to a healthier life-style. The conversion of negative energy arisen from the setbacks into positive learning would have raised soul frequency to a higher grade. The soul arising from setbacks would be wiser and healthier, by choice.

So, the plan needs to be subdued such that the difficulties encountered are spaced out well and lead to learning of the emotional lessons, rather than giving up on them as usually happens when the soul ends up with suicide or death. The Council makes suggestions on how the plan can be mellowed down so that the soul is able to achieve his/her evolutionary purpose of life.

The final decision, however, lies with the soul. The soul may/may not accept the Council's suggestions.

THE HALL OF RECORDS

The Hall of Records, also called the Hall of Akashic Records, is the hall where the records about all our lives are stored in full detail. In simple terms, it is like a Karmic library in heaven. All our experiences from the point of conception, as a soul are systematically recorded at an energy level in the form of feelings, thoughts and creations in separate files for each soul. Karma is a measure of energy exchange and the records have details of each event which had an impact on the soul as a complete visual and sensory experience and the positive or negative energy emanating due to the soul's activity. Any life we need to review can be found there.

The lives are stored systematically. Each theme of life has a separate record book. For example, if our main soul lesson is learning to cultivate patience, then there would be a separate record book which shows the number of lives we have lived to learn patience.

During a hypnotic session, the records can be visualized in the form of doorways to make the process easier. When a person goes into the Hall of Doorways, he sees the records of his lives in the form of separate doors. There are a number of doors, indicating the number of lives the person has already lived for achieving the purpose of life which the soul wants to achieve in this present life. Usually, people live four to twelve lives in one theme. Hence, they may see several doors there.

DEV'S FIRST LIFE BETWEEN LIFE SESSION

We continue with the previous session.

Since it was clear that Dev's bleeding heart would not completely heal until he helped the Greek soldier achieve his purpose of life, I next took Dev to the pre-life-planning stage of his current life to help him find out about his life purpose more specifically. As I decided that I had to take him on the spur of the moment in the middle of this session I had no time to educate him about what to expect there. He knew the concept of a life-plan but he had no idea about the Council or the work it does. I had not ever before mentioned it as I did not think it was needed. I did not expect that he would meet the Council members. I first planned to ask him to go to the Hall of Doorways and then I planned to guide him to enter the Life between Life space from a door which opened there from the Hall of Doorways.

Thus, I said to Dev, in continuation of the session.

"Ok, then, we will go to the Life-between-Life space to find out how your purpose of life can be achieved. Go to the Hall of Doorways. You will see yourself in a hall with a number of doors. When you see yourself there, say 'yes.'"

"Yes," he replied.

"Ok, how many doors do you see there?"

"Twelve," he replied.

"Ok, now go to a door which opens to the pre-life-planning stage of your current life. When you see yourself outside a particular door, say yes."

"Yes," he replied.

"How does the door look like?" I asked him details so that he would get more intensely involved in the experience.

"Regular," he shrugged.

"What is it made of?"

"Wood," he said.

"Ok, now as I count 5 to 1, open the door and be in the pre-life-planning stage of your current life – 5, 4, 3, 2, 1. NOW! Be there."

"Yes," he replied.

"Close the door behind you. What do you see?"

In the pre-life-planning stage, at this point, people usually say they see themselves in clouds, in a beautiful garden or in nothingness. They feel light and relaxed. The expression on their face soothes down as they imbibe the purity of the place. The celestial dimension is rejuvenating for the soul. They sometimes also find their spirit friends around them who are guiding them in their present life. They have complete details of the life-plan and answer the questions. Nobody, I knew had seen themselves in front of the Council. The Council is a high authority body. One has to ask specifically to be taken there, if needed. Since I had no plans to take Dev to the Council, as usual, I expected Dev's guides to answer our questions.

"I see some people sitting around a table," Dev replied.

I was surprised. Dev seemed to have reached the Council.

However, I wasn't sure this was the Council yet. Dev had no idea that something like the Council existed. How could he reach there when I had not even instructed him to?

"How many are there? How do they look?"

"…Twelve," he paused for less than a second and replied. He could not have known there are twelve members in the Council because I had never told him so. Nor was he the kind who read books on Spirituality.

"They look old," he continued. That confirmed that this was the Council.

"One old man is talking to me," Dev continued further.

I was again surprised… I had not yet directed him to ask questions. It seemed they were waiting for him in the Council.

"What is he saying?"

"Ma-gsi-mus," Dev replied. "I can't follow clearly. He is Greek. He is speaking with a strong accent."

"What is that?"

"It seems to be my name," he paused and said. "Maybe that was the name of the Greek soldier."

"Okay. Is it Maximus?"

"Something like that…" he concentrated and replied.

"Focus," I touched him on the third eye so that he could get his name clearly.

"The g and s are together. It is not separate…I can't pronounce it…It's in their language…it is spoken differently…" Dev shrugged his shoulders.

"Ok, shall we let it be Maximus?"
"Yes..." he nodded.
"What does the Old Man look like? Focus!"
"He's like ...the Greeks... Like Maximus ... He is talking his language."
"Okay, he must be coming from that life. How does he look?"
"He is very fair, almost white. Old, tall, skinny... Bald with long hair at the back. ...He is wearing a long white robe, talks with an accent," Dev replied in pauses.
"Okay. What is he saying? Focus!"
"The purpose of this life is victory," Dev replied in a heavier voice as if someone else was speaking through him. *"Maximus, you have to heal several people with whom you did injustice because your heart was full of revenge,"* Dev was addressing himself as YOU meaning the Old Man was speaking through him. "Your suffering of the life of the Greek soldier continues because of the injustice you did in earlier lives," he continued.
"What does he mean by injustice? Ask?"
"If a person dies a planned death, it is not injustice but if it is forced before exit time, then it is injustice," Dev replied on behalf of the Old Man.
(Dev himself had no idea that death, accidents and illnesses are planned, or that there is a time for death. I had not discussed the concept of the life-plan with him in detail yet. Moreover, when I did discuss it with him later, when he was in a fully conscious state, he was not completely convinced by the concept.)
"Does that mean that you forced people to die before their planned time?"
"Yes. After the life of Maximus, you lived several lives where you killed other souls. You were given several chances to heal those souls but each time, you ruined your chances. Earlier you killed because your heart was full of revenge. Later you killed for pleasure," Dev continued. His voice was heavier than usual and had a slower pitch.

"Ok, ask, how can you heal the souls you have already killed in earlier lives now?"

"You have to give back the purpose of life to those souls whom you took it away from," Dev continued to speak in a heavy voice.

"How can you do that?"

"Doing what you are good at. You have to heal or destroy other people who are doing substance or actions to harm their own souls." Dev answered. "What does that mean?"

"There are people using violence like you did in earlier lives. They are doing injustice to other souls while their own souls are suffering. You have to get victory over those souls. You have to fight for the truth. When you heal those souls, your own soul would be healed," he continued.

"How can you fight for the truth? Ask? By what means?"

"You have been given the means. You have to do what you are good at," he replied on behalf of the Old man.

"What are you good at? Ask?"

"Fighting," Dev replied.

"Fighting how, by what means? Ask?"

"By means where the intention is to fight for the truth and not destruction. You have got this chance after several lives to make up for all the lives where you were full of revenge and did injustice," continued the Old man through Dev. *"After this chance, you won't get another chance for several life-times. Whatever you do in this life will come back to you in this life itself,"* Dev spoke.

"Does that mean that if you use violence for destruction it will come back to you in this life itself?"

"*Yes, it does,*" Dev said heavily. *Since his conscious mind was obsessed with using violence for destruction, it was a shock for him to hear the opposite from his subconscious.* His conscious mind took a much longer time to accept these words of wisdom or incorporate them as a way of life.

"So, ask him what can you do to be on the right track?"

"You will be given continuous guidance," Dev replied for the Old Man. *"You will be given messages. You were given guidance in earlier*

lives also but you did not heed those messages," he continued.

"So, what can you do now to ensure you would heed those messages? Ask?"

"Listen. The message is given to you before the anger comes... You have to listen to the voice in your head before the feeling of rage consumes you," said the Old Man.

"What can you do to train your mind to listen? Ask?"

"You need to be calm first thing in the morning." said the Old Man

"How can you do that? Ask. Can they be more specific?"

"Exercise and meditation. When you are calm, you will hear what your heart speaks," Dev said.

(Dev used to practice yoga in the mornings which included meditation too. Yoga used to effectively calm him down but he wasn't a regular. Often, he used to skip to body building exercises like dumbbells, which somehow fuelled his needs for indulging in violence. The Old Man was suggesting Yoga exercise since he mentioned meditation with exercise, but he could not be more specific. The exact choice of the path was Dev's own.

"What else can you do? Ask?"

"You have to forgive some people, Maximus," said the Old Man.

"Can he be more specific? Ask?"

"You have to forgive your father and your sister. You have to forgive all the people you did injustice to and who killed you in successive lives," said the Old man.

(The Old Man was probably referring to the life where Dev as the tribal Roman soldier had killed his own king for money. In his next life as the Greek soldier, Maximus, the same king was his father who had got him killed.)

"Okay and what about the woman you loved in that life. Is she there in your present life also?"

"She is there. She has been there all along," replied the Old Man.

"How will you recognize her? Ask if he can give a clue?"

"You will recognize her when you see her. But she is not the purpose of this life. She is waiting for you to heal. The love was

pure. Because of that love, you have been given another chance," said the Old Man.

Dev looked relieved to hear that. For him, that was something to look forward to. Otherwise, he was being asked to leave the path of violence and destruction when these were the only things he found thrilling in his life.

"What is your purpose of this life? Ask?"

"*The purpose is to heal your heart by healing the people whose purpose of life you took away in earlier lives,*" said the Old Man.

"Which path do you have to follow to achieve this purpose? Ask?"

"*You are a soldier. You have to be a soldier. You can follow your own path or you can follow the path of Maximus,*" replied the Old Man.

"What does that mean? Can he be more specific? Ask?"

"*You are our soldier of justice. The path is not important. How it is followed is important. You have got carried away in earlier life-times. You were a soldier in the army. You were sent to prevent them but you joined with them,*" said Dev on behalf of the Old Man.

"Yes... So, which path can you follow? Are the police better or the army or is there any other path?"

"*It is your choice. You can follow the path of Maximus or follow the path where killing is the last resort,*" the Old Man repeated. "*You started killing to obey orders and later you killed anyone who came in front of you. You took several innocent lives. You have to heal those souls. That is your purpose. What you do to achieve that purpose does not matter. The intention behind it matters.*"

That was as specific as they could get. At the level of feelings, the army or the police did not matter. The important message was that Dev was being asked to change his whole pattern of thinking. He had to forgive his parents and not get carried away into a life of crime, which he often mused upon.

"Is there anyone on Earth who can guide you? Ask?"

"*The girl... She knows the path. She is the only one who knows,*" said the Old Man.

"When will you find her?"

"*You will find her when the time comes. You will get one chance to be with her. If you don't take it, she will go again,*" said the Old Man. After that, there was a long pause in which Dev was quiet.

"Okay. Is there anything else he is saying?"

"No," Dev replied, now, in his own voice.

"Is there anything the other council members are saying?"

"No." Only one Old Man from the Council had spoken to him. Maybe he was his guide in charge.

"Anything else you need to ask about your purpose of life?"

"No," he said affirmatively, indicating he had got enough information.

"Okay, then thank the Council members and the Old Man and come back to the Hall of Doorways."

"Yes, I am there," he replied when he was out.

"Now, Go out of the Hall of doorways."

"Yes… The Greek soldier is there," he said suddenly.

"What is he saying?"

"*You have to finish my purpose of life. When you do that, only then my heart will be healed.*" Dev spoke on behalf of Maximus, the Greek soldier.

"How does his heart look now?"

"It is half healed now… He is saying something more."

"What?"

"*The path you follow has to be righteous,*" Dev continued in the Greek soldier's authoritative voice.

"Is he giving any guidance on which path to follow? Ask?"

"*The path will be shown to you when the time is right. You have to follow your heart. Do what feels right in your heart,*" Dev continued.

"When will the right time come? Ask?"

"*Two years from now. You will take two years to find the right path,*" replied the Greek soldier.

"Okay… Is there anything else he wants to say?"

"No," replied Dev in his own voice.

"Okay, then ask him to go back to heaven. See him going in the Light."

"Yes... He is gone now."

"Okay, then I'll count you up...1, 2...20. Let all this be integrated in your mind when you sleep tonight. Feel light, refreshed and relaxed as you get up... 1, 2, 3, 4, and 5 – Eyes Open, wide awake."

Dev took some time to get up since he had been in a state of deep trance.

We discussed the messages he had received when he woke up.

CONCLUSION OF THE SESSION

Dev was virtually suggested a whole shift in his thinking patterns, which also included forgiving people he held deep grudges against. He wasn't convinced by that argument as he still felt deeply betrayed by them. However, it was a new perspective opening up to him.

He agreed that forgiveness and discretion concerning which cause is just and which is unjust, were his two main life-lessons. He could not join the army and blindly follow orders as the political decisions taken, may not have been for giving justice to people; there may be several innocent lives lost. He had to decide by himself that the work he did would lead to justice, and not depend on hearsay or orders given by others. If he spread injustice again for whatever external reason, his soul would not be able to get the peace it desired. His decision to opt for the army could not help him achieve his soul purpose, as he would have to obey orders blindly; whereas, an alternative profession of being soldier-like as in the police system, could offer him more room for decision-making.

We ended our discussion at that, planning to do a Parts Integration between the police and the army in the next session. His desire to be in the army was obsessively strong. We had to find out more about why it was so strong.

CHAPTER 13

SENT OUT FROM HEAVEN

DEV WAS IN A jubilant mood as he sat down for his next session.

"I have decided to join the army. I am sure now."

I was perturbed on hearing that, since in the previous session, he had been warned against joining the army by the Council.

"Why? In the last session, you were told that you took several innocent lives while serving in the army. Isn't it better to choose a profession where killing is the last resort?"

"Come On...You can't blame me for those lives. That is not my fault. I was just doing my job. I was given orders. I just obeyed them," he said in a casual tone.

"They don't think so up there. You have to heal all those souls in this life whose purpose of life you took away by killing them before time. In the army, you may again indulge in unjustified violence."

"I will not. I will destroy all the enemies of my country. I will fight for Mother India."

"You can do the same while working in the police as well. In the police, you will have more powers. You can choose where you need to fight, for justice."

"Yeah...but...the police is not the main fighting force..." he shrugged, "there is not much thrill in that... they use small pistols. I want military action, adventure. I will join the army," he spoke assertively, with his fists clenched, a grin on his face at the anticipated power of being in the army.

While in the earlier session, Dev was convinced after a lot of explanation that the police service is suitable for his personality, in this session he went back to his fascination of joining the army.

He did not seem to care about the fact that he may make the same mistakes again that he did in earlier lives. Probably because he could not yet agree that it was a mistake. According to him, he sacrificed his life for his country in his earlier lives and if people lost their lives in the process of him becoming a powerful soldier, it was just too bad but he could not be blamed for it personally. It was part of his job. "By wearing the uniform, you may believe you are working for justice but you may again fail to work for the weak and oppressed in a meaningful manner. If you use your strength unjustly again, it will come back to you in this same life. The Old Man told you that was the life-plan."

"I won't. I am sure. I will die for my country fighting in war... How great is that?" he looked at me with a twinkle in his eye, nodding his head assertively. "Yes... I will be a great soldier."

The feeling of success as a soldier from earlier lives was pulling him.

"Ok, let's do a parts integration. We will talk to the part that wants to be a soldier and the other part inside you which wants you to consider other options like the police..."

"Ok..." he replied with a resigned tone. "Let's try that but I am more or less sure," he said. "Are you willing to try with an open mind?"

"Yes, I am," he replied with more vigour this time.

PARTS INTEGRATION

In the process of Parts Integration, as explained in detail in chapter 6 *(Towards a life of crime),* we basically start interrogating two opposing personalities of the client's soul by asking WHY questions. Then we keep adding questions to the statements each personality makes subconsciously, until we understand the core intentions behind each choice.

I helped Dev get into the semi-trance by suspending his hands from the elbows. His palms were stretched out, straight and open.

"Ok, now call the personality which wants to go in the army on your left hand."

"Yes," he nodded indicating it was there.

"Who does this personality look, feel and speak like?"

"It is the guy who killed the lions," he replied.

"Maximus…now call the personality which wants you to consider other options like the police on your right hand."

"Yes," he replied again indicating that a personality had shown up.

"Who does this personality look, feel and sound like?"

"It's me," he replied.

That was interesting. The personality who wanted to go in the army was that of Maximus, not Dev's own, whereas his own self wanted to join other professions.

"Ok, let's talk to the person on the left hand. Shall I address him as Maximus?"

"Yes," Dev replied in a louder pitch, the change in tone indicating Maximus was taking over. The personality liked being addressed by his name.

"Maximus, why do you want to go in the army?"

"I belong there. I have always been a soldier and always will be a soldier," Dev replied in the Greek soldier's accent.

"You have always been a soldier, why do you want to be one now?"

"I am good at fighting… I have never been defeated," he replied.

"Why do you want to continue being good at fighting?"

"It makes me strong," he replied.

"Why do you want to be strong?"

"I want to fight for justice," he replied.

"Why do you want to fight for justice?"

"I have to take revenge." His tone was loud and aggressive now. *Fighting for justice and taking revenge were two separate intentions which he seemed to consider as synonymous.*

"Take revenge from whom?'

"From all those who inflicted injustice on me," he replied in an aggressive tone.

"Who inflicted injustice on you?"

"The people who betrayed me," he replied.

"Who betrayed you?"

"My father and my sister and others," he replied. His tone still reflected anger.

"You want to go in the army to take revenge on them?"

"Yes! I will destroy all," he said decisively.

Maximus wanted to join the army to take personal revenge. That was disturbing because, unlike the primeval times when personal revenge was warranted, in modern times, one doesn't join the army to take personal revenge. Maximus was trying to apply the rules of ancient civilizations, onto the present age, as he thought that as a soldier, he could take personal revenge without getting punished.

"How will joining the army help you take revenge from those people?"

"I will kill them," he replied in a high-pitch tone.

"How will you kill them?"

"I will have weapons," he replied.

"Yes, but your father and sister are your parents in your current life. How will you destroy them?"

"I will destroy anybody who comes in my way…all those who cause injustice are my enemies," he replied.

"In the army, you are supposed to work for the country. How will you destroy your personal enemies? There are rules against using public weapons for personal gains."

"Rules can be bent. I will cause so much mass destruction that everyone will be destroyed," he replied.

"That may lead to unjust destruction."

"I don't care. I will kill all those who do injustice. I will be the biggest destroyer ever," he replied with a thrill in his tone

"What about fighting for justice? You said you wanted to fight for justice?"

"I will be fighting for justice…I will destroy each and every enemy of this country," he clarified.

"How will you know who is the enemy and who is innocent?"

"Anybody who is not on our side is my enemy," he replied.

"How will you know who is actually harming the country and who is not?"

"That is not my job. I take orders," he replied in a matter-of-fact tone.

"Even if you take orders, the onus of innumerable deaths lie on you."

"That is my job…My job is to destroy… I will destroy all the enemies. Nobody would dare come my way again," he replied in a soldier's tone, assertively.

"Do you know that Dev has been told that if he takes away people's lives, unjustly he will have to pay for it in this same life?"

"Let him pay for it. He will suffer, not I. I will take my revenge…I will burn this world," Maximus said in a sadistic tone.

It is possible that it was Maximus who was driving Dev to join the army in his previous lives as well. He had already caused massive destruction in previous lives but he wanted to repeat the same sequence in this life. Apparently, he was not concerned that he would hurt Dev, in the process. This was the dichotomy between the soul and spirit, the stuck soul fragment. The Greek soldier was misusing his negative power to rule over Dev, even if it destroyed his very essence of light, a possibility Dev had not realized up till now. I had to revive the part of his soul which was still connected to the Light by reviving his ability to feel.

"Do you like the sight of blood? How do you feel when you kill?"

"It makes me feel bad. It is as if a part of me has died," he replied.

"Then, why do you want to kill?"

"That is what soldiers do. Soldiers are not supposed to have feelings," he pointed out to me.

"If soldiers had feelings, would you still want to join the army?"

"No," he replied.

"So, if you had feelings you would rather use killing as the last resort. Is that right?"

"Yes," he replied, though he sounded confused.

"Ok, now, we will call the personality on the other hand, Dev."

"Ok," he replied in his own voice.

"Why do you consider other options like the police?"

"I want to do God's work to create and not destroy," he replied.

"How will you create and not destroy?"

"By choosing a profession where I can serve my country," he stated.

"What kind of profession?"

"Where I can work with loyalty and honesty, where killing is the last resort." he stated.

"Ok, so now both the parts want a profession where killing is the last resort. We have integration. Join both hands and take in the integrated energy in your heart."

"Yes," he nodded.

I guided him to join both his fists together, take them to his heart, open them and put them on his heart. "Take a deep breath and breathe in the integrated energies."

"Yes," he took a deep breath and relaxed.

"Both your personalities are integrated at a subconscious level and would work in consensus now. Now, keep your hands down. As I count you up, open your eyes. Feel refreshed, integrated and relaxed and let clarity come to your mind. 1, 2, 3, 4, 5. Eyes open! Wide awake."

DEV'S REALIZATION

Dev looked puzzled when he opened his eyes.

"This Maximus guy is evil," was his first statement. "He doesn't care if I suffer."

The parts integration process had helped him realize the distinction between his own and the Greek personality's mind.

CONCLUSION OF THE SESSION – SENT OUT FROM HEAVEN

Maximus, the Greek soldier had been sent to heaven with the girl he loved during our last session. However, after this session, it appears he was sent out of heaven again. He was consumed with feelings of revenge and these negative feelings could not be allowed in heaven which does not tolerate any negative frequencies. He chose to remain with those negative energies rather than stay with his lover in heaven. He was subsequently banned from entering heaven and had to meet the Council's Old Man from another route. We were also told in a subsequent session that he abandoned the woman he loved and died for, as the Greek soldier, in his subsequent lives. She was his lover in several of his later lives as well, but each time they got separated, because he got preoccupied with his pursuit for revenge.

She did not like unjust violence. He chose violence over her wisdom repeatedly, initially insisting he had to fight to earn money for her. He thought that he went to wars for achieving his soul purpose; but all he did was spread destruction and got killed at a young age, each time. Thus, he could never achieve the purpose of his life of fighting for justice. The cycle of rebirth kept repeating. His claim of fighting for justice was actually a need to avenge himself which never got satiated. However much he killed in subsequent lives, as a criminal or a soldier, he could not bring back the honour he had lost as the Greek soldier. That moment never came again in the literal, physical sense. Hence, he kept fighting life after life, wanting to prove himself. The need was to let go of the energy of betrayal and revenge which consumed him, and to rise to a higher dimension of evolution. But all he did was to keep circling around in the same whirlpool of negativity, unable to break free as the spirit.

GENERAL AWARENESS – HOW SANE IS ASKING TO KILL ON ORDER?

In this session, we discovered that Dev was driven to go in the army because of an inner need for revenge and destruction, and not to serve the nation as he often claimed, at the conscious level. This session has a serious message because it makes us wonder about the number of soldiers recruited, having similar intentions at the subconscious level. Are the soldiers themselves aware that they may have inner selves, which can drive them insane in moments of action? There have been several cases where soldiers have killed indiscriminately. Some soldiers have also been put on trial and suspended. Yet, suspending a soldier after the deed is done doesn't help save innocent lives.

The core question, from the soul's perspective, is that if men are encouraged to suppress their compassion for fellow humans and kill on order, how can the system ensure that violence would not subsequently become a negative addiction. Why would men not use it to vent their frustration, whenever they have a weapon which can cause destruction?

Aren't we living in confused times where men are told that it is okay to kill if ordered, but otherwise they have to suppress their cultivated brutality. We first aggravate the violent tendencies and then ask the trainees to control it.

> *At an individual level, this amounts to a mother telling her child that, "it is okay to hit your younger brother when I say so but otherwise you can't." However, the child would hit his younger brother whenever he is angry with him whether it is justified or not, because he has seen that using brute strength works. As Maximus said – 'rules can be bent for convenience.'*

How much do we promote logical thinking in our children by teaching them different ways of reaction for the same cause? In a society where war heroes are historically glorified, a teenager who suffers from injustice instinctively hits back. The teenager feels like a war hero, who is fighting against injustice, but he gets rebuked by a society conscious of law and order.

The teenager then rebels because the reactions of people go against what has been taught to him since childhood. He feels betrayed by his education. Is the teenager at fault here, or is his education at fault?

Dev was clearly told by his spirit guide that *Violence should only be used as a last resort when there is no other way of curbing souls with a negative intention.* From soul evolution perspective, violence is not a means to suppress logical thinking. It is a tool for reinforcing a positive intention, to be used, as sparingly as possible, when nothing else works to stop the spread of negativity. As a tool for healing souls, violence needs to be used only as sparingly as doctors use surgery in place of medicines as a last resort to healing. As surgery can create more side effects than medicines, violence also leaves residue which is best avoided. Crushing of injustice through violence can lead to revengeful feelings, long term brutal behaviour, and escape from growth of intellect.

As the Old man indicated, violence can be used only with a very pure positive intention as in cases of self-defence, without any desire to gain self-respect or negative power from the act.

Otherwise, as in Dev's case, it leads to irresponsible thought and action, deviation from learning of soul lessons, and carries over negative karma which has to be subsequently repaid. When we ask people to obey orders blindly, we actually ask them to put a part of their brain in a freezer and not use it, and then when they behave like little kids in other aspects of life, we get upset. How sane are we in our expectations?

INTERPRETING A MESSAGE BY JESUS CHRIST

It's often appalling to note that though we live in a technically advanced civilization, our level of emotional training is still similar to the ancient man. At the level of emotional advancement, we still face the same issues, which we did when Jesus Christ was alive more than two thousand years ago. He spoke of peace and went unheard as a soul. He lives among us still, as a spirit, trying to get across the messages of God he came to spread. His messages were misinterpreted because humanity was not willing to evolve its consciousness. People wanted him to heal them, but did not learn from him and raise their consciousness to heal themselves. He became more a servant of mankind than a teacher, and therefore, could not change people's thought patterns from the core. In spite of all his service, whenever there was violence, we resorted to our animal instincts. We either chose to hit back or became meek and tolerated injustice. We saw fight or flight, but were not willing to let healing take root.

For example, when Jesus Christ said, *"If someone slaps you on your cheek, show him the other cheek,"* he most likely meant that we should build in ourselves the power to face negativity, ignore it as if it does not hurt and stick to our sense of right. The sentence suggests an act of defiance against bull strength. It does not ask us to tolerate hitting and run away; nor is it a command that one must be weak or humiliated.

For the chain of violence to break, it has to be confronted with a different line of thought, that is, the negative energy of violence should not be fuelled by our participation.

When negativity is confronted and ignored as foolishness, we detach from it. Negative thought cannot multiply when its existence gets threatened at the energy level. Conquering negativity at the level of thought or energy manifestation and not necessarily at the physical level, helps in soul evolution.

CHAPTER 14

SALVATION

DESIRE TO BECOME A MONK

WHEN DEV CAME IN for the next session, he was in a calmer mood.

He sat with his head down, a contemplative look on his face.

"So, how have you been?" I asked him, probingly.

"Good, I've been thinking," he looked up and replied.

"About what?"

"I am thinking of becoming a monk," he spoke with a resigned tone.

That was an interesting development, from a soldier to a mafia don to a monk!

I decided to probe further, so that we could reach that which lay beneath the surface.

"Why?"

"I want to join the army. That is my passion. Other than that, nothing pulls me," he shrugged.

"Yeah, but you heard Maximus in your last session He may again push you into unjust violence. If you do unjust violence in this life it will come back to you in this same life. That is why police was a safer option. You will be more responsible for the decisions you take."

"Yeah, but I want a life of strength and honour… In the police … you're not looked up to as a soldier in the army is, the privileges are less, you don't get free rum," he said sceptically.

"You want to join the army to get free rum?"

"That's a part of it. What else is there to life there…It is just fighting otherwise?" He reflected and elaborated. "…The passion is missing. I want to kill all the enemies of my country even if I die…

The soldier who dies in war and gets a medal for his bravery… That is who I want to be."

"What is the point in getting a medal after you die… why can't you do something where you live and get fame?"

He looked surprised on hearing that, as if he had never come across that view. He often gave the impression that he wanted to run away from life through death.

He nodded, thoughtfully. "Yeah! I never looked at it that way. That makes sense…"

He rubbed his chin considering that view for a moment, then shook his head in a resigned manner. "Nothing else gives me that kind of rush," he said. "If I don't get in the army, I could go to Tibet," he replied thoughtfully.

"Why Tibet?"

"To be a monk. There are good monasteries there," he replied.

"Why do you want to be a monk?"

"I want peace. I don't belong here… I don't have a desire to live in this world… If I could go in the army, I could have fought for my country. At least, that way I could have contributed," he paused, musingly.

"Yeah! It is good that you want to contribute meaningfully. If you want a job where you use your fighting skills…You can contribute very meaningfully being in the police, in helping the weak and oppressed. The idea is to use your fighting skills to get justice to the weak and oppressed, not to defend your country against enemies."

"It's the same… A terrorist is an enemy." He replied.

"It is not the same. …the poor, exploited people may become terrorists because they haven't got justice…"

"A terrorist is a terrorist and he has to be killed…" he said with fists clenched.

"You may kill the person who needs justice than the person who is the oppressor while obeying orders blindly… The Old Man warned you."

"He speaks from up there ... Here, on Earth... it is not possible," he replied.

"It is, if you don't join the army... You would have more independence to think and act."

He shrugged off my argument with a shake of his head, "I don't want to ... my core skill is in being a soldier."

"The soldier of today, is not the same as in the Middle Ages. You felt powerful as a soldier in a past life. You may not feel the same now. These times are different. Power is with people who control the economy. Are you good with numbers?"

"Yes, that is my core-skill... but I excel at fighting," he pointed out. "I want military and action...If I don't get that, I can be a monk as well...live away from the world, it's beautiful up there... Peace," he said looking up, with longing in his eyes.

"Yeah... That does sound good. It is finally your decision. Are you sure you want to be away from the world?"

"Yes, I don't want to stay here... I don't feel at home anywhere." He repeated. "A monk's life is peaceful...I'll be fine being a monk."

"You have a purpose. You have to heal all those souls, the Old Man said doing what you are good at. Then only you will get peace. Becoming a monk is like running away."

"How does it matter?" he shrugged and asked.

"You are choosing two extreme options...Let's go to the Life-between-life space again and ask the Old Man."

"Can we go there again?" He looked up, suddenly more interested. Obviously, he had liked his first Life between Life sessions.

"Yes, we can go there as often as we want. They are there to guide us."

"Ok, let's go then," he agreed readily.

I took Dev into the semi-hypnotic trance. Within five minutes, he involuntarily started seeing images.

STUCK IN 'NOWHERE ZONE'

"What do you see?"

"Its Maximus... his heart is bleeding heavily," Dev replied.

I was surprised to hear that. We had half-healed Maximus's heart before sending him to heaven. Now, after our previous session and the aggressive conversation on causing destruction through the army, his heart seemed to be bleeding profusely again.

"Is he in heaven?"

"No," Dev focused and replied.

"Then, where is he?"

"He's ... He's held in some place in between," he replied.

"Which place?"

"It's no-where. It's an empty place..." Dev said.

"What kind of place?"

"He's in some kind of a glass box. There is red energy around him...he can't get out of there," Dev said.

"What does that mean... he can't get out of there?"

"He has been kept there so that he does not use his powers unjustly..." Dev said.

"What will happen if he uses his powers unjustly?"

"He will be stuck there forever," Dev replied.

"How does he look?"

"Sad," he focused. "He is saying something."

"What?"

"I am sorry," Dev replied in the voice of Maximus.

"Okay, does he want to say something else?"

"No," Dev replied.

"Ok, then move on... Ask that image to go where it came from and keep going deeper in your own mind."

"Yes," Dev nodded and allowed himself to go deeper in trance.

It was only after we reached the life-between-life stage that we understood why all this was shown to him now.

THE POINT OF SALVATION

As I was counting him down the stairs, to take him deeper into trance, he saw another involuntary picture.

"What are you seeing?"

"I am going down the stairs of a castle," he replied.

"Which castle? Is it a past life? What are the surroundings like?"

"It's all in ruins… I am old," Dev said in a surprised tone.

"Old? Look at your clothes? What are you wearing?"

"Regular clothes…it's that same picture, which came earlier," he replied.

"Ok. Focus on it. What are you doing walking down the stairs?"

"I have a book in my hand," he replied.

"Which book? Focus."

"It's about Buddha," he spoke in a surprised tone, surprised that he was reading on Buddha. Dev did not like reading any books other than his study course material.

"Which time is it? Can you make out?"

"It's me… Now, when I am old…I look peaceful," he said in a surprised tone.

"How old? How do you look?"

"Around sixty… my hair is white…I am the same…glasses, shoes, a regular shirt-pant," he replied, surprised at seeing himself at sixty.

I was wondering why he was being shown a future picture of his present life. What could be its relevance now?

"Why have you gone there? Focus."

"I don't know…" he replied.

"Move to a point just before this scene. What do you see?"

"I'm in the castle now… there's a small window. I can hear the sea… It's Greece," he said.

"Why are you in Greece? Focus on how you reached there?"

"Just happened to go there. I seem to be visiting," he replied.

"Can you be in the body? Be in the body. Now."

"No," he shook his head. "I can't get in his body."

He could always get in the body from a past life experience but he could not get into this body from his future. Something was blocking him. It could be that he had never experienced that kind of peace till now and, probably, he could not get into that feeling till he was subconsciously ready to experience it.

"Why are you being shown this future picture? Ask."

"*This is where you have to reach. This is the salvation point.*" he spoke, suddenly in a heavier tone.

"Who said that?"

"There's a bright light above. The voice came from there," Dev replied.

"Ok, when do you have to reach there? Ask."

"*When you have healed all the souls you took away the purpose of life from, is when you will reach the salvation point. It will be the final destination point.*" He said in the same voice.

"Ok, is it saying something else?"

"No, it is gone now." Dev replied in his own voice.

"Ok, then let's go to the Life between Life space as we planned."

"Okay." He nodded and allowed himself to go deeper in trance.

BARRED FROM HEAVEN

I again counted him down the stairs. Then, I planned to take him to the Life-between-Life space, through the door of heaven.

"Now, that you are at the bottom of the stairs, see yourself outside a big, beautiful door which opens to the garden of heaven."

"Yes," he nodded.

"Now, open the door and step into the garden of heaven."

"I can't," Dev replied, after a pause.

"Why not? You were able to visit heaven in the last session… you saw Maximus sitting there with his lover?"

"Now, I am not allowed to go there," he replied.

"Why?"

"I don't know," Dev shook his head.

"Is Maximus in heaven now?"

"No, he was sent out…He is in the nowhere zone now," Dev replied.

> This was the first time I realized that because of the session we had with Maximus on Earth, where he had proudly acclaimed his desire to join the army to become the biggest destroyer ever, he had been sent out of heaven.

It was surprising to note that what happened on Earth was noted in the zone of heaven almost instantaneously. This was a new experience for me…I knew the other dimensions existed at a theoretical level but had never actually experienced their involvement. With no other client, had they been so visibly interactive yet.

DEV'S SECOND LIFE BETWEEN LIFE SESSION

"Ok, then directly go to the Hall of doorways. Turn to your left. You'll find the Hall of doorways. Do you see it?"

"Yes," he replied.

"Now, go to the door which opens to the pre-life-planning stage of your current life,"

"Yes," he nodded.

"Open the door and step inside."

"Yes, I am there," he said.

"What do you see?"

"I'm in the clouds…" he said.

"In the clouds? Do you see any spirit guide?"

"I'm going down a hill…He is there," he replied.

"Who?"

"The Old Man from the Council," he said.

Since Dev could no longer enter the Council which was in heaven, the Old Man had come outside to meet him.

"Okay, thank him for coming and ask your questions."

"Yes," he nodded and waited for me to guide him.

I decided to go with my intuition and ask questions…

"Ask him where is Maximus…what is that empty space?"

"It is...Hell," Dev replied in a heavier tone, on behalf of the Old Man.

"Is Maximus in hell?"

"*A part of his energy have been locked in a glass bottle and kept there. He is not in hell. A part of him is kept there,*" replied Dev in the same voice.

"Why?"

"*From there, that part can't communicate with anyone...It is blocked from communicating with anyone,*" said the Old Man.

"Why?"

"*It is too impatient...and too powerful... if left loose, it can cause mass destruction,*" replied the Old Man.

"How does that affect you?"

"*Maximus and you are the same soul,*" replied the Old Man.

"So, while Maximus is in hell, will you experience the same anguish? Is there any way to heal this anguish now so that you can move towards the purpose of your life faster?"

"*Maximus has not joined the dark forces yet...So, he is not yet in hell...he has only been kept there so that he cannot communicate with anyone,*" continued Dev, in the heavy voice of the Old Man.

"Why can he not communicate with anyone from there?"

"*He is in a box... the frequencies around him are too low... he can't get out,*" replied the Old Man.

"Is there a way in which he can be healed?"

"*You can't give him peace now...You need that spirit to fight the dark forces to achieve your purpose...that is your strength,*" stated the Old Man.

"What dark forces?"

"*There are dark forces which are trying to pull him... they have been trying to pull him since a long time... since he came on Earth,*" replied the Old Man.

"Why have they been trying to pull him?"

"*He is a very powerful soul. They want to use his energies to cause destruction on Earth,*" he replied.

"So, has he not joined them yet?"

"No, he came on Earth to do the work of light...Once on Earth, he got carried away...But, a spark of that light is still there in him... he can still join the right path," said the Old Man.

"What if he doesn't? What if he gets carried away again?"

"Then the dark forces will win...he will cause heavy destruction..." the Old Man replied.

"How?"

"He is saying, *Through me*," replied Dev.

"What about the personality of Maximus wanting you to join the army?"

"*You may cause mass destruction if you go in the army... destruction as has never been seen before,*" said the Old Man in a warning tone.

I was half inclined to shrug such extreme statements off as Dev's imagination. But intuitively, I was worried that the warning may be true, probably, even if, not in the literal physical sense but, at the level of thought or energy creation. "How can you prevent that?"

"*Failure arouses Maximus... Defeat makes you get overtaken by the negative in his personality...You need his powers to achieve your purpose...you can follow his path or you have to find your path... You have to use the powers of Maximus in the right way,*" said the Old Man.

"Would it be easier for you if you find a path different from that of Maximus?"

"*Yes, it will be...the pull will be more in the path of Maximus... but, the choice is yours,*" replied the Old Man.

"If Maximus again pushes you on his path, and you get carried away again, what will happen to you?"

"*There will be no salvation...this is your last life on Earth...We have not yet decided on your fate, yet if you fail again...You cannot be allowed to go back to your planet, till you balance the destruction you caused here,*" said the Old Man.

"Which planet is that?"

"*The planet that you came from,*" replied the Old Man.

"Which planet did you come from? Are you not from Earth?"

"*No, you were called from another planet… you came to do some work…Once that work is complete, you will get salvation. That is the reward…After your work is done, you can go back to your planet,*" replied the Old Man.

"How will you know you are on the right path?"

"*On the right path, you will get peace with each step you take… otherwise, your own thought process will be your biggest enemy,*" said the Old Man.

"What about choosing to be a monk in this life?"

"*You have to achieve your purpose in this life…if you run away… you will never find peace…You will find peace when you reach the place which you were shown today… If you reach that place, you will get salvation,*" said the Old Man.

So, that was the relevance of the place he was shown today. He wanted to find peace by becoming a monk but he was being told that he would find peace only after he achieved the purpose of this life, not before that.

"Why do you say if?"

"*There are chances that you would get carried away again…If you don't, the dark forces will create obstructions…Now, they will create temptations for you to leave the right path, Later they will try to prevent you from reaching that point …*" said the Old Man.

"What if you die before you reach that point?"

"*Death before achieving the purpose of this life means suffering for several future lives… You will not get another chance to find peace for several lives to come,*" clarified the Old Man.

"So, if you join the army and die… the soul will suffer for several lives? Is that right?"

"*Yes,*" drawled the Old Man. "*The soul has been suffering…*"

(So, army was ruled out once more if Dev wanted peace. Dying mid-way may worsen the scenario for him, as a soul.)

"What is the right path?"

"*Don't kill unless you have to…Violence is justified when used for justice, not for money or power,*" said the Old Man.

"What can you do now to choose the right path?"

"*Right actions will help…*" said the Old Man.

"What does he mean by right actions? Can he give examples?"

"*Studying,*" replied the Old Man.

"Does studying help you feel at peace,"

"Yes… It gives me peace," replied Dev in affirmative,

"What does he mean by right actions?"

"*Where the intention is to create and not destroy,*" specified the Old Man.

"When will Dev find the right path? How many months or years?"

"*Two,*" replied Dev.

"Two what? Months or years?"

Dev was silent. Since time is not a factor on the celestial plane, it cannot be accurately predicted.

"*You will take two years to find the right path…two years is the training period, then the real tests will start,*" continued Dev, in the voice of the Old Man.

"What tests?"

"*Tests where you have to fight for justice… the pull from the dark forces will keep coming…if you pass the tests, the plan would keep moving up as we have planned it,*" said the Old Man.

"What about your soul mate?"

"*She is there… a part of her is stuck in heaven as a part of you is stuck in hell…*" said the Old Man.

"How will she guide you?"

"*… There are many mountains to climb… she knows which one to climb…*" replied the Old Man.

"So, you have to heed her?"

"*Yes… in earlier lives, you blocked her from coming close to you because of your desire for revenge … She will stay for two years…After that, you have a choice,*" said the Old Man.

"What choice?"

"Whether she stays or not ... she may stay or she will go forever," replied the Old Man.

"Okay, is there anything else you want to ask?"

"No," replied Dev.

"Is there anything he is saying?"

"Yes," he replied.

"Okay, hear what is it? Focus"

"You have caused massive destruction in earlier lives...This is your last chance of finding peace." Dev spoke on behalf of the Old Man.

"Does he mean the lives we have already seen or are there other lives as well?"

"There are other lives ..." replied the Old Man.

"Can we see those lives?"

"No..." replied the Old Man

"Why not?"

"You cannot enter that body... that is the part which is in hell. We cannot allow that part to come up again," replied the Old Man.

"Ok, but can you see them as an observer if it comes up during therapy?"

"Yes," he replied.

"Ok, is there anything else he is saying?"

"No," replied Dev.

"Then, thank the Old Man and come back to the door where you entered from."

"Yes," he replied.

"Are you there?"

"Yes," he nodded.

"Then, open the door and be back under the stairs."

"Yes," he replied.

"Ok, I'll climb you up the stairs from 1-25... when you wake up, feel light and refreshed and let all this be integrated in your mind when you sleep tonight."

When he woke up, he looked refreshed; and curious.

CONCLUSION OF THE SESSION

Dev started understanding his trauma of feeling that he did not belong anywhere, after this session as he was told he was from another planet. He liked that idea and felt an inner desire to go back to his planet. That he had come to do some work, gave some meaning to his existence, while, being told that he could leave for good after he finished his work in this life, relieved him. Eventually, he was less insecure about not belonging or not performing.

GENERAL AWARENESS: A UNIVERSAL INTERPRETATION OF THE OLD MAN'S MESSAGES

This was the most dramatic session I had experienced as a therapist till then. When interpreted, in everyday language, whatever was told by the Old Man to Dev for his life applies to our lives equally well, as elaborated below.

> "You can't give him peace now. You need that spirit to fight the dark forces to achieve your purpose…that is your strength."

Dev was told he has a purpose. If he moves towards it in the right way, he would find himself with greater levels of peace with each step he takes, but he won't get peace till he achieves his life purpose. His past life spirit and its anxieties were needed to fight the dark forces.

This is true for all human beings as each person has a unique life purpose. If s/he pursues it such that soul needs are satisfied in the process, that person reaches greater levels of emotional happiness with each step. If he does not follow the purpose, at the level of feelings, then the mind is in conflict with each new step he has to take. Dark forces become stronger as the levels of anxiety and stress-related diseases increase – it is an indication of a conflict in the subconscious mind. For overcoming stress, one has to choose the right direction, that is, the direction which leads to peace along with achievement of life purpose.

> 'If you do not follow the right path, your own thought process would be your biggest enemy.'

This also applies to all of us. When we are doing work which causes us more stress than peace, then we keep creating more negative energy for ourselves and others. Though, sometimes, we inherently know what to do to find peace, we can't get ourselves to do it, because of undue fears of survival based on a negative conditioning. We are not able to change our negative beliefs and patterns because we are afraid to let go of the conventional routes to success. Our own rational mind defeats us, preventing us from reaching the level of satisfaction or happiness which our soul desires.

When we can control our negative thought process, we defeat our biggest enemy: our own negative mind. Then, we can bring ourselves to believe in the positive. Thus, we are able to grow faster to achieve our purpose, because when our inner frequencies are positive, negative energies do not affect us as much anymore. When we are positive in balance, we can craft our own route to success without being blocked by doubts and fears created by the dark force of nature.

> *'Dark forces would pull you. The test is to resist that pull and keep moving ahead on the right path.'*

Like Dev, all of us have to give tests on Earth. The test is to resist the pull of negative thinking. The pull keeps coming our way but as we keep resisting it, we keep passing our tests and moving forward with our life-plan. Dark forces imply negative thinking patterns. People who get influenced by the dark forces are essentially, those who are focused on the negative aspects of life. They believe that the world is a bad place and hence, unhappiness has to be tolerated to survive here. Whatever they choose to do, they end up creating more negative energy than positive. They always seem to be cribbing, angry and suffering however successful or rich they may become.

All of us are constantly pulled by dark forces on Earth. When we feel depressed and low, it is a pull of the dark forces. If we feel tempted to use wrong means to make money or to get other pleasures, it is because of an inherent belief that we can't get what we desire by using the right means, which is again a pull of dark energies. The test for each of us is to change our way of thinking so that we can achieve all that we desire by using unscrupulous means that can ensure us peace within. We have to follow methods of living, which inherently lead to soul evolution.

If we get pulled in the energy of darkness, we get into a vicious circle of negative thinking wherein we lose our peace as well as the purpose of life. Like Dev, each of us suffers for several subsequent lives when we fail to achieve our soul's purpose in the present life because the soul dies feeling negative.

'Failure arouses Maximus ...The feeling of defeat, is overtaken by the negative in the personality ... you have to use the powers of Maximus in the right way.'

The feeling of defeat or failure overtakes Dev when he is unable to perform as expected by others or is unable to come up to the standards of success he set for himself. The feeling of defeat causes Maximus to rise within him. We all fall prey to feelings of being a failure, off and on, and a negative personality within us may rise when we feel defeated. We may tend to get diverted from a positive path of life in these weak moments.

To prevent losing control over our senses we have to train ourselves to remain focused and not let our self-esteem get negatively affected by external judgments. Our self-esteem falls when we feel unsuccessful. Yet, very often, the goals of success that we set up for ourselves may not be realistic from the perspective of meeting our soul needs of evolution. Success on Earth does not mean success from the universe's perspective.

Until we learn the emotional lesson attached, the desired material success as well as emotional satisfaction cannot take place. As we see in Dev's case, if material success is not accompanied with emotional satisfaction, it becomes almost futile to achieve it as it is not recognized at the soul level as meaningful.

> *'The right direction is where the intention is to create and not to destroy.'*

The intention to create means to indulge in acts, which generate positive feelings like happiness, love etc. It also means to transcend the existing negative energy into positive by choosing to focus on thoughts and actions, which make us feel positive.

Destruction happens by spread of negative energy. Negative energy spreads through focus on negative feelings. The intention to destroy means to indulge in acts which spread negative feelings such as hatred, anger etc. It also entails choosing to aggravate the existing negative energy by continuing with the same thinking patterns and doing things that continue to harbor negativity in our lives. These may include situations such as staying on in unhappy marriages and professions – the inability to muster courage to break institutions that only bring us more suffering and so on. Making choices that make us feel low or create emptiness in our lives or in others' lives, drift us away from the positive frequency of the Creator, thus, preventing our souls from evolving. For our efforts to bear fruit at the soul level, whenever we choose to do something, our intention must be to create more positive energy rather than destroy it.

> *'You can choose your own path or follow the path of Maximus... the pull (from the dark forces) will be more in the path of Maximus.'*

This also applies to each one of us. The path of Maximus represents the path of a past-life personality. Maximus was successful in his path on Earth, but failed to achieve the purpose of his life as a soul. Similarly, we are all pulled by paths in which we have been successful in previous lives in Earthly terms. But, we may have failed to achieve our purpose of life as souls in that path. Maybe, we got caught in negative thinking and got carried away by the pull of dark forces, away from the path of soul evolution. Hence, the soul creates circumstances in the life-plan, which prevents us from pursuing that path.

If the soul does not want the person to follow a path, the person may have all the abilities to pursue his/her preferred profession but the circumstances will prevent him/her in strange manners.

> *E.g. Dev was physically fit to be a soldier. He was well-built. People who met him told him he walked and talked like a soldier. He liked guns and fighting and he wanted to serve his country. Everything seemed to be perfect on the exterior but yet he is prevented from pursuing the army because of his circumstances.*

When we face difficult circumstances, we can try to find different paths for achieving our ambitions by focusing on satisfying the emotional need, which the ambition entails, rather than just focusing on the material profession. The following example would clarify this concept further:

A CASE OF AMBITION: DESIRE TO BE AN ACTRESS

> *A girl may have an intense desire to be an actress, but her circumstances may not allow her to be one. If the soul prevents this path, it is possible that, in a past life, she was a successful actress but instead of being appreciated for her contribution to evolution through acting, she had been acknowledged for her beauty or sexuality. She may have been unable to contribute to acting in roles she would have liked to, because she got pulled by material considerations and chose popular roles. Instead of helping society break rigid, negative patterns of thinking, she may have contributed to reinforcing them. If she chooses the path which she pursued in her past life, there are greater chances that she will again be pulled by negative thinking and make choices for gaining material success than for satisfying soul needs.*

In other words, in this life she may still be as beautiful and with perseverance may even overcome her difficult circumstances and become an actress again; but then, she may again be acknowledged for her beauty and not her soul evolution. However, if she can discover other skills that she possesses, which can give her more emotional satisfaction with success, then there are greater chances that her mind would not repeat the same old negative patterns of thinking.

However, breaking mind patterns requires time, energy and effort in a direction we need educational training in, for more awareness. Depressed, negative thinkers too keep worrying, eventually becoming more sick and depressed. Our energy gets locked in self destructive, energy circles instead of being free to create happy, emotionally satisfying, productive realities. Yet, the pull from the dark forces is lesser and the level of satisfaction more, whenever we are able to break free and find the right path.

Thus, the words that poured out of Dev's subconscious mind made profound sense for the entire human race. Either it was because he was a much evolved soul who had got diverted from its path, or it was his spirit guide warning him in clear terms so that there were leser chances of him causing destruction again.

CHAPTER 15

THE FANATIC GENERAL

DEV HAD A SERIOUS, contemplative expression today as he came in for his session. He greeted me with a smile and sat on his chair, looking down, as usual.

"How are you?"

"I'm good," he replied with a nod, still looking down.

His tone was confident as he said that. This was a pleasant change from his previous sessions, where there used to be suppressed disappointment in his tone.

"I was wondering about your depression. You haven't mentioned it since some time. Do you still feel that way?"

"I think I'm not much depressed now," he replied.

"That means? You are a little depressed?"

"Maybe. I'm not sure anymore. It seems to have gone. Maybe, depression was never there," he replied, off-handedly as if it did not concern him at all now.

I was happy to hear that. Usually, when a person gets well through hypnotherapy, his thinking pattern changes to the extent that the old thinking pattern is forgotten. When healing occurs, it appears to the person as if the problem never existed or that they were misunderstanding it.

"...I thought it was but now I feel it was something else," he continued and paused not sure whether he should speak it out.

"What was it?"

"I used to feel I don't belong here," he paused and looked up, unsure of himself.

"Could be... the Old Man told you that you came to this planet to heal some problems which existed here, and were supposed to go back after the work was done, but couldn't. Maybe, that is why you feel you don't belong here."

"Maybe..." he contemplated, trying to find more tangible explanations. "It's this place... when I was small my parents had gone to London for a year. I was happy there. I felt it is home. But, they didn't like it there so they came back... I did not want to come back," he paused, looking up questioningly.

"That could be because you have had several past lives in Europe, as you have seen... You identify more with the culture there maybe... Maybe, you haven't had many past lives in India."

"I haven't had any lives here," he said in a decisive tone.

"One can't be sure. Maybe, you had some. There must be some reason why you chose this country in your life-plan. But if you feel like it, you can always emigrate." I suggested. His answer to this was startling: "Here, I will kill all the enemies of this country... We will make this country a Hindurashtra[1]," he said in an authoritative tone.

TOWARDS FANATICISM

"A Hindurashtra? I didn't know you felt that way. You never mentioned it earlier."

"I do...I talk about it a lot...I have convinced all my friends," he elaborated.

"About what?"

"That we have to destroy them and reclaim our land," he said, assertively, with his fist clenched.

"Who is 'them'? Reclaim which land?"

"Our mother land from the enemies," he spoke with dramatic passion.

"You keep talking of enemies. Who specifically are the enemies?"

"Those who do injustice," he replied.

---

[1] Hindurashtra means a Hindu country

"How can you decide who does injustice? When you say enemies, whom do you have in mind?"

"The neighbours and those who support them," he replied.

"Which neighbours and who supports?"

"The neighbours who keep threatening us. If we decide on war, they will be defeated…I am going to prove it to them…" he said vehemently,

"To who?" I wanted him to spell it out before jumping to assumptions.

"…the Muslims. This country needs a champion to protect it."

"That is politics…the neighbours are also threatened by India."

"It is not only from their country… it's the ones who live here… They are our enemies," he persisted.

"But don't they belong here?

"Muslims will always destroy Hindus, they are traitors," he replied in a firm voice.

"Why do you think so?"

"Muslims want to take over…if we don't push them out, they will push us out," he continued.

"No, they can't…Ours is a secular country. People of all religions live here."

"This is not their home. This is our home. …If this was their home, why were they given a separate country?" He asked, but he was disconcerted again, his eyes moving continuously from left to right.

"That was a political decision…So much anger against one race…these are fanatic tendencies, aren't they? It is not secularism. Where did you pick them up?"

"I am an atheist… I don't believe in God," he stated defiantly.

The thought of destroying people from this community seemed to excite him. I asked him if he was such a devout Hindu.

"I am an atheist…I don't believe in God."

"You don't seem like an atheist …"

"I don't?" He asked me incredulously.

"In the life of Maximus, you were actually angry with God. You can't be angry with God if you think God doesn't exist… Maybe you don't like following rituals."

"Yes… I don't think God exists that way… God is everywhere… You can't say God will be happy through this and not that," he mused, contemplating.

"If you don't believe in traditional rituals, what is your problem with Muslims? Why do you talk like a fanatic religious leader?"

"Yes. I will join them. I will be the soldier of justice. I will establish the supremacy of Hindus," he said.

"Again, soldier?" I asked him.

"What's your problem with soldiers?"

Before I could think of an answer, he answered his own question.

"Soldiers kill without asking questions," he stated.

"Yes, they do. You've answered your question yourself."

"But they are terrorists and they have to be destroyed," he said, insisting that his antagonism was justified.

"All countries support terrorism. It is power play…in politics; they don't care about the soul needs. People are made terrorists by leaders who fuel their feelings of dissatisfaction by blaming it on religious differences. The soul has no religion. Being in one religion is an experience for the soul. The soul changes its religion in every life. The God you worship is a symbol of an invisible power. The symbol can change depending on your upbringing in that life. But, the symbol you use doesn't change the soul within you, the energy, who you are, your essence or the essence of the Creator."

He was not listening to logic or reason. He was just fuelling the energy of anger. I decided to interrupt his thought pattern and move towards some serious therapy with his subconscious.

"Here, we have been trying to remove your pull towards violence so that you find peace… how will you find peace with such thoughts in your mind?"

He paused contemplating.

"Yes, that is there," he nodded. "These thoughts keep coming... When I exercise for some time, I calm down. But again it starts." I want to destroy all those who cause injustice," he continued.

"We are going around in circles... You can't decide whether a person is a friend or an enemy on the basis of which God he worships."

"Yes," he nodded and agreed.

"You saw yourself as a Christian in some past lives, as the European soldier and a German soldier in some another. And you still call yourself an Aryan..."

"Yes, I am Aryan. Aryan blood is superior," he replied.

"That is Nazi thinking. Besides, how are you an Aryan in this life? There is no Aryan lineage. That is coming from a past life too."

"No, it is not... I have sharp features, like an Aryan," he replied.

"That is fanaticism again, one way or another... you took so many lives as the German soldier. You want to repeat it again. We are trying to help you find peace here. You need to find what your problem with Muslims is. What have they done to you personally? Why are you so much against them?"

"Nothing," he shrugged. "These are nationalist feelings. Everyone has these," he replied in a calmer tone

"Everyone? I don't know many people who feel so strongly about it. I don't. Why do you feel so strongly about it?"

"I don't know. It's just there," he shrugged.

"You need to free yourself from these destructive thoughts," I told him. "You said you wanted to find peace. But all you are doing is finding reasons to feel violent... we should try to talk with your subconscious mind now."

"Yeah ... I do want to find peace," he agreed finally. "Okay."

"Let me frame the root cause of why we want to find the life. Framing it correctly will enable to open up the relevant life. Tell me if it sounds okay to your mind. If any word sounds out of place, tell me."

"Okay," he nodded.

I was relieved. After an exasperatingly long discussion, more than half of which has not been narrated here, I was finally able to break through into his conscious mind. Now, I hoped his subconscious mind would do my work.

DEV'S EIGHTH PAST LIFE: THE FANATIC GENERAL

I took Dev into a semi-trance state. He went in fast, as usual. We did not see the Greek soldier appearing uncalled this time.

"Now, that you are relaxed, walk a few steps... You'll find a door which opens to the Garden of Heaven. Open the door and enter the Garden of Heaven."

"I can't," he said. He was still locked out of heaven.

"Okay, then be back under the stairs. Look to your right and you'll find a door which opens to the Hall of Doorways. As I count 5-0, open the door. Once in the hall, you'll find several doors on your left and right. These indicate your lives that have been and will be. Go to the door which is the root cause of you wanting to give justice to Hindus by killing Muslims. Now. 5, 4,3,2,1 and 0. Are you in the Hall of Doorways?"

"Yes," he replied.

"Okay, now go to the life which is the root cause of you wanting to give justice to Hindus by killing Muslims. Go to any door which pulls you and enter the door. If you don't see anything, imagine you are walking in white light. Slowly, images will start opening, now, as I count 5-0, open the door and be in the life... 5, 4, 2, 1 and 0. NOW!"

In the trance, Dev again saw himself as a soldier, but this time he was an Afghan Muslim, fighting for Mohammed Ghazni. He was very strong, powerful and much feared. His ferocity and loyalty as a soldier earned him the place of a general in Ghazni's army. However, he followed the same pattern seen in Dev's other lives; he turned fanatical and excessively violent. He encouraged his soldiers to indulge in all kinds of atrocities in the name of religion. He went so far as to disobey his king's orders and ended up being betrayed and assassinated by his own king.

At the end of Dev's narration, Maximus appeared with his bleeding heart again, to remind Dev that he had been unsuccessful in achieving his life's purpose as the Afghan General as well. I asked him to send Maximus away and disconnect from that life and come back to the present. I decided to take him into the Life-between-Life space to find out the significance of that life.

DEV'S THIRD LIFE-BETWEEN-LIFE SESSION

"Go to the door which opens to the pre-life-planning stage of your current life... Are you there?"

"Yes," he replied.

"Now, as I count from 5-0 open the door and be in the pre-life-planning stage of your current life. 5, 4, 3, 2, 1 and 0. NOW!"

"Yes," he replied.

"What do you see there?"

"There's a hill... its beautiful," he nodded in appreciation.

"Do you see any spirit guide there... anyone?"

"The Old Man is standing at the bottom of the hill... I am with him now," he replied.

"Okay, is he saying anything?"

"He is asking, '*why are you here?*'" He replied, imitating the surprise in the Old Man's tone.

"Ok, tell him that you want to ask him whether killing Muslims in India would give justice to the people and help you achieve the purpose of your life."

"*Every time you ended up protecting the people you were supposed to fight against,*" replied Dev, in the voice of the Old Man, addressing himself as YOU.

This reply obviously indicated that killing Muslims would not serve his purpose of life. However, I asked more questions so that he could get more clarity in his mind.

"What about you thinking Muslims are enemies?"

"For you, *anybody who doesn't agree with your thought process is the enemy*," replied the Old Man.

I was amused at the answers, which were coming from his subconscious mind, which completely contradicted the statements given by him in his conscious self. The answers were indirect but had profound wisdom when interpreted.

"What about his thinking that his purpose is to establish the supremacy of the Hindu race?"

"*Your own thought process is your biggest enemy,*" replied the Old Man.

"What does he need to think instead?"

"*The lesson is to realize that power should not be centred on one person,*" came the reply from the Old Man.

In all his previous lives, Dev had fought as a soldier to establish the supremacy of his religion under a king. Since he wanted to be a soldier again in this life, he thought it was his duty to protect a religion like in old times. However, his soul lesson was to understand that power could not be centred under one king or one religion.

"What is the reason for the anger against Muslims?"

"*It is the soul taking revenge against itself,*" replied the Old Man.

The soul as the Muslim General had probably felt guilt and wanted to repay karma by seeking forgiveness from Hindus in the present life. However, Dev did not realize that he was repeating exactly the same feelings of fanaticism in his mind though it was from the other side now. Instead of repaying karma, he was likely to increase it this way.

"How will he find peace if he retains these negative feelings?"

"*He has to heal those souls whose purpose of life he took away,*" replied the Old Man. "*Those souls have to forgive him.*"

"Will he find peace when those souls forgive him?"

"*He will find peace when he forgives the people who did injustice to him and when he receives forgiveness from the people who suffered injustice at his hands,*" replied the Old Man.

"Why was India chosen to be the country for him to achieve his purpose?"

"*Because he caused maximum destruction here,*" explained the Old Man.

"Is there a definite plan by which he can achieve his life purpose? What is the plan?"

"*He is our champion against the dark forces,*" replied the Old Man in a commanding voice.

"Champion in what?"

"*There is a war between the good and evil. He has to destroy evil forces by fighting them,*" stated the Old Man.

"Is there any other way he can do it other than fighting?"

"*He is a soldier, he has always been a soldier… he has to achieve his purpose doing what he is good at… the path is too big for him to complete, if he tries any other method,*" he replied.

"What role does he have to play in this war?"

"*He is the deciding factor,*" replied the Old Man.

"Deciding factor in what?"

"*There will be a series of events, which can escalate into a war,*" replied the Old Man.

"What does that mean? Is there a war expected here?"

"*A number of small events will take place all over the world… There is an army of the good forces and an army of the evil forces…*" replied the Old Man.

"Which side is he on?"

"*He can join any side… the dark forces are trying to pull him on their side,*" replied the Old Man.

"What do you mean when you say that he is the deciding factor?"

"*The side he joins will win,*" replied the Old Man.

"What if he joins the dark forces?"

"*If he is allowed to go on the wrong track, he can cause mass destruction, destruction as has never been seen before. We cannot allow that to happen. We will kill him before that. We cannot take another chance,"* replied Dev in the voice of the Old Man, which sounded fatalistic.

"So, a war is expected? Could this be a third world war?"

"A series of events will take place which can escalate into a war," replied the Old Man.

"Will the destruction not be there if he doesn't join the dark forces?"

"Unless the old is destroyed, the new can't be created," replied the Old Man.

"So, there would be destruction?"

"Yes," replied the Old Man. *"But it will be kept to the minimum."*

Apparently, Dev's role was to help the Light forces by using his aggression. If that was so, Dev could be an Indigo. There are several indigos on Earth now as the planet is going through a transition on the astronomical planes, towards the New Age. Dev felt like a misfit in society. He was rebellious and he had unchannelized strength which made him restless to the extent of being destructive. He had all the characteristics of an Indigo child.

Though Dev did not know who Indigos were since we had never discussed about them, I anyway decided to ask the Old Man about them.

"Is he an Indigo?"

There was a pause as Dev looked confused by the question. Then, he replied on behalf of the Old Man.

"Yes… he has always been an indigo…he was called to do the work of Light but he got carried away…This is his last chance to go back to his planet," replied the Old Man.

"If he fails this time, then where will the soul go?"

"The fate of the soul has not been decided yet. It got carried away in earlier lives…We are hoping that this plan will be successful…I agreed to intervene… Because the soul is good," replied the Old Man, explaining why Dev was getting more guidance than usual.

"Are there other indigos involved in this plan?"

"Indigos are the deciding factors," he replied as the Old Man.

"Deciding factors in what?"

"They will decide who will win the war," replied the Old Man.

"Where are they placed?"

"We have Indigos who make decisions in the key areas…they will get together and decide who will win the war," the Old Man explained.

"Are other Indigos also pulled by the dark forces?"

"Yes…if the Indigos are carried away, the level of destruction will be huge," replied the Old Man.

"Have any got carried away?"

"Yes… the dark forces have their champions as well," he replied.

"So, if they are all powerful, how can you be sure the forces of Light will win?"

"There are several on our side still…the ones who go on the other side will cause mass destruction. They will have to be stopped," he replied.

"So, is Dev one of the factors in deciding which side wins?"

"Yes …He is," replied the Old Man.

"Will he be guided? How will he know he is on the path of the Light?"

"Do not kill unless you have to," replied the Old Man.

"Anything else?"

"Marriage will help him," replied the Old Man.

I assumed this was marriage to that girl who was his girlfriend in the life of Maximus. The Old Man had said that she knew the plan.

"What about him feeling that this country needs a champion to defend it against its enemies?"

"The concept of countries is the root cause of all destruction," stated the Old Man.

"What do you mean by that statement?"

"The country is the root cause of all evil," said the Old Man again.

This was completely against what Dev believed in his conscious mind. Dev wanted to be the champion for his country whereas the Old Man indicated that his role was that of a champion of the forces of Light. The concept of the country was destructive, according to the Old Man.

"What role do you suggest for him then? Which path should he follow?"

"*The role will come to him,*" replied the Old Man.

"When will it come?"

"*When the time comes,*" replied the Old Man.

"Okay, is there anything else you want to ask the Old Man?"

"No," he replied.

"Okay, then thank him and come back."

"Yes," Dev replied.

I woke him up from trance.

DEV'S PERSPECTIVE

Dev looked thrilled when he sat up.

"Did you know about Indigos earlier?"

"No," he replied and looked up curiously.

"Indigos are interplanetary beings who have come from another planet to help Earth. They have been coming since a long time but at this time, they are here in far more numbers than usual. Since the Old Man said you are from another planet and you are aggressive, I thought you might be an Indigo. Indigos are aggressive. They are from more advanced civilizations and can't put up with the slow way things happen here. They can't put up with rituals and doing things just because they are told so. They question the system. Hence they are rebellious. They are here to break old systems. They are supposed to be very intelligent also. Indigo kids are usually put on medications by psychiatrists to help slow them down so that they can fit in human society. Otherwise, they keep fighting and getting into trouble."

"You know... this makes sense..." He nodded as if something has suddenly struck him, "I can feel it."

"Why do you think he said the country is the root cause of all destruction?"

There was no reply but I knew from the slight flicker of his eyes that he knew.

"It came from your mind...You know the answer," I prodded.

"Okay, but, I don't want anyone to know that I think this way," he replied.

"Okay, I don't know anybody you know. So, you need not worry...if I write a book, I'll quote you,"

"He said the country is the root cause of all evil, because...humanity has been divided into boxes which are not relevant," explained Dev.

"Why do you say not relevant? Each country has a different culture."

"Culture is to be shared," he replied.

"You said earlier that you don't want Muslims to live here because our culture gets corrupted."

He shook his head and replied, *"Each person adjusts to a new culture easily."*

"Millions of dollars are being spent on amassing weapons... (pause) which can be used for ensuring nobody goes hungry," he continued. *"If we take the defence expenditure of the world for one day... it is sufficient to wipe out all the diseases of the world."*

"What about terrorism?"

"Terrorism is funded...If there is no country, there is no need to fund terrorism," he continued. *"Labour can move freely... Now, because of these boundaries, world productivity suffers..."*

"How?"

"Like unskilled labour is needed in Germany... It is not available there... there are millions starving in another country...who are willing to work...They can't go there and work," he replied.

"What about protecting honour of the country?"

"Honour is a created phenomenon," he stated and continued. *"It is the oppressor who has to realize...not use his powers unjustly... because his soul pays for it. He is creating walls and terrorists where none existed..."* he elaborated.

"And worshipping one God over another?"

"Each God represents a different type of energy in the universe," he replied.

That Dev realized all this in his subconscious mind and yet was ready to support political parties on the basis of religion at the conscious level, shows how mass thinking can corrupt the individual and rational mind. *Or it was possible that the soul of Maximus was speaking through him since he was just out of trance.* The moment I asked him directly, he went back on his old track.

"When you know all this, why do you keep speaking against Muslims?"

"They kept Hindus in slavery...they have to pay for it," he replied back to his old self.

"You know you are saying this because you were one of the Muslim generals who raided India... You want to get Hindus justice now to make up for that life...but it is the same thing... If you kill again, using religion as an excuse, your soul will again feel remorse."

He did not reply.

"You can help Hindus without harming Muslims."

"Maybe..." He paused and contemplated grimly. "I will think about it ..."

Apparently, there were two parts of his personality and he needed time to integrate them.

We ended the session at that.

THE SOUL'S PERSPECTIVE

The Old Man explained Dev's fanatic tendencies as, *'It is the soul taking revenge against itself.'* Dev became a fanatic Hindu in this life to make up for the atrocities done by him when he was a fanatic Muslim. It is clearly revealed in this session that it is not the soul which is fanatic; it is in fact the mind that interprets the need of the soul to do justice to one particular race while breeding hatred for another. The soul does not belong to any religion. The same soul can be born as a Hindu, a Christian, a Muslim or any other as it wants to have different experiences. Each religion uses a different way to express the same feeling. It is like using different kinds of vehicles to reach the same place.

Each God represents a distinct type of energy and yet, energy is one whole. It cannot be divided as it merges as one, just as all colours merge as one in white light. Spending a life and dying as a fanatic is a wasted effort from the soul's perspective because in the celestial realms, God is not divided. Metaphorically, the celestial realms may be viewed as corporate houses where each type of God works to bring harmony in the lives of people who follow its ideology. However, the Gods don't fight against each other as there is a power of Oneness above the division of labour. It is the human mind that wants to be one up on others in its zeal to compete, which creates division. Humans have branded everything as superior or inferior in the spirit of competition including God. Under the robe of competition, only one God can be superior. Irrespective of which race the soul is born in, it wants the God of that race to be superior. *For example, Dev was a fanatic whether he was a Muslim, a German or a Hindu.*

Our souls would find it easier to deal with negative emotions and evolve if developing emotional maturity is given a priority on Earth. From Dev's example, fanaticism appears to be a mental disease for a reincarnating soul. The fanatic thought process, continues life after life irrespective of the fact that the soul is born into a different religion in each life. The pull towards fanaticism is a test for our soul. The test is to resist the temptation of proving oneself, one's religion or one's view as more powerful than others and instead, integrate viewpoints.

> *Dev's soul wanted him to realize that he has to fight against its rigid thought process, which makes him want to make one race supreme or one perspective supreme.*

When we use the doctrine of 'survival of the fittest,' as Dev did while trying to prove the superiority of his race, we devolve to animal consciousness where we kill another to eat ourselves. Killing for fear or food raises animal instincts. As humans, we have to rise above competition and violence, as we have the brains to develop technology wherein we can survive as a whole, and not in exchange of one another. Dev was told during the session that he would get peace of mind if he heals the souls whose purpose of life he took away; what he was not told was that he has to kill other souls to repay his karmic debt.

Fanaticism is a by-product of a competitive social structure which says, *"my shirt is better than yours, my car is brighter than yours and My God is wiser than yours."* It reflects emotional degradation of the human mind. We think as God does when our soul upholds goodness, love and peace, and not violence, or ego supremacy. God is one and evolves through incarnating in different forms and colours/religions. Needs vary from one individual to another, based on which, they evolve differently in different socio-cultural contexts. Given the diverse cultures and way of life around the world, God too is defined or interpreted differently across different regions, climates and languages. From the soul's perspective, there is a common thread in all religions. The teachings radiate the same types of meanings, though the words and rituals used are different.

Religion aims at merging the soul's thinking with the Creator's for increasing positive light, but fanatics make the whole process of merging with God negative, thus devolving the soul to a lower, negative frequency. A fanatic soul is a failure from the soul's perspective of ascension.

CONCLUSION OF THE SESSION

Dev became less fanatical after this session. The rigid thought pattern was attacked and hence, had broken. However, the negative energy had not gone yet. His negative energy circuit had loosened, but it would take him time to release it completely. It was clear that the guidance from the celestial planes did not agree with killing souls on the pretext of safeguarding methods of worship. Evolution of the soul entails bettering what already exists; not proving one superior over another. From the soul's perspective, we can work in union with the ideologies of the Gods we worship. It is only then that we manifest peace and happiness instead of negative whirlpools, resulting from feelings of competition, inferiority or fanaticism.

GENERAL AWARENESS: IS THE CONCEPT OF THE COUNTRY, THE ROOT CAUSE OF ALL EVIL?

The Old Man raised some questions about the fabric of the structure of human society, when he said: *the concept of countries is the root cause of all evil and destruction.* Dev further elaborated on this message by interpreting it as: *Human beings have been divided into irrelevant boxes. There are walls where none existed.*

We, in the human society, are so conditioned into being divided by the illusory walls of countries that we never question ourselves on whether the concept is relevant in today's society or not. The concept of boundaries started in the primitive civilization and extended to countries over time. The primitive man needed the boundaries to save his belongings. He had a dearth of resources because he did not have the means to exploit nature's gifts. That is why it was felt that there was a scarcity of resources, that there was not enough for all. Today, with so much scientific development, there is no dearth of resources and yet human beings continue to feel threatened. All our lives, we keep practically manifesting the scarcity due to our negative focus even when essential resources are no longer as scarce.

This happens because we focus so much on competition now, that we keep feeling deprived in comparison to others. Thus, resources continue to appear scarce at an individual level because we cannot share them. Metaphorically, if a poor man becomes rich, he may always remain afraid of not having money. He may hoard money because of his fear of losing it. Similarly, though, we now have access to far more resources than we ever did earlier, we continue to build upon similar fears through illusory walls of division on who can own and exploit them.

Because of these illusory divisions, there is lack of mechanism to spread the benefits of scientific development. Food is excess and can be disposed of by some countries, whereas in others, people starve. Rich people feel despair without constant flow of riches into their lives including new cars and diamonds while the poor have nothing to lose. Further destruction is caused by wars and fanaticism. Wars are fought for economic reasons but sold to the public as being for the country's honour and self-respect.

Like Dev said, *Honour is a created phenomenon.*

Instead, if we could focus our mind on the feeling that there is abundance for all, we would multiply the energies of prosperity and abundance of resources. We no longer need to spend on armies for protecting the concept of countries. We need to spend on developing bridges which can help spread the benefits of economic development. We also need to spend on developing human intellect so that we can rise above the need for using violence because when we kill others, we also devolve ourselves, as souls, and deprive ourselves of peace and happiness.

As Dev said: *"It is the oppressor who has to realize."*

People who fund terrorism to increase their wealth and power, do not realize that they are losing their own peace of mind in the process. They live in fear and insecurity more than others. The need to be rich, powerful or fanatic for the sake of being so comes without realization that satisfying such needs is not directly contributing to an increased well-being. The stress and negativity involved in staying competitive increase unhappiness, trauma and pain. We seek to create happiness, good health and peace with the abundance we manifest. However, the creation of an emotional reality opposite to that intended, reflects a lack of educational training in understanding cause-effect relationships between actions and resulting emotions.

As souls, our energy moves in circles and we automatically multiply the feelings we focus upon. That is the LAW OF CREATION, as explained in my other books in detail. When we are aware that, energies multiply in areas we focus upon, positive or negative, would we endorse the negative energies of threats and division by maintaining armies?

Instead of teaching little kids in schools about countries and divisions, emotional training in oneness, love and compassion must be inculcated...This would condition our future generations into creating abundance, peace and happiness from childhood, taking the world as ONE whole.

CHAPTER 16

THE MIND OF A KILLER

DEV'S MOTHER HAD TOLD me that he had tried to kill her about three years back. She had not got over the shock, nor had been able to forgive him. She said he had almost strangled her. The trauma seemed to be fresh in her mind; she appeared to be scared that he was likely to do it again. Their relationship had turned from bad to worse since that incident. I wondered what had driven him to that extent and whether there was any possibility of this extreme behaviour recurring. Though Dev did find violence a just means to aggressively gain power, he had never mentioned a desire to use aggression against his family. He felt betrayed by his parents, but, there was never any indication, whatsoever that he would try to kill his mother.

Also, I had to take into account that the incident was reported by his mother, and she had a tendency to ignore the other person's perspective. So, whenever his mother complained, I always cross-checked with Dev, to get a grasp of his perspective, as well. Thus, I had found that what she called episodes of him beating up his younger brother and the house dog, were, in fact, brotherly games, according to him. I had ruled out those behaviours for intervention, since they seemed to be exaggerated by his mother. I had not yet asked him about his wanting to kill his mother, largely because it was a sensitive issue. In fact, I was waiting for the right moment to bring it up.

Now, that we had covered some significant ground in therapy and he said he was getting over the depression, I thought I would broach the subject of him trying to kill his mother.

DISCOVERING A KILLER WITHIN

Dev walked in a good mood. He sat down with a relaxed look on his face.

"How are you?"

"Good," he nodded.

I listened to his general concerns about his career for some time. Then, I said with some anticipation, "I need to ask you something your mother spoke about."

As soon as I mentioned his mother, he suddenly became cautious. "Okay," he nodded.

"She told me you tried to kill her once."

He turned pale. There was no reply. He just sat there clenching his fists and his face started turning red with anger. I was worried this might affect his trust in me as a therapist.

"Well, did you?"

"Why do you want to know?" He asked grudgingly, looking sideways.

"It is important. There may be something we have missed out."

Again he made no attempt to reply.

"What are you thinking? Tell me…You can trust me."

"You won't understand," he shook his head.

"How can you say that?"

"Only she understood…" he replied. (From the look of longing in his eyes as he said *She,* he was obviously referring to his dead girlfriend.)

"You can try explaining…maybe I would…what do you lose?"

He contemplated for some time, before deciding to reply.

"I have that," he explained, with a bewildered look.

"What do you have?"

"I know how to do it. I don't know how… It is there in me," he replied now with a touch of arrogance, in his voice.

"What is there in you?"

"I know how to kill," he said in a serious tone.

"What do you mean?"

"When a killer looks at a victim, he doesn't see him/her as a person. He sees it like a prey, like a lion looks at the animal it wants to kill. It is totally focused on that person, blind to everything else except the target, and then it kills it," he explained. "It is easy."

"And how do you know that?"

"I don't know. It just happened at that time. It used to take me over," he replied.

"When?"

"When I came back from the engineering college. I used to be depressed all the time. My state of mind wasn't right," he said.

"Ok…does it still take you over?"

"It is there," he said casually, indicating that it was dormant but there in his mind.

"You do realize human beings are not lions…? If you kill somebody, you will be caught and put in jail."

"You don't need to get caught, once you kill. I don't know why people should get caught," he shrugged.

"You are the first person I have heard saying that. How?"

"Just burn the body and clear the ashes. How will anybody know?" He replied confidently, in a tone which indicated that he thought he was a genius.

For a minute, I felt helpless that I couldn't arouse his emotions. So, I approached more directly. "That does not explain why you tried to kill your mom?"

He paused and his face turned redder in self-defence. "Yeah… I would have killed her. But here, it wasn't safe. Where could I burn the body? This place is not right for that… And then she is a woman… I don't hit women… So, I left her." He said condoning, shaking his head.

"That is very good but why would you want to kill her? How do you think of killing anybody?"

"That's very easy… you just focus…" he replied, and again demonstrated it, by showing me how he focused his hands and eyes simultaneously, like a lion.

"We are talking about the emotional side of killing here? How can you take a life?"

"That is nothing... She'll just go and come back," he replied casually.

"What does that mean?"

"Human beings are like worms... they live like worms, then they die and again they come here and live like worms..." he replied.

"That is true... a soul never dies, but can that justify killing?"

"It is a game... one can do anything... it doesn't matter," he replied, shrugging his shoulders.

"I know it is a game but you can't take away a soul's free will. I still don't understand why you wanted to kill her?"

"You won't understand," he replied, shaking his head in disappointment.

"Why?"

"You are a parent," he replied.

"Yes, I am...But that does not mean that I won't understand your perspective..." He was again silent for a minute before deciding to speak.

"Ok...When I came back mid-way from college, she used to call up all her friends and ask if someone could get me admitted to an engineering college again through special reference. I hated that but I didn't say anything, I just listened to it and ignored it..." He paused. "That day I felt really betrayed." He spoke in a low, angry, disheartened tone; his fists clenching as he uttered the word *Betrayed*.

"Why?"

"She was speaking about me on the phone, to her father... that how much they have suffered because of me. She went on and on. I was hearing from the other room. Until then, I thought she understood," he said shaking his head.

"For the first time you heard her complaining about you to her father?"

"Until then…I thought at least they liked me but…" He shook his head in dismay.

"…She said I was born to kill them," he replied, in a low, angry tone.

"What else was she saying?"

"That I came back from the engineering college, how much money was wasted on my admission…then she said that they are taking me to a psychiatrist so that he can convince me to go back to college… that put me off," his fists clenched.

"Why?"

"Because until that day, I trusted her. I trusted her too much," he replied. "She had promised me that once I completed school, she will talk to my dad and let me join the army. I agreed thinking that she wanted to help me. Then, when the time came near, they wanted me to pursue engineering. This was deceit. As she went on speaking, I was feeling miserable. Nothing was working out. I was in a bad mood. I had a fight that day… When I came home in the evening, I heard her…I listened for some time. Then, when I heard about the psychiatrist, something just took me over. I could not control myself. I would have killed her if she wasn't a woman."

"Something took you over? What was that something?"

"I don't know," he replied shrugging.

"Maybe, it was a personality inside you."

"I don't know and I don't care," he replied, still angry.

"I understand. Your mother should not have spoken like that. People don't always exactly mean what they say."

He sat silently, looking down. His face was red indicating his anger and conflict.

"But, you can't lose your cool. That worsens your position."

"I won't do it again… I could have… but what is the point…I don't hit women," he said, shaking his head in disappointment.

"Do you feel justified in what you did?"

"Yes, I do," he replied.

"Why?"

"I want justice," he replied.

"Does wanting justice justify killing?"

"Yes... I think it does," he replied.

"Maybe from a soldier's perspective, it could..."

"Yes... it does," he reinstated.

"What does justice mean?"

"Revenge," he replied in a firm voice.

"How can justice and revenge mean the same for you? Justice is a positive emotion. Revenge is negative."

"Justice means revenge against those who do injustice. Rage becomes a source of power," he replied clenching his fists, explaining why revenge was a positive emotion for him.

"The purpose of your life is to get justice to souls who are weak and oppressed. Your personal revenge may not be a part of that purpose. Revenge was an emotion which Maximus died with. To him, rage was a source of power... There could be more to this than what you see... The personality of Maximus takes you over without you realizing it."

"I don't know... could be," he replied.

"But, even then, that does not explain the method you describe. Maximus was a soldier. He wanted to take revenge... But do you think he would know to kill this way? He was a soldier, not a contract killer. What you describe is different... It is cold-blooded... It could be the personality of Maximus or there could be something else. Maybe another life."

"Maybe... I don't know how I know it, but I can do it," he replied contemplating, looking up. As he looked up, I noticed how emotionless his eyes had become. They were red and blank, almost the eyes of a killer. It could be because he was angry with his mother or it was a personality from within, which had woken up.

"We do need to know how you know this... You don't know where it is coming from. We could find out. At least, you would know."

"How?" he replied, contemplating.

"We can ask the Old Man ... If there was a life where you have killed like that he would tell us."

"Maybe," he nodded

"We can also ask why you chose this mother. You will understand your life situation better then."

"Okay," he agreed...

DEV'S FOURTH LIFE BETWEEN LIFE SESSION

I took Dev into the hypnotic trance state. Then, I took him down the stairs and into the Hall of Doorways.

"Are you in the Hall of Doorways?"

"Yes," he replied.

"Then, go to the door which leads to the Pre-life-planning stage of the current life. Are you there?"

"Yes," he replied.

"Now, open the door and be there."

"Yes," he replied.

"What do you see?"

"The Old Man is there," he replied.

"How does he look?"

"He looks the same. Thin, tall, in a white robe, bald with little hair on his sides," he replied.

"Okay, ask him how you know so much about the mind of a professional killer,"

"Because you were one," Dev replied in the voice of the Old man.

"In which life?"

There was no reply.

"Where was this life?"

"In Italy..." he replied.

"How did you become a professional killer? Ask."

"You started killing for money. But, later you killed for pleasure. You were given the job to kill one person but instead you killed the whole family. You went on and on. You started deriving thrills from

killing. There were several families destroyed," replied the Old Man in a gruff voice.

"What about the soul?"

"The soul suffered each time you killed. It became smaller and smaller," replied the Old Man.

"What does that mean?"

"You did not listen to the soul... It became insignificant," explained the Old Man.

"Is there anything else we need to know about this life? Ask?"

"Nothing," replied Dev.

"Okay, then ask why did you choose this mother for this lifetime?"

"You had a limited number of choices. You were given a very short period. You did not get time to recoup from your previous life. We had to send you back early because of the role you had to play...In this family, you could get all the resources you needed to each the right path," replied the Old Man.

"Which was the life before this?"

"You were a Don in Italy. You became very powerful. The government had to intervene to kill you...We chose you because you were a part of those who destroy their own souls as they destroy others... Since you were an assassin yourself, you would know how the mind of an assassin works. You can use that life to destroy people who use substance to kill others ...," replied the Old Man.

I wondered how they (on the celestial plane) could be sure he would join the path of Light when he had been a Don and an assassin in his previous life. As if reading my thoughts, the Old Man replied,

> *"I agreed to intervene in this case because the soul is good,"* said Dev on behalf of the Old Man and continued. *"He had been getting carried away and causing destruction for several lifetimes. We could not allow that to happen again. There is hope that the soul will get redemption this time."*

"And, what if he doesn't?"

"*If he fails again, he will not get a chance of redemption for several lifetimes. We cannot give him another chance…*" replied the Old Man.

"What will happen to the soul?"

"*The fate of the soul has not been decided yet,*" replied the Old Man.

"Why did his mother choose him?"

"*She had to pay for some things,*" replied the Old Man.

"You trying to kill your mom… was this a planned event?"

"*Yes…*" replied the Old Man.

"Why was it planned?"

"*This was the event which signalled to us that the negative personalities were taking over. At this point, we had to start our intervention. If we had not intervened at this point, you would have joined the mafia,*" answered the Old Man.

"Okay…that makes sense. Is there anything else you want to ask?"

"*No,*" replied Dev.

"Okay, I want to ask something. Why does a person become a serial killer?"

"*They are people who have had pain, they get relief when they inflict pain on others,*" replied the Old Man.

"You mean they have had pain themselves, hence they need to kill others? What do they feel at soul level?"

"*They feel worthless. They want to ensure success by beating someone weaker than them. It is like a lion hunting for food,*" replied Dev on behalf of the Old Man.

A lion kills for food. The Old Man had used the metaphor of lion hunting for food, referring to a survival instinct. The emotional hunger indicated that as the lion could not live without food, this person could not live without killing. The killer's emotional deprivation had to be very deep if his survival was dependent on killing.

"Okay, I thank him for that answer. Is there anything else he wants to say?"

"No," he replied.

"Okay, then thank the Old Man and be back in the Hall of Doorways."

"Yes," replied Dev.

I woke him up out of the semi-trance state.

DEV'S PERSPECTIVE

"How do you feel?"

"Okay," he nodded. He looked refreshed but still a bit sullen.

"Now, you know why you know how to kill."

"Yes," he nodded contemplating.

"Do you understand it was a planned event now?"

"Yeah," he shrugged, still angry with his mother.

"Did they intervene after that? Did you start hearing voices or something?"

"Yes, they did... Anya came in my life. I fell in love... If I hadn't, I would have joined the mafia then. Next year, I was again thinking of it. I could have become a drug dealer. There is good money in that," he mused, "then, she started taking drugs. So, I beat up a drug dealer because of her... and I decided I could not be what I despised him for."

"Good... So, your girlfriend had a purpose, too. She saved you while she died."

He was silent. It appeared that idea had never flashed on him earlier.

"I don't know... maybe," he replied slowly, looking up at the sky.

"Maybe, your mother had to pay for the life when she betrayed you as your sister...At least, we know of that life. That can be an explanation of why she chose you...There you trusted her and she got you killed. Here, it was the reverse... Maybe, she had to feel the same pain as Maximus felt."

He shrugged on that.

We ended the session at that.

His mother had panicked and insisted that he meet a psychiatrist after this incident. Thus, his psychiatric treatment also began around the same time. He was given medications, which, according to his mother, curtailed his violence. They also kept him feeling sleepy, low and depressed. To overcome his low energy levels, he started learning Yoga and going for rock climbing. Those activities helped him get back in control and also connect to his subconscious more. It might be that the psychiatric drug intervention was a part of the life-plan.

THE SOUL'S PERSPECTIVE

Dev's Mother's Soul Perspective

There was karmic balancing, involved in the incident of Dev, threatening to kill his mother. His mother had to bear the suffering because she had to pay for some things, as the Old Man said. According to regression analysis, karmic debt can be personal or impersonal. If a person looks in the other's eyes and kills, then there is personal contact. So the soul would want to be victimized by the soul it abused in the earlier life, as in Dev's mother's case. She had to pay back a karmic debt to him, in particular. If the soul just kills randomly, there is no personal contact. This soul will pay back his karma to humanity, in general, as in Dev's case.

DEV'S SOUL PERSPECTIVE

The Old Man compared the soul of a killer to lion hunting. He meant that the soul of the killer becomes so small that it is like an animal's soul, without a human conscience. The comparison was particularly apt in Dev's case because for nine lives Dev had been killing to earn his bread. In seven lives he was a soldier, and in two lives he was a criminal. Just like a lion has to kill to eat; as the soldier and assassin, Dev too had to kill to survive. In all his previous lives, he literally earned money and rewards when another person died. Since he was in professions where he had to kill on order, he may have trained his mind to *not allow contradictions*. Like Dev developed emotional blindness due to training his mind to not question authority, it is probable that any psychopath or serial killer cannot feel emotions; because in his childhood and previous lives, his professional success demanded blind obedience over development of reasoning, thinking or questioning skills.

Had he actually killed in his present life, he would have been punished. However, punishment could not have healed him because for punishment to work, the victim has to understand what he is being punished for. Dev only obeyed orders in his previous lives. He did not allow his intellect to grow enough to understand cause and effect because he did not want to question authority. In all his past lives, he was conditioned into believing that killing is justified. If he was now told, that killing is not justified and been punished he may have blamed the punishers instead of realizing his own mistake, as most criminals do.

It is tragic that in our society, such professions flourish, where killing other souls becomes a necessity for one's own success. Subsequently, when we try to heal our society by means such as capital punishment, it does not help remove negativity in the soul's mind. Punishment, by any means, does not address the root cause; it only destroys the body, while the soul lives on, with even more negativity. Usually, when a person dies feeling negative, the soul keeps coming back life after life and causes more destruction than ever before. Such a soul needs Positive Reinforcement therapy. It needs to be taught how to find satisfaction in using methods other than killing, to earn its livelihood. The person needs to train his mind to seek better means to gain power, which lead to more emotional fulfilment, than killing. The soul can then be induced to find pleasure in positivity by creating work.

Realization of cause and effect has to come from one's own mind. The intellect cannot be super imposed by preaching or punishment. When the soul realizes that killing another soul harms his own happiness, he would understand that using animal strength doesn't lead to contentment.

Dev's Higher Self was trying to show him the futility of using violence as a means of gaining power. This emotional training, which his spiritual guides had given, needs to be a part of our educational development curriculum on Earth as well.

CONCLUSION OF THE SESSION

Dev never tried to kill again. As he understood more about his mind and the hidden personalities, he could understand and control his impulsive personalities better. Upon reflecting on his repeated encounter with negative people, he once said that – *'A thought process cannot be destroyed by killing. Even if you kill that person, the same energy would come back in another form.'* That was a profound statement though I was not yet convinced that he completely imbibed it, but that he could state this truth indicated that an old, experienced soul in him, was aware. Probably, the Old Man was right in saying that he was a good soul. Subsequently, we came across Dev's past life wherein he was a Mafia Don, in three more sessions, that were to help us significantly in dealing with the emotional issues.

CHAPTER 17

THE NINTH LIFE: A MAFIA DON

DEV WALKED IN A terrible mood for our next session. Anger radiated from his body language... "You seem to be upset today. What happened?"

As he looked up, I noticed that there was an expression of hurt in his eyes, as well.

"I have been betrayed," he declared, in a low tone.

"Betrayed?"

"Yes... I have no alternative left now," he continued, talking more to himself than to me.

"Betrayed by whom?"

"It doesn't matter. I need money and I have to take it from my friend, now," he said defiantly.

"Which friend?"

"The one with the mafia... he owes me money," he clarified.

"Which money?"

"I beat up some people for him... I never took money for that," he replied.

"But, you said you don't want to take that money?"

"There is no other way... I am not going to beg to these people," he replied angrily.

"Which people?"

"I needed money to pay fees. My mother's father had promised me that he would give it," he replied and paused, shaking his head in anger.

"Then?"

"He says he doesn't have the money now... Bloody liar!" he spoke in anger.

"Now I have no choice but to take money from the friend in the mafia. He owes me this for a job I did for him," Dev replied, eyes blazing.

"If you take it from your friend, will you have to return the favour?"

"Yes," he replied.

"By beating up somebody?"

"Yes...he wants me to help with his drug business also," he elaborated.

Dev was talking almost insanely. He seemed to be again looking for an excuse to join the criminal profession. However, the fact that he was talking with me about it meant that he was unable to justify it himself. His mind was going around in circles. Betrayal was the main trigger point for Dev. He spoke of wanting to join the mafia only when he felt betrayed and felt having been repeatedly betrayed, particularly by his family members. Since betrayal was a pattern in his present life and had been in several previous lives, evolving above it had to be a part of his life-plan.

There was obviously a specific soul lesson attached with the feeling of betrayal (as is behind any repeated negative experience); identifying these, could control the negative personality within him. Maybe, the lesson was to understand other people's perspectives or to plan better and believe less blindly in promises, so that he would not feel betrayed. Or there were more karmic issues involved, which we had not looked into yet.

"People sometimes break promises...maybe your grandfather had a genuine problem."

"It'll be good if I join the mafia. I can become a big and powerful Don. Then, I won't have to bother about all these people," he declared confidently.

The peculiarity about this negative personality within him was that it was convinced that if Dev joined the mafia he would become a successful Don. That was not a regular thinking pattern.

"Your girlfriend died because of drugs. You had a fight with the dealer who supplied drugs to her. You despised him. Do you want to become him?"

He paused, as if there was sudden jolt in his mind.

"Yes…" he replied slowly, and looked up. "I won't join the mafia. I have decided on that now."

"Are you sure?"

"I only decide once," he stated. "But, maybe, I'll take the money from my friend. It is my due, anyway. I will just take what is my due, nothing more," he said, contemplating.

"Maybe, it is an acid test situation. We can ask the Old Man for guidance."

"Okay," he shrugged.

"There is another thing here. Being betrayed is a pattern in your life."

"Yes," he shrugged, gritting his teeth.

"And each time you feel betrayed, you want to join the mafia."

He paused contemplating. It had never struck him earlier.

"You think so?" He asked me quizzically.

"The last time you were intent on joining the mafia, you were feeling betrayed by your mother. Now, it is your grandfather. It seems to be coming from close relatives."

"Maybe," he agreed.

"You also seem to feel that whenever you need money, it should be available to you…

You seem to have a problem understanding another person's perspective?"

"Could be," he shrugged, now much calmer.

"Let's go to the Old Man and ask. Before that, we can do a past life regression to see why you feel your need for money is more justified than others' need for it."

"Everyone feels that way," he replied, disagreeing.

"Not everyone but if you are not willing, we can reframe it…

let's find out why you feel betrayed when it concerns money. Maybe, you betrayed somebody the same way in a past life."

"I could never have done that," he stated defiantly.

"There is no harm in finding out… If it is not there, it won't come up."

"Okay," he nodded, seemingly sure that it won't come up.

"So, we will go to a past life which is the root cause of you feeling betrayed regarding money by close relatives and/or when you betrayed somebody in a similar way. Does that sound Okay to you?"

"Yes," he nodded.

DEV'S NINTH LIFE: A MAFIA DON

I took him into the hypnotic trance state. Once in trance, I asked him to go down the twenty stairs, then through the Hall of Doorways to the door which opened to the life which we were looking for, thus:

"Go to the door which pulls you the most."

"Yes," he replied when he was at the door.

"Now, open the door and be in the event, which is the root cause of you having felt betrayed, in money matters by close relatives and/or when you too have similarly betrayed somebody."

"Yes," he replied.

"Are you there?"

There was no reply, but his eyeballs were moving under his closed lids. This is an indication that the person is seeing something. "What do you see?"

"I am killing someone," he replied.

"Who is it? Focus!"

"It is my brother," he replied.

"Why are you killing your brother?"

"He wants money," he replied.

"Why is that a reason to kill him?"

"He wants his share. I don't want to give it," he replied.

"His share of what?"

"From a family business," he replied.

"Why don't you want to give it?"
"I need that money," he replied.
"Why do you need that money?"
"I need it to put in my liquor business. I have to buy distilleries to expand my business," he replied.
"What do you do? What is your profession?"
"I am in the mafia," he replied.
"Okay, what happens next?"
"I kill my brother," he replied.
"Okay, move to the next significant event. What happens next?"
"I buy the distilleries," he replied.
"Did that help you expand your business?"
"Yes, I become powerful," he replied.
"Okay, then? What happens next?"
"I go on to become the Don," he replied.
"How do you become the Don?"
"I kill my boss," he replied.
"Okay, what happens next?"
"Nothing…" he paused, "I become more powerful."
"Okay, move to the next significant event."
"I am in my house, drinking…scotch," he replied and continued. "I have a gun. I am planning to go and kill somebody."
"Okay, move to the next significant event. What happens?"
"I move on to the drug business… I expand it."
"Okay, move to the next significant event?"
"It is the same… The Don has become very powerful," he replied.

Dev had used 'I' throughout this session. It implied that he was still associating with the Don. The personality of the Don was very much a part of him, unlike that of the fanatic Muslim General, where he had used, 'He,' throughout.

"Okay, move to the scene just before you die. What is happening?"

"I have come to visit my girlfriend. She betrays me to the government. The cops have come. They seize the house. I am shot in the back of my head," he replied.

"How do you feel?"

"I feel bad," he replied.

"Why?"

"I failed in my purpose," he replied.

"What was the purpose?"

"The purpose of the soul was to become a big businessman but you ended up becoming a mafia don," he replied. He had addressed himself as YOU.

"Who said that?"

"It came from the Light above," he replied.

"Do you see someone there? Ask who it is."

"I see the Old Man," he replied.

"Okay, ask the Old Man why you became a Don, instead of a businessman."

"You killed somebody in rage. Then, you started killing for money," replied the Old Man, in his gruff voice.

"Is this the same life that he spoke of earlier, in Italy, where you were a professional killer and went on to become the Don?"

"Yes..." drawled the Old Man.

"Okay, ask the Old Man whether we can send the personality of the Don to the Light so that it doesn't affect you anymore."

"You cannot send it away. You need it in this life to achieve your purpose," replied the Old Man.

"How can this personality help?"

"It knows how the mind of a criminal works. You have to use this energy to tactfully destroy the demons," stated the Old Man.

"But, it pulls you in negative directions. What about that?"

"You have the power to fight for justice," replied the Old Man.

"Okay, ask if you can take money from your friend."

"You cannot do anything that can take you in the wrong path," replied the Old Man.

"So, taking money from his friend can put him in the wrong path?"

"The dark forces are trying to pull him on their side. Satan is testing worthiness," replied the Old Man.

"What if he gets pulled into it?"

"Whatever injustice he does to others will come back to him in this life-time. That is the deal. He cannot be allowed more lives," replied the Old Man.

"Okay, is there anything else you want to ask?"

"*No*," replied Dev.

"Okay, then thank him and tell him he can leave to where he came from."

"Yes…" paused Dev, "he has gone."

"Let the sprit go to where it belongs."

"It has joined Maximus," replied Dev.

"How is he?"

"*His heart is bleeding… Otherwise, he is okay,*" he replied.

"Okay, then disconnect from that life and come back to your body."

"Yes," drawled Dev, "his energies are there with me as I need them in this life."

"Okay… you need them to understand the criminal mind in this life so that you can destroy it, as the Old Man said."

"Yes," he replied agreeing.

I woke him up.

DEV'S PERSPECTIVE

Dev was elated to see himself as a powerful Don. I gently reminded him that a Don's success was devoid of any kind of happiness.

"Maybe, you had to face your girlfriend's death in this life, because so many people would have died because of the drugs you supplied in the Don's life… Their families would have suffered then, as you did now."

"Maybe," he nodded grimly.

"Has seeing your life as the Don helped? Has the desire to be in the same role again, reduced?"

"Yes…that was great. But his soul became very insignificant," he said.

"Yes, and maybe he never was happy in that life, in spite of all the power."

"Yeah! He never looked happy," he contemplated. "He killed because he had no choice."

"Do you still feel bad on being betrayed?"

"Nah! I don't care about these people." He said cheerfully.

"Good… You are getting it now. If you are indifferent to hurt, they can't hurt you. They have their own problems. …But, it is not your problem."

"Yes," he nodded.

We ended the session at that.

THE SOUL'S PERSPECTIVE

Dev's life-plan in the life of the Don had been to become a big businessman. Hence, subconsciously, he was driven to build a big business. The life-plan is made from the perspective of feelings, and at the level of feelings, the experience of a big businessman and a Don can be very similar. Both strive for money and power. Yet, there is a critical difference in understanding the right path and the wrong path. In the right path, the soul would be responsible for creation of positive energy in his life and the life of others. Whereas, in the wrong path, the soul would always feel dissatisfied and create the same destructive, negative energy in the life of others. The Don's soul was never happy because he tried to thrive by creating negative energy.

Another reason why Dev as the Don was driven to kill could be that the soul's life purpose was to fight against injustice. It was found in a later session that at the beginning of his journey as an assassin, Dev had killed two men who had raped his girlfriend.

(His girlfriend was the same soul as Maximus's girlfriend.) After that incident, he had run away from law and become an assassin. She had become a nun and never returned to him, partly, because of his profession. The Don became very rich and powerful, and had several mistresses, but he could never forget the girl he loved and craved for her until his death. Hence, he could never be happy. At the death point, he apologizes to her soul. It is possible that the Don killed the two men because his mission was to fight against injustice and since he had been a soldier in several lives, the only way he knew he had to fight against injustice was by killing. As Dev reflected, he had no choice but to become a Don.

The Don was killed by the government. Yet, Dev considered his death as a proud moment than a moment of shame. He recalled that the government had to intervene because the Don was very powerful. That means that he still did not realize that the Don was wrong. According to Dev, the Don protected the people of Italy from an oppressive socialist government. Punishment did not help the soul (that was attached to Maximus), repent. Even now, Dev feels that the Don was justified.

The only reason why Dev does not want to repeat the experience in his present life is because he never saw the Don look happy. He realizes that the original soul had become very insignificant, and that he had failed to achieve his purpose of life. This is a clear illustration of the fact that punishment does not help the soul evolve. Punishment may temporarily solve the problem on Earth but has no long-term impact because death does not exist at the soul level. Punishment is unable to revive the soul within the criminal. The negativity comes back as the conscience lies dead. Use of any kind of force cannot re-direct a person's thoughts to positivity. Instead of using shortcuts to curb criminal acts, we need to find ways to develop people's emotional reasoning and ability to empathize. Metaphorically speaking, using pesticides to kill insects in crops is not enough to ensure good crops. We also need to put fertilizers to improve the soil base. In everyday course of life, people may not become mafia dons but they still pursue power through means which cause them to be more negative than positive. The human race needs to comprehend the futility of staying negative or pursuing negative forms of power as a means to happiness.

CONCLUSION OF THE SESSION

Strangely, Dev's self-esteem rose multi-fold after this session. He felt inherently powerful. Yet, his desire to join the mafia to prove his power, reduced since he had seen himself unhappy as the Don. Dev realizes now, that though he felt powerful, he did not feel content… It was as if he kept striving for something but could never achieve that, in spite of working all his life. That life was futile because the soul suffered and continues to suffer. To evolve again, Dev wanted to use this life to accomplish the purpose of his life as a soul. However, as the Old Man (his spirit guide) kept warning him: –

'The pull of the dark forces remains, and each choice he makes is a test of his worthiness.'

CHAPTER 18

THE WARNING

THE WARNING

As he sat down for his next session, Dev seemed absorbed in his own thoughts. Something was bothering him. He had woken up from sleep last night to see the old man instructing him.

I asked him what the matter was.

"Something weird happened last night," he replied, looking up.

"What happened?"

"It's kind of weird…I don't know whether you would believe me…" he paused, as he spoke. "I suddenly woke up in the middle of the night and I saw the Old Man. He was saying something."

"What was he saying?"

"It was something like– *'If you continue like this, you would be killed,*" he replied, looking at me with questioning eyes.

"Why would he say that? Did he say anything else?"

"No, after that he went away," he replied.

"What do you think he meant? Continue like what?"

He paused and contemplated.

"It could be," he said and stopped hesitantly.

"What? Did you do anything he had warned you against?"

"It could be that. I was drinking last evening," he paused and continued, "two friends called up. They wanted me to help them."

"Help?"

"They had got into an argument with some older guys who were threatening to beat them up," he paused.

"So?"

"They wanted me to go and help them. So, I went," he stated.

"You went to fight some street guys, when the Old man has been warning you not to misuse your fighting skills? It was their fight. Why did you get involved?"

"I could not say NO. Those guys are cowardly. I had to help them," he replied with a grimace.

"Then, why are you feeling bad?"

"I beat up those guys very badly," he said in an exasperated tone. "It was not needed. They had collapsed long back. I just went on hitting …on and on, till they said a cop is coming," he said in a self-reproaching tone.

"So, it was unjustified. What happened when the cop came?"

"We ran away…I wanted to drink, but those guys were not ready for even that. So, I went alone," he said, shaking his head.

"So, you did not even get appreciation for going out of your way?"

"They thanked me…but, yeah," he mused.

"Is that what is worrying you?"

"No," he said shrugging. "It's what the Old Man said. I thought I was helping those guys… that it was justified, but…"

"He did not seem to think that way…Besides, before helping anybody you should look at the cause…You can't just help anyone who may be shedding crocodile tears… It affects you badly…The Old Man told you that whatever injustice you do in this life, will come back to you in this same life."

"Yeah… But, I was helping… how can I know? They're my friends. How could I have said No?" he mused again.

"If you have problems in saying NO, we can desensitize that through therapy."

"I don't know…Why did he come? It was scary," he said, looking up.

"I cannot give you a sure answer on his behalf. We can ask the Old Man why he came."

"I'm not sure whether it was real or not. Do you think it came or whether it was something I dreamt?" he asked.

"I don't know. There is no harm in talking to your subconscious mind, if it wants to tell you something. Maybe, the Old Man is saying what you already know at a subconscious level."

He shook his head. "It was too real to be imagination, " he contemplated.

"I am not saying it was imagination. Let us go to the Old Man and ask."

"Okay," he nodded.

DEV'S SIXTH LIFE BETWEEN LIFE SESSION

I took Dev into the hypnotic trance. I started with breathing relaxation and moved on to light visualization. While in the middle of Light visualization, his eyes were distracted.

"Do you see anything?"

"I am walking down the stairs of an old building," he said.

"Where?"

"It is that same place… I look old," he replied.

"Is this the salvation point?"

"Yes," he replied.

"Why are you being shown that? Is anyone saying anything?"

"*You have to reach that place…*" he spoke in a gruff voice, and paused. "It is gone now," he concluded in his own voice. The voice had come from above. It was some kind of message being given to him, probably by his Higher Self.

I continued with the induction into trance state. I next took him down the stairs, through the Hall of Doorways, and in through the door which opened to the Pre-Life-planning stage of the current life.

"Are you in the Life between Life space?"

"Yes," he replied.

"What do you see?"

"I am going down a slope," he replied.

"How does it look?"

"It's like a small hill. It is green," he nodded, an expression of appreciation on his face.

"Ok, where are you going?"

"The Old Man is standing at the end of the slope," he replied.

"Okay, when you are with him, let me know."

"Yes," he nodded, indicating he was with him.

"Okay, ask him what he was trying to tell you last night?"

"If you continue the same way, you will be killed," replied Dev in the gruff voice of the Old Man.

"Why did he say that?"

"We gave you a test. You failed in that," replied the Old Man.

"Which test? The urge to fight for your friends? Was that a test?"

"Yes… If you continue like this, we will have to kill you," Dev spoke in a flat tone, but the warning intonation was clear.

"Continue like what? What does he mean? Ask."

"You have to choose who to fight and who not to fight. You have to unlearn to learn," explained the Old Man.

"Does this mean there was no need to fight for his friends?"

"They were cowards. The road to redemption is tough. You will have to give one test after another," continued the Old Man in his gruff, slow tone.

"Have your tests begun already? He earlier said this was the training period?"

> *"The real tests will begin in two years. Those tests will be far more severe," he paused and continued. "Yesterday's test was an example. You failed in that test. If you fail in those tests, you will go in the wrong path. Once you join the negative forces, there is no redemption for you."*

"If you are in the profession of violence, you may get carried away. Can you join any other profession? How about scuba diving or management? You keep thinking of joining those?"

"You have to heal all the souls whose purpose of life the soul of Maximus took away, You have to sacrifice this life to make up for the crimes that soul committed …pursue anything you desire, after you finish that purpose.," reinstated the Old Man.

"Does this mean he cannot choose an alternate profession?"

"*You can choose any path that would help you use the powers of Maximus in the right way,*" replied the Old Man.

"Would more tests come his way?"

"*The next two years is the training period. All the difficulties now are in preparation for the major tests which lie ahead. Concentrate on learning,*" replied the Old Man.

"What if he fails again?"

"*In these two years, if he tries to go in the wrong path, we will have to take the extreme step to stop him. Once the tests begin, he will become too powerful,*" replied Dev on behalf of the Old Man

"Ask how will you know when to use violence and when not to?"

"*There will be no situation in the next two years, where hitting would be required to attain justice,*" replied the Old Man. "*If he gets into a fight before the actual tests begin, he will be killed. Once the training period is over, he will become too powerful. We will have to stop him before that.*"

The Old Man spoke addressing Dev as *HE*, which indicated that he was speaking directly to me, than to him. When he spoke to him directly, he addressed him as *YOU*.

"Can you take a life like that?"

"*Usually, we don't intervene. Here, we have a deal. This soul wanted redemption so that he could return to his planet. We wanted a soldier for The Light. If he breaks that deal, we can make ONE attempt to kill him, before the actual tests began,*" replied the Old Man.

"Before the actual tests begin? What does that mean?"

"*He will have the choice to join the dark forces, after his tests begin. We cannot allow him that as he is capable of causing mass destruction. We will make an attempt before the tests begin,*" explained the Old Man.

"Will he get redemption then?"

"*If he fails to achieve his purpose this time, there is no redemption for the soul. For several life-times he will not get another chance,*" said the Old Man.

"But, if you kill him before he gives the tests, then what happens to the soul? Can he come back to Earth and try again to achieve his purpose?"

"*The fate of the soul has not been decided yet,*" replied the Old Man.

"Okay… So, you can make one attempt to kill him, before his actual tests begin, if you feel he is likely to join the dark forces. Is that right?"

"*Yes,*" replied the Old Man.

"Ok, do you need to ask anything else?"

"No," replied Dev.

"Then, thank the Old Man and come back to the Hall of Doorways."

"Yes," he replied when he was back.

"Now, be back under the stairs and I'll wake you up."

I woke him up from his trance.

DEV'S PERSPECTIVE

Dev now understood why the Old Man appeared in his dream, but he still did not completely believe it. He did not want to take advice from anybody about what he should do or should not do. Most importantly, he wasn't yet convinced about not using violence as a means of coercion or gaining power to spread justice.

The Old Man had repeatedly told him that violence could only be used as a last resort when the cause was justice and not his popularity being at stake. However, Dev chose to ignore the Old man as a dream sequence. A week later, another incident of a similar nature occurred, which led to the Old Man intervening visibly, that is, through his conscious mind. Subsequently, there were counter attacks by the dark forces on Dev.

CONCLUSION OF THE SESSION

Up until now, I was not convinced whether the Old Man was an entity in his own right or a personality of Dev's subconscious mind that he could access during his hypnosis sessions. This was the first apparent intervention by the Old Man during the course of Dev's therapy who appeared in his dream, without being summoned; Dev was able to see him when he was not in a hypnotic trance. That meant that the Old Man had a mind of his own and that he existed beyond Dev's mind. With this incident and the next, Dev and I were more convinced that an alternate reality exists.

CHAPTER 19

SATAN'S PULL – ANGER, TEMPTATION AND…

"*SATAN PULLS THROUGH ANGER, temptation and negative form of power,*" said the Old Man, while Dev was in trance.

Dev had an accident, that morning before he came in for the session. He almost got run over by a bus. The peculiarity was that the Old Man had appeared before the accident to warn him not to go in that direction. He had believed it to be a delusion and gone ahead on the road where he was warned not to go. A bus had come suddenly from an opposite direction; he had managed to turn just in the nick of time to miss the bus.

He walked in confidently for the session, and proudly told me how he had saved himself from getting killed under the bus. "The Old Man had appeared when I was thinking to go that side or not. It was weird."

"How did he appear?"

"I was driving and he just appeared, in front of me. He said – *don't go there,*" Dev said, looking perplexed.

"Then?"

"He disappeared," he shrugged.

"You did not heed his warning?"

"No, I had to go there for some work." he said.

"Anyway, I am alive now," he continued, relaxed. "It could have been bad but I escaped it."

"Yes…but, we will have to ask the Old Man what this was about."

"Okay," he agreed.

"You haven't got into any fights since he warned you not to?"

"No, yesterday I almost got into a fight. But, I didn't," he replied.

"Okay, that's good. How come?"

"I just didn't feel like it. The argument was foolish. I thought I should support my friend. I was going to but…" he shrugged. "Suddenly, I felt calm so I just ignored the urge to fight."

I was impressed by this sudden change in his thinking. However, I did not realize then that it had occurred due to an intervention by the Old Man in his mind.

DEV`S SEVENTH LIFE BETWEEN LIFE SESSION

I took Dev into trance by starting with the breathing relaxation. Then, we moved on to the Light Visualization process.

"Now imagine a light entering from the top of your head. It can be any colour you see. What colour comes to your mind, first?"

Usually, he saw BLUE colour – which is the colour of an Indigo soul. He always said that it's nice. But this time he gave a different answer which appeared strange.

"Red," he replied, a little surprised himself.

"Red? How does it feel?"

"It doesn't feel good," he replied and paused. "It is blue on top. The bottom one-third is red. It is shaped like a spear. Here!" He indicated the space above the top of his head.

He looked worried.

"Okay, just let the Red stay there. Don't let it enter you. Just concentrate on the top of your head and feel relaxed. As you exhale, you exhale out dark smoke and as you inhale, you inhale pure oxygen. With each breath, keep going deeper and deeper, until you reach the deepest levels of your subconscious mind."

Thus, I continued taking him deeper without the actual light visualization process. I did not ask him to visualize Light because he was seeing RED colour and wasn't feeling comfortable about it. Dev went deep in trance again.

Next, I took him through the Hall of Doorways into the Life-between-Life space.

"What do you see?"

"The Old Man is there," replied Dev.

"Okay, ask him why the red colour is there?"

"The pull of the dark forces has become strong. Satan is testing worthiness," replied the Old Man, in his gruff voice.

"How is he testing worthiness?"

"Anger, temptation, negative form of power," replied the Old Man.

"What are those?"

"That is how Satan pulls. The pull from the dark forces will be through temptation or through anger," replied the Old Man.

"So, Satan pulls by working on the mind? Ask."

"Yes," replied the Old Man.

"How would you know if it is Satan pulling?"

"The urge for power is always external. Whatever rewards the evil forces give will be external. They will be transitory in nature," replied the Old Man.

"How are those rewards transitory in nature?"

"It is not about doing the job that is important; it is how you do it," replied the Old Man.

"What does he mean by that? Ask."

"There will be no lasting sense of satisfaction once the job is completed. The peace I give is internal. It is long lasting," replied the Old Man.

"How would you know the difference?"

"You can make out the difference in your mind," stated Dev on behalf of the Old Man.

"Why has Satan's pull become stronger now? Ask?"

"I had to intervene…We could not allow you to fight. Before the spark reaches the oil, it has to be prevented," replied the Old Man.

"How did you intervene?"

"I gave you calm when you were going to fight. You almost slipped yesterday," replied the Old Man.

"How has that led to Satan's pull becoming stronger?"

"Because I intervened when I was not supposed to. We had to give them two attempts," replied the Old Man.

"What does that mean? Two attempts?"

"If I had not intervened, you would have been killed...Now, they can try to kill you. They have got two chances to kill you," replied the Old Man.

"Okay...So, the dark forces would try to kill you? Is that what the Old Man is saying?"

"Yes," confirmed Dev in the Old Man's gruff voice.

"Is today's accident connected to that?"

"Yes. They made one attempt today. They will make another in the next 15 days," stated the Old Man.

"What can you do so that their attempt fails? Ask."

"Their attempts are weak...Satan will work through the mind. Resist the pull," replied the Old Man.

"How can you do that?"

"You have to avoid going to those places," replied the Old Man.

"Which places?"

"Where the pull is strong," replied the Old Man.

"Okay or if you do go to those places, you can choose not to fight. Would desensitizing your resistance to say NO help?"

"Yes... you have to learn to say NO," replied the Old Man, *"You need to control your heart. If you learn to control your egoistic part, half of the work is done."*

The heart symbolized Dev's emotional impulses. This message held a deep meaning for Dev whose egoistic part was Maximus who influenced his heart which represented his emotional impulses the most. Maximus, in his heart, was bleeding with a desire for revenge. The Old Man was saying that if Dev could control the personality of Maximus, half of the work was done.

"Okay... we will desensitize your resistance to say NO. You

can say NO whenever the pull is from the dark forces. Ask, how can you distinguish between fighting for dark forces and fighting for the Light?"

> *"The pull from the forces of Light would ask you to use violence for reasons which would require honesty and courage to fight injustice...,"* explained the Old Man. *"The pull from the dark forces will be through temptation or through anger. The need to fight would be to suppress the argument by a show of power. There would not be any real need for violence and nothing would be lost if it is not used."*

"Okay...thank you for that guidance... Can we also remove his negative feelings of anger, fear, guilt, hurt and sadness over a period of time so that the pull of the dark forces is much lower?"

"You cannot remove guilt. He has to heal those souls whose purpose of life he took away. They have to forgive him," replied the Old Man.

"Can we, anyway, try to heal him now, so that he is not tempted again?"

"You haven't seen the destruction he has caused... the villages he destroyed...We cannot allow that to happen again," replied the Old Man.

"Can we remove the other negative emotions like anger and fear?"

"You can," replied the Old Man, after a pause.

"Okay, thank you...Is there anything else you want to ask him?"

"No," replied Dev.

"Okay, then thank him and be back in the Hall of Doorways."

I woke him up from trance.

THE TIMELINE

"He has warned you not to go to those places. They will make another attempt to kill you."

"Yeah!" Dev shrugged. His expression showed that he did not take the Old Man seriously.

"If we check your Timeline now, it may help."

"What is the Timeline?"

"The Timeline is an energy line which goes through your subconscious mind. It connects your past, present and future in a linear manner. You can't actually see the line but in trance you can feel it…

When there is a difficulty, there is an unfinished soul lesson. The subconscious mind always works for a positive intention. It stores that memory of fear or hurt because it wants you to learn that lesson, so that you do not repeat the mistake. Through the timeline, we find the first incident which caused the problem."

"I don't have fear," he replied, unwilling to think of himself as afraid of anything.

"Okay, just find the Timeline. We can go back and see the first incident your mind has recorded of your visit on Earth. You will know how old you are as a soul, on Earth."

"How old a soul are you?" he asked me, with a half-grin.

"When I first saw my TimeLine, I saw an incident which was two thousand years old. Then, when I saw it again for healing an emotion, I saw another incident which was five thousand years old… I am a very old soul… With each emotion, you would see a different date, depending on the first incident since it is unhealed."

"Okay," he nodded.

"The first event where you encountered the negative emotion is like a big rock in the subconscious mind. In a drain, a rock prevents water to flow freely; similarly, this negative memory prevents free energy flow in the body. Any new incident which creates a similar negative emotion is pulled by this rock and gets attached to it. The negative emotions stored, act like poisonous acid in the body, causing continued stress."

"Healing that negative emotion is like removing a big rock stuck in the drain. Once the big rock is gone, the smaller rocks dissolve fast and water can flow freely."

"Okay," he nodded.

I helped Dev discover his Time-Line. The Time-Line extends way back in the past and way ahead in the future. *If somebody's Time-Line for the future appears blocked, curled or small, then that person can be suicidal or approaching death.*

To help Dev see the first incident recorded, he had to be taken towards the past on the Time-Line.

"Go back on the line. Keep going towards the past. See how far it extends. How far back do you go? What do you see?"

"I see that Roman soldier who betrayed his king," replied Dev.

"Beyond that?"

"I can vaguely see my planet... but I can't go beyond that point," he replied.

"Ask your subconscious mind if you can go there?"

"No... I am not allowed to go there now," replied Dev.

"Okay, then brighten up your line. See your bright past, as bright as you can. What do you see?"

"Yes, it is brighter," he replied.

"Come back to the present... and go towards the future. How far can you go? How big is your future line?"

"It is very small," he replied.

"How small?"

"About one-two centimetres," he replied.

That was worrying. Usually, a Time-Line is, at least, a few inches long.

"Okay, then extend it. Make it longer."

"Why?" he asked. "It is fine."

"It is important. I will explain. Just trust me once and make it longer."

"Okay," he replied and paused, trying to make it long. "It is not happening."

"Ask it why? Ask your mind what can you do to make it long?"

"It says I have to change my path," he paused and focused again, "if I go down left, it is short but if I turn up right, it is long."

"Okay, then turn it up right. Make it as long as you can."

"Yes, it is done," he nodded.

"Good... now see the line bright. Look back and see the present also brighter. Make the whole line bright."

"Yes," he replied.

I was relieved that he had made his Time-Line longer. I did not anticipate how much more relieved I would be until his next session.

"Okay, you can open your eyes now? How does it feel?"

"Good," he nodded.

"If the Time-Line is too short, it means you are not anticipating a future in your mind. It can mean death...or at least that you have no clear goal, no direction for the soul. Now, your line is longer. You have a path ahead of you."

"Yes," he nodded.

We ended the session at that.

THE SECOND ATTEMPT: DEV'S EIGHTH LIFE BETWEEN LIFE SESSION

The next day he had another accident where he just missed being killed.

One day before we had extended his Time-Line. Probably, if we had not extended his Time-Line, he may have been killed.

Dev said it was a minor accident, though it could have been fatal. *The coincidence with the Old Man's warning was too glaringly obvious to be ignored.*

We again went to the Life-between-Life space to ask the Old Man. During induction, he again saw the red colour above his head, in the form of a spear.

"Whom do you see?"

"The Old Man is there," replied Dev, once he had reached the Life Between Life space.

"Was the accident you had today connected to the dark forces? Ask."

"*It was the second attempt,*" replied Dev, on behalf of the Old Man, "*the attempts are over now.*"

"The red colour is still there. Is there any more threat? Ask."

"*Satan will continue to prevent you from going in the right path. Later, they would try to prevent you from reaching the salvation point,*" replied the Old Man.

"What can you do to stay on the right path?"

"*Stop going to those places, where the pull is strong,*" replied the Old Man, "*if you go in the wrong path again, we would have to stop you.*"

"What would they do to stop you? Ask."

"*We would have to make one attempt to kill you. Our attempt would be much stronger. It would be one attempt for their twenty attempts,*" replied the Old Man

"Does alcohol affect temptation to fight?"

"*Yes, drinking makes Satan more powerful in that instant,*" replied the Old Man, and continued, "*Satan works through his mind. When he is drinking, he is not in touch with his own mind. The dark forces can slip in then.*"

"What if he gets tempted again? What can he do to resist that pull?"

"*He has to avoid going to places where it comes,*" replied the Old Man again. "*Right actions will help.*"

"What do you mean by right actions?"

"*Studying would help him,*" replied the Old Man.

"What else can help him?"

"*Exercise …*" replied the Old Man, in a vague tone.

The Old Man was giving suggestions, which would help Dev generate a positive feeling. From the soul's perspective, by right actions, the Old Man meant that Dev could do whatever gave him a right feeling.

"Would removing the need to drink help as well?"

"*Yes, that would help him resist the pull,*" replied the Old Man.

"What if he continues to drink as much as he does?"

"We would not be able to help him, if he slips again," replied the Old Man.

"Okay, so if we desensitize the inability to say NO ...so that you can say NO to your friends when they want you to fight, and you reduce the need to drink, then you would be less dependent on them. Ask the Old Man if that is okay?"

"Satan will fail. Redemption will be complete," stated the Old Man explicitly.

"Okay, is there anything else you need to ask the Old Man?"

"No," replied Dev

"Okay, then thank the Old Man and be back in the Hall Of Doorways."

I woke him up from his trance.

CONCLUSION OF THE SESSION

The Old Man clearly said that dark forces are thought forms which enter a person's mind when his conscious mind is not in control. He also said that the dark forces' influence could be reduced by resisting the pull towards negative thinking. Due to the Time-Line coincidence, and the logistic explanation given of the dark forces, Dev's belief in the existence of the unseen realm grew further, which speeded up his healing.

Subsequently, we did several sessions where we desensitized his resistance to say NO and also worked on his need to drink. Once he found the ability to say NO, he never fought for his friends again. He did get pulled into one fight where the cause was just. However, there were no dire consequences of that. Some amusing yet perplexing values he had stored in his subconscious mind came up from his life as the Greek soldier, Maximus, during the process of de-addicting him from drinking in the next session.

CHAPTER 20

WHAT KINGS AND SOLDIERS DO...

WHEN DEV CAME FOR the next session, I reminded him that we needed to de-addict him from drinking so that the pull of dark forces would reduce.

"I am not an addict. I don't drink every day," he said defiantly.

"I don't have a problem with it... The Old Man said it is safer for you if you avoid drinking... But, you don't seem to want to quit drinking?"

"No, I don't," he agreed.

"Why not?"

"It feels good," he replied.

"What do you mean by feeling good?"

"... Not feeling bad," he paused and replied.

"What do you mean by not feeling bad?"

"Being able to study," he replied, in a low self-reproaching tone.

"So, how is drinking helping you in that?"

"It makes me think less about the problem which prevents me from studying," he replied.

"But, it also gives you a hangover because of which you cannot study even more. How does it help you not think of your other problems? Does it help you relax? Does it give you a high?"

"It does give me some high later after I have around 10-11 pegs," he stated.

"10-11 pegs! Some high...it doesn't help you relax. Does it give you any pleasure at all?"

"No... actually it doesn't," he shrugged, contemplating, "It's just that... everyone does it."

"Everyone? You are not everyone. You can't choose your actions based on what everyone does. Different people have different reasons for doing the same things...Decide what makes YOU want to drink... Why do you drink?"

"I'm a man; a man drinks," he declared, in an assertive tone.

"Women also drink. Drinking is no longer associated with being a man..."

"Yeah...maybe," he said doubtfully.

"Okay...From what I understand, one part of you wants to drink, but another part of you doesn't get a high from drinking. So, there is a conflict in your mind?"

"Yes," he nodded, agreeing.

"So, we could try parts integration between these two parts... just to find out if there can be a consensus between these two parts?"

"I don't see a need to stop drinking," he replied, resisting the idea of quitting drinking.

"You don't need to stop it. You can reduce it...You know the pull of the dark forces becomes strong when you are drinking."

"Bah... I will destroy all of them. I'm a soldier," he said.

"You can destroy them only when you are in control of your own mind. They enter when you are not in control of your own mind... What's the harm in doing a parts integration? You can continue drinking if you still want to. We are only trying to understand your subconscious mind."

"Okay," he nodded, contemplating. "Let's do it."

PARTS INTEGRATION: UNDERSTANDING THE NEED FOR DRINKING

I relaxed Dev through the breathing exercise and light visualization.

He again saw the colour RED on top of his head.

"The Red is still there," he said pointing to the top of his head.

"How does it look?"

"It's the same, like a spear at the end," he replied.

"Okay, let it remain. You don't need to take it inside. Just focus on your breathing."

"Okay," he nodded, and continued with the relaxing process.

Once he was relaxed, I asked him to extend both his hands, bent from the elbow.

"Ok, now call the personality which wants you to drink. Is it there?"

"Yes," he replied instantly.

"What does it look, feel and sound like? Anybody you know?"

"Yes, it's Maximus," he replied.

"Ok, the Greek soldier…Now…call the personality which doesn't like to drink. Is it there?"

"Yes," he replied again immediately.

"Who does it look, feel and sound like?"

"It's a Blue Light," he replied.

"Is there any person there?"

"No, it's just a bright light," he replied.

The bright light could be his Soul energy in its pure form. It was obvious that the Greek soldier was responsible for most of his negative addictions.

"Okay, thank them both for coming."

"Yes," he nodded.

"We will start asking questions from the personality which likes to drink, first. Give me the first answers which come to your mind."

"Yes," he nodded.

I started asking questions from the personality which liked to drink. Dev was in a light hypnotic trance. The answers were coming directly from his subconscious mind.

"What is the intention behind wanting to drink?"

"That is what kings and soldiers do," declared Dev, in the heavy voice of the Greek soldier…

It was a queer answer. It sounded strange because it was coming from Dev, though the Greek soldier spoke it. Dev, by himself, did not any way look like a person who would want to drink because that is what kings and soldiers did.

He was a boy from the 21st century. The answer was coming directly from the Greek soldier who was a personality frozen in bygone eras of kings and soldiers. There was no point in telling him that kings no longer existed.

"What is the positive intention behind drinking because that is what kings and soldiers do?"

"It is glamorous," he replied.

"What is the positive intention behind drinking, because it is glamorous?"

"It is associated with being a man," replied the Greek soldier.

"Who associates it with being a man? Which other man drinks?"

"My father, the king," he declared in his heavy, commanding voice.

"But you don't like him. What is the positive intention behind drinking because it is associated with being a man?"

"Other Generals drink. My teachers drink. My soldiers drink… I drink with them," replied the Greek soldier.

"What is the positive intention behind doing what they all do?"

"They are all strong men; all strong men drink," he replied.

"What is the positive intention behind believing that all strong men drink?"

"Accrymese used to drink," replied the Greek soldier.

"Who's Accrymese?"

"He is a great soldier, all great soldiers drink," replied Maximus.

"What will happen if you don't drink?"

"I won't become a great soldier," replied Maximus.

"Is there any other positive intention for drinking?"

"That is a style…" replied the Greek soldier.

"What do you mean by style?"

"It makes me strong and aggressive," replied the Greek soldier.

"What is the intention behind wanting to be strong and aggressive?"

"So that I can kill the enemy," replied Maximus.

"Why do you need to kill?"

"That is what everyone does," replied Maximus.

"You kill because that is what everyone does? Who is everyone?"

"Everyone…only saints and monks don't kill. And they are not powerful," replied the Geek soldier.

"What is the positive intention behind wanting to be powerful?"

"To fight against injustice," replied Maximus.

"Injustice against who?"

"The weak and the oppressed," replied the Greek soldier.

"Is there any other positive intention for drinking? Does your girlfriend get impressed by your drinking?"

"No," he replied. "When love is there, I don't need to drink."

"So, when she is there with you, you don't drink?"

"Nah… I don't," replied Maximus

"So, you actually desire love…Is love the positive intention behind wanting to be powerful?"

"Maybe," he replied.

"So, does drinking make you feel more accepted?"

"Yes," he replied.

"So, the positive intention behind drinking is to feel powerful and accepted. What is the intention behind being wanting to feel powerful and accepted?"

"So that I can fight for justice," replied Dev.

"What is the positive intention of fighting for justice?"

"I am a soldier… That is my identity," he replied.

"Okay, so, you are drinking to save your identity, because you feel it makes you strong and aggressive and helps you fight for justice?"

"Yes," he replied.

"But, when love is there, you don't need to drink to feel powerful. You feel you have your identity, even without drinking, and you can do your job as a soldier?"

"Yes, when love is there, I don't need anything else," he replied.

So, the personality within Dev – that of Maximus, was actually craving for love. He needed to drink when the woman who loved him wasn't around because he did not feel accepted otherwise. When he found the love he was seeking, he did not need alcohol as an escape.

Dev was carrying the thought pattern of the Greek soldier. The main reason for Dev's drinking in the present time was that he wanted to do what everyone does, to feel respected in the society. The Greek soldier felt strong and aggressive after drinking, which made him want to kill the enemy. The same thing happened with Dev. After drinking, he wanted to hit somebody. The problem was that this kind of aggression was inappropriate.

"Okay, so, now let's talk to the personality on your other hand, the Blue Light. Is it ready to talk?"

"Yes," replied Dev.

"What is your positive intention behind not wanting to drink?"

"It doesn't give me a high," replied the Blue Light.

"What is the positive intention behind it not giving you a high?"

There was no reply. I repeated the question.

"What is the positive intention behind it not giving you a high?"

"You don't get a high because we prevent it. We do not let drinks affect your mind," replied Dev in a gruff voice.

"Who said that?"

"There was a light above, which answered," replied Dev.

"Do you see anyone there?"

"No, just a bright light…blue," replied Dev.

"Okay, so you don't get a high because it is prevented. What is their positive intention in preventing you from getting a high?"

"So that you do not depend on external things for strength," replied Dev again in the voice of the Old Man. It was either his Higher Self or the Old Man, who seemed to be speaking from the Light.

"What is the positive intention behind not depending on external things for strength?"

"*Strength will come from within, when you need it to fight for the cause,*" replied Dev in the same slow, gruff voice.

"What is the positive intention behind not drinking and wanting the strength to come from within?"

"*Drinking is not helping the cause,*" replied the voice from the Blue Light.

"What is the positive intention behind believing that drinking is not helping the cause?"

"That I don't become an alcoholic," replied Dev.

"What is the positive intention behind not becoming an alcoholic?"

"Not losing control," replied Dev.

"What is the positive intention behind not wanting to lose control?"

"*If I lose control, there is a threat to my existence,*" replied Dev.

"And, you don't want to drink because you don't want to lose control?"

"Yes," replied the Blue Light.

"Also, you don't want to drink because drinking can be a threat to your existence?"

"Yes," replied Dev.

"And you don't want to drink because you want to fight for the cause without depending on external things?"

"Yes," replied Dev.

His hands, bent straight from the elbow, were coming closer now. This indicated that the two personalities within his subconscious mind were reaching a consensus.

"So, you feel you can fight for the cause with your internal strength, without needing to drink?"

"Yes."

"When you have internal strength you don't need to drink?"

"Yes," replied Dev. His hands were very close now.

"Okay, so both the personalities agree that when they feel strong, loved and accepted from within, they don't need to drink?"

"Yes," nodded Dev in an affirmative voice.

"Okay, now, thank the two personalities for having reached a mutual consent on not drinking."

"Yes," replied Dev.

"Now, join both the palms together in a fist and integrate the energies."

"Yes," Dev joined both the hands together, in a fist.

"Now, move your palms to your chest and take the energies into your heart. Which colour do you see going into your heart?"

"Blue," replied Dev.

"Okay, good. You can put your hands down now. Open your eyes, and come back to your conscious state."

Dev opened his eyes and came back to his normal conscious state.

THE SOUL'S PERSPECTIVE

It was clear that Dev's two personalities: his Higher Self, represented by the Blue Light and the personality of the Greek soldier had disparate intentions. The Blue Light wanted Dev to rely on his inner strengths to attain power whereas the personality of the Greek soldier, Maximus, wanted him to attain power through imitating what other powerful men did. The soul had a positive need for power. The soul energy never used negative words, like 'enemy,' or 'kill.' It said it wanted to use its strengths to fight for a just cause. However, Dev continued to live with the beliefs held by Maximus. Apparently, there was no change in the thinking or evolution of his soul since the last two thousand years. He was still so much focused on getting success and approval in the external world, that he could not focus on what his soul was seeking at the emotional/evolutionary level. Whenever a conflict arose in his mind, he thought it was a desire to fight against the injustice done to him because of which he felt like a failure. It was a battle with himself; a battle of personalities between the vengeful intentions of Maximus and the pure intentions of the Blue Light.

The Blue Light, his Higher Self always pulled him away from negative paths, while the Earth-bound vengeful spirit coaxed him to follow his urges towards violence, alcohol and being destructive. The meaningless success he got, led to instant gratification but increased anxiety later. He pursued negative means to bring in the hope of raising his positivity by establishing justice but since the causes he fought for were unjust, he failed and therefore felt betrayed often.

However, at the subconscious level, we had found that he felt that injustice was done to him by other people, because he did not feel loved by them. Thus, the desire, from the soul's perspective, was not just to fight against injustice, but to feel loved as well.

Dev thought that power and position were needed to feel loved, but by seeking power in a way which caused him to think negatively, he was going against his soul. As the Old Man told him, *'right actions would help,'* had he pursued power in a way that it helped him get justice for the truly weak and oppressed, he would have felt loved by them naturally. This session made me realize, once again, how much we get influenced by other people.

In the process of satisfying an external desire, we stop focusing on the feeling we seek to satisfy, at the soul level, through pursuing external desires.

Like Dev, we all carry over values and beliefs from previous lives. The biggest conflicts in our mind arise because of our conditioning which makes us hold onto beliefs, which have become redundant in our present circumstances. These make us feel negative, instead of helping in our growth. Instead, we could focus on achieving the positive feelings that we desire, and at the same time take actions. This is better than dwelling on preconceived notions of being conventionally rich or successful. Just pursuing external appreciation often leads us into a trap of a negative cycle as we may strive to imitate a superficial lifestyle, wherein the masses are internally unhappy, materialistically competitive and angry.

A positive inner focus would multiply good energies in our lives, creating the desired happy future with inner feelings of peace, self-approval and being loved. This would also help us understand and achieve our soul's purpose more effectively.

CONCLUSION OF THE SESSION

Dev understood his need for drinking but he had not got over the habit yet. He did not feel loved and hence felt the need for acceptance through drinking. Drinking made him feel one with men who exhibited power. However, a mutual consensus was reached between the two personalities; that of Maximus and the Blue Light. The personality of Maximus, which had been coaxing Dev to drink, was now ready to explore ways to quit drinking. The personality understood that the real soul need was to develop his core strengths and not depend on instant gratification to feel powerful. Dev was thus ready to undergo therapeutic sessions, through which, we recovered the most recent past life that was the start point of his present drinking habits. We also healed childhood emotional deprivations that significantly helped in reducing his need for drinking.

CHAPTER 21

THE RACING HEART

DEV REACHED LATE FOR the session. Being late was unusual for him. He had been disturbed for the last few days because his heart was beating abnormally fast, again. The racing heart always worried him because it made him feel out of control. He was more disturbed because he had been taking psychiatric pills hoping that they would help in regulating his heartbeat but his heart still raced off and on. The pills he took had been given because he was suspected of suffering from borderline schizophrenia. However, he had agreed to take them due to his pounding heartbeat and when they did not help in controlling it, he thought they were ineffective. That made him feel helpless.

When he sat down, he looked depressed.
"What's on your mind?"
"Nothing," he said, looking down.
"You look tense. Why are you late today?"
"I went to the doctor," he said, looking up, his eyes tense.
"Why?"
"It's my heart… It is beating very fast," he replied.
"What did the doctor say?"
"He said it's nothing… It is just that way," he replied.
"But, why does it happen on certain days and not others? What have you been doing differently?"
"Nothing," he replied again, shaking his head nonchalantly.
"Have you been drinking?"
"Yeah…" he nodded.
"Drinking could be causing your heart problem."

"That is just coincidence. It doesn't always race because of drinking," he stated.

"Yes, but when it races you are drinking."

"Nobody's heart races because of drinking," he replied.

"You can't generalize. Other peoples' past lives may not have a bleeding heart either."

"But, this is a purely physical problem. It is not affecting the soul," he replied.

"Then what else have you been doing differently? Think."

"Dumbbells. I was doing Yoga, but that gets boring. I like doing dumbbells. It makes me feel Strong," he said, emphasizing how he felt.

"Strong? How do you feel after doing dumbbells? Do you feel relaxed?"

"No… Actually, it gets disturbing. I have this strong urge to go and hit somebody," he replied.

"You feel relaxed after you do Yoga. Why don't you stick to that?"

"Nah, weak men do all that. I want to be Strong," he said again.

"Strong and aggressive? You have been drinking and doing dumbbells. That combination could be a reason for your racing heartbeat. Maximus is resurfacing."

"Nah…this is a medical problem," he stated, shaking his head.

"How do you know that the soul is not connected to your body?"

"Everything is not connected to the soul. The soul is above all this. It feels no pain. These are problems of this world and they need to be solved by means available in *this* world," he said contemplatively.

"Yes, but there is a specific thought pattern, that is causing these problems in you. Problems don't manifest out of the blue. The subconscious mind runs the body according to instructions given by the conscious mind. A negative situation occurs in your body only when you focus on a negative feeling repeatedly in your mind. Maybe, you need to change some patterns in your life."

Dev however, was still convinced that another check-up of

the heart was what he needed. I suggested we go back to a past life and check if this problem has its roots there. He agreed, reluctantly.

UNCOVERING THE PAST-LIFE CONNECTION OF THE RACING HEART

We started the Hypnotic process.

During Light Visualization, Dev once again, saw the red colour.

"Now, visualize a light on top of your head. It can be any colour you choose it to be."

"I see the red colour," he replied.

We continued the induction. Once Dev was relaxed, I took him down the staircase, into the Hall of Doorways.

"Now as I count from 5 to 1, enter the door which pulls you the most. As you enter the door, you will be in another life, another time, in the event, which can explain your racing heartbeat, and or the event where you experienced the racing heartbeat for the first time…NOW! 5, 4, 3, 2, 1 and 0. Are you there?"

"Yes," he replied, once he was through the door.

"What is the first impression you get?"

"It's the Don," he replied.

"What is he doing?" I asked him.

"Drinking," replied Dev.

"What is he drinking?"

"Scotch," he replied. Scotch was Dev's preferred drink in his present life.

"How is he feeling?"

"He has a gun in his hand. He is going to kill someone," he replied.

"Kill who?"

"I can't make out who it is," he replied, focusing, "it's part of his job."

"Okay… So, he is drinking before going to kill someone?"

"Yes," replied Dev.

"Does he always do that? Focus."

"Yes... He drinks a lot," he replied.

"Who else is with him when he is drinking?"

"There is no one. He lives alone... He is sitting ... There is a gun in his hand," he replied.

"Can you feel his heart? How does it feel?"

"Okay," he shrugged and replied. He could not enter his body, since he was addressing the Don as HE and not I.

"Do you feel it could be racing?"

"Maybe," he focused and replied.

"So, how does he deal with it?"

"Nothing...He is used to it," he replied, "there are other things which concern him more."

"Okay...So, he drinks, and then he goes to kill someone. Is that a pattern in his life?"

"Yes... He is lonely... he is thinking of the girl he loved," he continued.

"Okay...where is she now?"

"She became a nun," he replied.

"Okay...So, he is drinking, and he is lonely, and he is going to kill someone. Is that right?"

"Yes," replied Dev.

"And how does he feel when he kills someone?"

"Powerful," replied Dev.

The same pattern had emerged, when we were working with the personality of Maximus. He drank to feel strong and aggressive, so that he could kill the enemy. He felt powerful when he killed the enemy. However, he also felt that if the woman he loved was there with him, he would not need to drink. The need to be strong, aggressive and powerful was connected with drinking; so was the need to be loved.

The external lives of the Greek soldier Maximus and the Don, were very different. For example, Maximus was a soldier, whereas this guy was a Don; one worked for the law, the other against the law. However, at the level of feelings, both felt the same. The Don was repeating the life of Maximus, at the level of feelings. The soul was actually stuck with the energies of violence and revenge that Maximus had died with, and in each life it kept reliving the same feelings.

"And how does the soul feel?"

"Bad," Dev replied in a rueful tone.

TALKING WITH THE LIGHT

We needed guidance from someone in the Life between Life space about his life-plan, and whether we could heal his drinking problem through past life re-scripting. Dev could get this guidance by merging his mind with The Light, as in the life-between-life session.

"Ask the Light whether we can re-script this life to get you out of the habit of drinking."

"*No… You cannot,*" replied Dev.

"Why not?"

"*You have to heal the souls whose purpose of life you took away. They have to forgive you,*" replied Dev in a slow, gruff voice. It was his Higher Self answering or the Old man from the Light since he was being addressed as YOU.

"But, can we heal this part which was drinking so much?"

"*No…You need this part to achieve the purpose of your life,*" replied the voice. "*He knows how the mind of a criminal works. You need this knowledge to destroy those souls who use substance to destroy other souls, and destroy their own souls in the process. His energies will give you the mental strength to fight the enemies of the Light.*"

"But, the drinking habit causes stress to his heart."

"*The negative part will come along with that personality… You have to learn to control it,*" replied the voice.

"Okay, then disconnect from that life."

"I can't do that," replied Dev.

"Why?"

"He is a part of me. I cannot disconnect from him," he replied.
"But, you disconnected from your earlier lives?"
"Yes," he replied.
"Can you disconnect from this one?"
"No," he replied.
"Okay. So, you may need those energies, as the Light is saying. Let it be there."
"Yes," replied Dev.
"Ok, then rise above that body. Let that body live that life, and you come back into your present life."
"Yes," he replied, after a pause.
"There is something else I want to ask the Light. Be in the Light. Are you there?"
"Yes," replied Dev.
"Okay, ask why do you have the red colour above your head still?"
"The pull of the dark forces became strong because of our intervention," came the answer from the Light.
"Now, the attempts by the dark forces are over but the red colour is still there. When will it go?"
"In two weeks," replied the voice.
"Okay, thank the Light for that answer. Is there anything else you want to ask?"
"No," replied Dev.
I woke Dev up from trance.

THE SOUL'S PERSPECTIVE

From the soul's perspective, the racing heart was a warning to Dev to not indulge in thoughts of violence. The heartbeat used to increase due to him feeling aggressive after drinking and doing dumbbells. Dev was sure that drinking was not causing an increase in his heartbeat. He could be correct in that reasoning because the heartbeat did not rise each time he drank. *However, drinking and doing dumbbells together, was causing an increase in his heartbeat.*

The four features of *drinking, dumbbells, thoughts of violence and the racing heartbeat* were a part of the same energy circuit in his subconscious mind, though he did not realize it at the conscious level. According to him, all four were individual, separate activities. The connection did not strike him because he drank in the evening and exercised in the morning. So, it did not appear to him that he was doing them together. Yet, this was cumulatively increasing his thoughts of violence. The combination made him feel strong and aggressive, more than he ever felt otherwise.

At the subconscious level, this pattern evoked the personality of Maximus to take over since he was strong and aggressive. Thus, he increasingly felt the heartbeat as he was focused on his injured heart that kept reminding him that he was a failure and had to prove himself successful again by any means. The Greek soldier's negative focus and the rapid pacing of Dev's heart was accompanied with vengeful feelings in his mind. At the conscious level, he felt restless, frustrated and depressed whenever his heart raced. He yearned to prove his strength that made him want to hit somebody, and whenever he *did* hit, he felt bad later.

However, the heart was racing for a positive intention like all negative feelings that have a positive intention. He was being told by his subconscious mind to not indulge in activities which increased aggressive thoughts.

> *The intention of the soul was to help him get rid of the urge for negative power that came into him with the personality of the Don. From the soul's perspective, whenever the heart raced, he had to control the personality of the Don from emerging further. The racing heartbeat slowed him down so that he could think before taking actions.*

To fulfil his soul's need, he needed to stop all those activities that increased negative thoughts and aggression in his mind, which caused the heart to race; these included dumbbells and drinking.

Though Dev was clear that he did not like the racing heartbeat, he did not want to let go of drinking and doing dumbbells. Next was Inner Child Healing for him that had a significant impact on reducing his drinking habits. Six months down the line Dev's drinking habits had substantially lowered and he also stopped doing the dumbbells. As a result, he did not feel negatively aggressive; the desire to hit others was no longer fuelled. The heartbeat came under control. Later when he restarted these activities with much lower intensity, the heartbeat did not race.

CONCLUSION OF THE SESSION

Like Dev, we all carry over personalities and diseases from past lives. Whenever we indulge in a thought pattern, which is similar to that of a negative personality from a past life, the physical problems we faced then, also crop up. From a soul's perspective, our physical aches and pains guide us to not indulge in feelings and thoughts, which are negative. The soul is like an energy ball in a package which glows with Light of the Creator. When we feel diseased, we must identify the packet which is spoilt, not the ball of energy. However, due to the spoilt packet, the energy of the ball cannot reflect outside in its complete radiance. Likewise, the soul is unable to radiate its energy to the parts of the body which are diseased due to accumulation of negative energy in those parts. Just as a bulb can't glow fully when its wall is damaged, the soul cannot spread its positive energy, when the body is damaged. Practically, this means that due to the person's negative focus on fears and betrayals, the involvement of the soul in the person's body and in his life, reduces. As the Old Man said, the soul becomes small and insignificant due to negative thinking. The soul stays involved in the body only when the person strives to stay positive and raise the soul's frequency. If the person becomes negative, the soul's priorities of evolving with the work it does in the world, no longer matter to the person. When the person consistently ignores his soul's needs, he loses his sense of priority and functions as a car without a sane driver at the steering wheel. The car just moves randomly and may reach nowhere near its desired destination.

Dev was far from his soul-purpose but it wasn't purely because he was a Don. The profession does not matter as much as the temperament of the person. Very successful doctors have been reported to die early from heart attacks, indicating that the soul chooses to leave the body when its evolutionary needs are ignored. Focusing on the body without healing the mind's negative, defeatist thinking habits, frustrate the soul, be it a doctor or a don. We can heal our physical bodies and mental traumas, if we let go of habits and feelings, which seem conventionally correct but cause negativity in the soul later. Similarly, to heal his racing heart, Dev had to finally let go of drinking and doing dumbbells. We all have to control our negative personalities just as Dev had to control the Don. If we cannot be at peace due to our focus on worrying, disappointments, anger, fear, loneliness, etc., we need to learn how to detach, forgive and let go.

CHAPTER 22

CONVERSATION WITH A SPIRIT

FEELING LONELY

DEV WALKED IN, LOOKING crestfallen.

"How are you?"

"Okay," he replied in a sad tone, looking down at his feet.

"Is there something bothering you? How is your heart?"

"It is better now," he replied, looking up at the ceiling, and then looking down again.

"You look sad."

"She said she won't be coming to meet me anymore," he said. As he looked up, it appeared that he was almost crying.

"Who?"

"Anya, my girlfriend," he explained, still looking down.

"You said she had died. You were still meeting her?"

"She used to come in the woods to meet me," he said.

"Which woods? There are no woods around here. Did you go there in your mind?"

"I went there and she came…She comes often," he replied, with a forlorn gaze, probably to indicate that he went there in his mind to meet her spirit.

I was reminded again of Dev's diagnosis of borderline schizophrenia. He was talking about a spirit as if she were a real person.

"How often did you go there?"

"Once in two weeks…" he replied, still in a low tone.

"What did you talk there?"

"We just talked…" he replied, not elaborating and still looking down.

Spirit communication is always more at a level of feeling than through words as the spirit is an energy form and cannot actually speak. Our mind converts the feelings into words to decipher their meaning at the conscious level. The first words coming to the mind are accepted as in real conversation, but arguments are not possible without training the mind in psychic abilities.

'Did she say why she won't come any more?"

"No," he shrugged. "I miss her."

"You could have asked why. She may have a genuine reason."

"She said she won't come anymore," he repeated and shook his head sadly. "She was all I had. There is nobody else I can talk to."

"You do have friends."

"They are not like her… I feel lonely without her," he explained. Then suddenly his teeth clenched,

"I am going to kill those bastards," he said aggressively.

"Who?"

"Her father and her brother," he said, clenching his fists.

"Why?"

"She died because of them. They killed her," he replied angrily.

"How did they kill her? You said she died because of drugs?"

"They did nothing to stop her," he replied.

"Did they know she was on drugs?"

"I told them," he said.

"But, I think you said that they did not believe you."

"Yes… They thought I was introducing her to drugs," he replied.

"So, they did not trust you."

"They tried to keep her away from me after that," he continued, still in a rebellious tone, "I was not even invited to her funeral."

"Why was it so important for you to be at her funeral? She was not there… They may be thinking she died because you introduced her to drugs."

"How could they think that? I loved her..." he said, shaking his head, in anger. "There is something I haven't told you."

"Okay. What is it?"

"She was my wife," he said in a grave tone.

"But you are twenty-one now. So you married her when you were nineteen? That is not even a legal age to get married. Did you tell anyone?"

"Only her cousin... She did not want to tell anyone else... But now... She is not there. I thought I should tell you," he said, close to tears now.

"So, that is why it was so important for you to be at her funeral."

"Yes," he nodded, gravely

"That explains a lot...your wife died. That is why you have not entered another relationship."

"Yes... I had decided that I won't get married again," he agreed.

"Okay...?"

"She is not coming anymore. I am going to beat up her father. I know how I'll do it... I'll call him out on a pretext..." he planned.

"He must be an old man, and he has already lost his daughter... Do you think he will realize his mistake if you beat him up?"

"That doesn't matter. He should be punished. He did not take care of her..." he said angrily.

"What about her mother?"

"Her parents separated long back. Her brother also is responsible. He is going to get it now," he said, his fists clenched, as if he was preparing for battle.

"Did they know you had married her?"

"No, I wanted to join the army and then tell them," he replied.

"Then...you did not live together ever, after you got married?"

"No, she continued to live in her parent's house. She did not talk much and after drugs, she talked even less. She was always in her own world," he said, recalling those memories.

"How often did you meet?"

"Once or twice in a week... Then, she went away. She did not even tell me she was going. There, she died of AIDS," he said, a sad look in his eyes.

"When did she get AIDS?"

"I don't know. We had stopped meeting in the last few months. I did not like to see her like that. I told her to choose between drugs and me. She chose the drugs," he said ruefully.

"So, you had grown apart before she died?"

"Yeah... She died because she injected cocaine through a syringe in her wrist. She knew that was fatal. I don't know why she did it," he said in a sorrowful tone.

"Yeah. It sounds suicidal... There seems to be a life-plan. We can talk to her and ask."

"She is not coming anymore," he repeated.

"Yes... but she is there in the Light, and she can see what you are doing. Maybe, her life-plan was like that. You need to talk to her. Don't do anything in anger which is not justified."

"This is justified... her brother and father have to be punished. They did wrong," he replied angrily.

"Yes... They could have saved her but it is not necessary that they did wrong. And if they did, maybe they are punished already or they will be punished... You don't need to take the responsibility of teaching everyone their lessons. It may not be your job to punish them. The Old Man warned you not to indulge impulsively in anger."

"But here the cause is just," he replied.

"She did not ask you to help her. Unless she does, you do not have a right to interfere. It is her family... Let us talk to her now... and maybe we can talk to the Old Man, as well, and ask if this cause is justified."

"Will she come? She said she won't," he asked again, still unsure.

"There is no harm in trying. After that, we can go to the Old Man, and ask whether you need to vent your anger against those people. We can also ask if this was a part of your life-plan and why, if so."

"Okay..." he agreed.

CONVERSATION WITH A SPIRIT

I took Dev into a semi-trance state. I was planning to call her once he was deep enough. I asked him to relax by focusing on his breathing and then used muscle relaxation, then, some other techniques of deepening the trance. When I asked him to visualize light on top of his head, he again saw RED. So, I just asked him to focus on each part of his body and release negative energy with each exhaling breath. Then I took him down the stairs. I was planning to call her once he was down the stairs.

"Imagine yourself on top of a staircase with twenty steps going down. When you have that image in your mind, say yes."

"Yes," he replied.

"Now, imagine a box next to you with a lock and a key. Open the box. Collect all your worries and questions in the form of a ball in front of you. Put the ball in the box. Lock the box and throw the key as far as you can because you won't need it again. When you have thrown away the key, say YES."

"Yes," replied Dev.

"Now, as I count twenty to zero, you have to go down the staircase in your mind. With each count, you will go a thousand times as deep in your mind. As you go down, your soul comes up... Allow yourself to go to the deepest levels of your subconscious mind, where your girlfriend's spirit can come and meet you... Now, starting with your left foot...20, 19...0! You are at the bottom of the stairs. Take a deep breath exhale and say RELAX to yourself. Feel light and relaxed...Are you at the bottom of the stairs?"

"Shhh," he said suddenly, "I am talking."

He was focusing on something or someone.

"To whom?"

"To her," he replied, in trance.

"Is she there?"

"Yes," he replied, flushing with happiness.

I had been planning to call her spirit by giving a command once he was down the stairs. Apparently, she had been waiting to meet him, since she had come without a direct command.

"Okay, talk to her. When you are done, tell me. Don't send her away. We need to ask her some questions. Let her be there."

He was silent. Apparently, he was focusing on her.

After a long pause, he spoke. "Okay, she wants to go now."

"Okay just ask her to wait a few moments. What did you talk about? Tell me only if it's not personal."

He was silent indicating it was personal. I let him be for some time, and then asked.

"Ok, how is she?"

"She is happy," he nodded.

"Okay, we need to ask some questions. Is she ready to answer them?"

"Yes," he replied.

"Ok, ask her why she decided to die at such a young age?"

"That was a life-plan," he replied after a short pause, as if he was waiting for her to answer. "She had come to prevent me from joining the drug mafia."

"Ok...Is she going to come to meet you?"

"No," he replied.

"Ok, ask her why?"

"She has to rest in peace now," he replied.

"Can she meet you sometimes? Ask?"

"No," he replied. "She has to rest in peace."

"What does that mean?"

"She goes where she belongs to. She wants to be free from the connections of this life, this world," he replied.

"Okay... But since you are going through a critical period, can she stay on a bit longer?"

"She says she can't," he replied.

"Why not?"

"She says that if she stays, I will block myself from other relationships, which are coming my way. Her memories have to go for a new relationship to come in. There is a girl, the girl whom the Greek soldier had to marry. She has to come in and show me the light. She will guide me on the path through which the purpose of life can be attained," he explained.

"But the Old Man said she would come in 2-3 years?"

"She says you misunderstood. She can take her place anytime in the next two years. You can meet her anytime now," he replied.

"Okay. Before she goes, ask her what you could have done to save her from dying?"

"Nothing, she says," he replied.

"But, you tried so hard and you still feel guilty. What does she say about that? Ask her?"

"She said *Thank You,* to me," Dev replied, blushing.

"Okay, that is nice. Thank her and ask her what should you do about her father and brother? Should you take your revenge upon them?"

"*Release that anger. It was their lesson,*" he replied, on her behalf.

"What was their lesson? What did they learn from her death?"

"*They learnt that they have to care more for people whom they love. They learnt their lesson,*" he replied.

"Okay, ask her how did she know she had to die?"

"It was her purpose. She knew her time was up," he replied.

"How did she come to know?"

"The Old Man told her and she killed herself," he replied.

"What were her last thoughts when she died?"

"She died with a feeling of satisfaction," he nodded and replied.

"Okay, how does she feel after her death?"

"She is happy that she achieved her purpose. The Old Man praised her, and said she will be complimented for it," he replied, and continued. "She has to go now."

"Okay, thank her and let her go."

"Yes," he nodded. It appeared that he was close to tears...

"Has she gone?"

"Yes," he replied.

"Okay, before you wake up, we can talk to the Old Man about her death as well, so that you are clear about the plan of your life. Are you ready for that now?"

"Yes," he replied.

DEV'S NINTH LIFE BETWEEN LIFE SESSION

Thus, we went into the Life-between-Life space to talk to the Old Man, about the Life-plan involved.

"Be in the Life-between-Life space. Whom do you see?"

"The Old Man," he replied.

"Ok, ask why did you choose to have a girlfriend who died of drugs?"

"In the life of the Don, you made money by selling drugs. Thousands died of drug abuse. People lost those they loved because of the business you spread. The soul had to pay for that," replied the Old Man, in his flat-toned, gruff voice.

"Okay, ask why did she have to die? You would have been in pain even by watching her suffer?"

"She was sent to prevent you from going into the drug business again. Seeing her suffer made you realize how painful it is. Her purpose was to distract you, at that moment," explained the Old Man.

"Was her death part of a life-plan?"

"Yes," replied the Old Man.

"Why did she choose such a life-plan?"

"He had to be prevented from joining the dark forces so that he would be our champion," replied the Old Man.

"So, she volunteered?"

"It was planned by her soul. It was part of a deal we had. She sacrificed her life for the purpose," replied the Old Man.

"What kind of deal?"

"*We had a deal. Her purpose was to distract you so that you don't get distracted from your main purpose of life,*" replied the Old Man, not divulging more.

"Was she rewarded for her sacrifice?"

"*Yes, her sacrifice was noble,*" replied the Old Man.

"Where is she now?"

"*She is in the Light among us,*" replied the Old Man. "*She is in heaven.*"

"What about her father and her brother on Earth? Why did they not heed you, when you warned them?"

"*They thought that you introduced her to drugs,*" replied the Old Man.

"Is your anger with them justified?"

"*They thought what they were doing was right,*" replied the Old Man.

"Does Dev need to take her revenge from them?"

"*No, justice will be done to them,*" replied the Old Man.

"What should Dev do about that anger?"

"*Lose that anger. With that anger, you burn yourself more. You will suffer more if you keep it. Release it. You have to use your power to fight for justice,*" replied the Old Man.

"Okay, thank him. Is there anything else you want to ask?"

"No," replied Dev.

"Okay, then thank the Old Man and come back to the Hall of Doorways and out of the Hall of Doorways. We need to release your anger now."

> *Subsequently, we did sessions for anger release, where Dev released the anger he was storing against his girlfriend's father and brother. We removed the negative energy and symbols of that anger from his subconscious mind. Dev willingly removed the anger after understanding her life-plan and that he was not required to teach those souls their lessons. Once the intense,*

pent-up anger was released, it was easier for him to shift his focus to the positive.

VIEWING PAST LIVES WITH THE SPIRIT

In spite of releasing the anger and understanding his life-plan, Dev was yet not completely over his regret at losing her. He often looked sad, and was unable to move on. So, I suggested that he view his past lives with her, so that he could feel her presence once more and understand that she will be there in other lives, as she was there in his past lives. Dev saw two past lives with his girlfriend:

The first life he saw was when he was the Muslim general from Afghanistan, who had raided India. He had caused the death of several Hindus, massacred villages and destroyed Hindu religious structures. His present-life girlfriend was his mistress in that life. She had travelled with him from Afghanistan. She used to instigate him to kill Hindus. She called Hindus 'Kafirs.' She was angry with Hindus because her father had been killed by 'Kafirs.'

The second life he saw with the same girl was the Don's life. She was his chief mistress in that life who had finally got him killed, by informing the government officials of his whereabouts. In the session, she said she had done so because she was angry that he had never married her. He said that he had not married her because he had always loved another woman (the Don had always loved his first girlfriend, who was the same soul as the Greek soldier's girlfriend).

After viewing these past lives, Dev realized that his former girlfriend had encouraged him to pursue a path of crime in his previous lives. It struck him that she had done so in his present life, as well. Since she was a drug addict, while she was alive, Dev had to fight several times with guys to whom she owed money and who threatened her. After viewing these past lives, Dev also realized that he had never loved this woman as he had loved the other girl. He now looked forward to meeting her in his present life. That realization helped him move on.

THE SOUL'S PERSPECTIVE

From the perspective of Karmic Balancing, the soul of Dev's girlfriend had repaid its karma, by stopping him from joining the mafia in this life. The realization of how painful it is to see someone you love, waste away her life due to drugs, dawned upon Dev, only when he saw his own girlfriend suffering. His life-plan also incorporated Karmic Balancing. Because she was a drug-addict, Dev had to fight the drug dealers who supplied her drugs and hence did not want to join them. Also, she was angry because he had not married her in the past life. In the present life, she had married him and then died. However, she was never attached to him after marriage, probably because as a soul she had detached from him in the previous life when she got him killed. Her desire for marriage that was left incomplete was accomplished in this life, as if to finish an unfinished ritual before death.

CONCLUSION OF THE SESSION

Dev was not ready to consciously accept that bad karma could cause present-life problems. However, as long as karmic balancing was being done at the level of the soul and he could view his problems as learning lessons, he did not need to have necessarily understood all the details involved in the concept of karma. He could move on with his evolution. From the soul's perspective, every experience gives a feedback, be it negative or positive. Creating bad karma is a learning experience in understanding the needs of the soul. For example, after the life of a Don, Dev understood that the soul is not happy by amassing wealth through creating negative energy.

Dev's life purpose was to feel powerful to spread justice for the weak but he only focused on amassing power and did not understand why power was important. Hence, his life purpose could not be completed by this method of pursuit. The soul lives several experiences before it finds a method by which it can achieve its purpose of life. Then, it lives several experiences to improve that method and achieve its desired positive soul frequency. That process of trial and error is needed for soul ascension. In this process of learning, a person needs to retain unpleasant memories and the negative feelings arising due to wrong choices, only so far as they can become learning experiences. Then he needs to let go of the focus on suffering, and shift focus to feeling positive. This would transform the negative energy earlier created, into positive energy. After conversing with Anya's spirit and the Old Man and viewing his past lives with her, Dev no longer felt like a victim. He was ready to move on.

CHAPTER 23

AN EMOTIONAL HUNGER (INNER CHILD HEALING)

HEALING AN EMOTIONAL HUNGER

WE NEEDED TO DO Inner Child Healing for Dev to heal his excessive need for alcohol addiction. The technique is based on the assumption, that the person is indulging in an addictive and undesirable behaviour because he has an inner emotional hunger, and the means that he is using to satisfy that emotional hunger is not serving its purpose. Since efforts directed to satisfy the addictive craving fails to bring contentment, there is a constant conflict ensuing in the mind because of the emotional deprivation in a person. The emotional hunger usually comes from childhood when the child feels intensely deprived over something. Because of this long-standing emotional hunger, negative energy in clusters, accumulate in the mind of the individual. These negative energy clusters keep pulling the person to indulge in the undesirable behaviour at an unconscious level. For the addictive or undesirable behaviour to subside, this cluster of negative energy needs to be broken down. Until a swamp-like amalgamation of negative energy exists in the mind, positive energy cannot make an impact.

At an energy level, the strong negative current overrides the small positive currents coming in. Therefore, all new positive thoughts get crushed or overruled by the existing swamp of sadness. Once negative energy ceases to exist in a concentrated form, the pull to indulge in the addictive behaviour subsides. There is an energy shift in the mind which causes a change in belief systems automatically. When long-held desires are loosened, any new energy or thought does not get swamped by a constant feeling of deprivation. It is healing that works because positive energy can flow smoothly, in and out of that area of the mind.

> *Inner Child Healing seeks to understand where exactly this emotional craving is coming from and aims to satisfy it at that point in the person's mind. The process works on changing energy concentration in the person's mind from negative to positive, which subsequently causes the undesirable craving or behaviour to subside or disappear.*

I reminded Dev that we needed to do his Inner Child Healing, as he sat down for the next session.

"It is necessary to heal childhood traumas to get peace of mind."

"I don't have any childhood traumas," he said bluntly.

"Everybody has some... at least one or two. We all feel afraid or suppressed at some point in the childhood, or witness a painful event, which leaves us in shock."

"I don't remember any," he replied.

"Now in your conscious state you don't. If nothing comes up, in your trance state, we will leave it."

"I am not sure. I find children scary and weird," he said, with a grimace.

I noticed that he was half willing. "This is not about children. It is your own soul."

All of a sudden he looked up at me, on hearing that, now attentive.

"We try to join soul fragments so that you feel complete, as a soul. If we imagine our soul energy as one full circle, then there are parts of this circle, which get cut off at different points of time. These are soul fragments, which get detached from the whole, due to an emotional trauma experienced by the soul. The incident may not be of much significance at an external level but if the feelings involved are intense, the soul cannot let go. So, this part of the soul becomes stuck at that point in life.

For example, if you were severely scolded by your parents when you were a five-year-old or you felt acutely deprived of food, milk, toys or love, then a part of the soul could have got cut off at that point. Though the rest of you has grown up to be an adult, that part of you is still just five. It has the same mind as that of a five-year-old. It cannot see or reason, as you can. It keeps asking for those things which it could not get then. So, if at five, you wanted a particular toy, then the feeling that you were seeking through that toy remains unfulfilled.

The need to fulfil that desire keeps coming up as a craving. That part makes you indulge in actions which can satiate that feeling. So, you indulge in buying things or doing things you don't really want at an adult and logical level. However, they feel the same as the toy did for the five-year-old. That child pulls down your energies and doesn't let you be all that you can be because it refuses to let go; it does not grow up.

You need to make that part feel that it belongs to the whole again. In the session, you will make it feel loved and give it all that it desires. Once it gets what it wants at the level of feelings, even if they are imaginary, it would feel happy. The subconscious mind does not distinguish between imagination and reality, as long as the experience is intense. The imagined satiation of its desires would make the stuck, lost soul feel positive at that point in your mind. That will break the negative loop it is in. Once the inner child is ready to come out, you can ask it to integrate with you."

"Okay," replied Dev.

"So, for that I will ask you to imagine yourself in the Hall of Records of your Inner child. The Hall of Records is the same as the Hall of Doorways. Only, instead of doors, you would see files of records. For each life you have lived, you would see separate records. We need to see the life, where there is an inner child who could be increasing your urge to drink. Go to the first record which pulls you. Then, enter it. Be that child. See it sitting in a dark room, or wherever it is. Next, you go to it as an adult and console it. Be affectionate and kind."

"Okay," he agreed ruefully, his expression still uncertain.

THE PROCESS OF INNER CHILD HEALING

I took Dev into a trance state.

During Light visualization, I checked if the red colour was still there. The Old Man had said it would take two weeks for the red colour to go. The two weeks were not over yet.

"Which colour do you see on top of your head now?"

"Red," he replied.

"So, the red is still there. How does it feel now?"

"Bad," he replied, with a grimace.

"Okay, then don't take it in."

"Yes," he replied.

We continued the induction. After Light visualization, I counted him down the flight of twenty stairs, and then took him to the Hall of Records.

"…20, 19, 18…2, 1, 0… Be at the bottom of the stairs. Take a deep breath; exhale and say relax to yourself. Allow yourself to feel light and relaxed, as if your whole body is made of light. Are you there?"

"Yes," he replied.

"Now, on your right, you would see a door which opens to the Hall of Records. You want to see the records of your inner child states. Open the door and be in the Hall of Records, where all your Inner Child soul fragments are stored. Are you there?"

"Yes," he replied.

"How many records do you see? Look around you."

"Thousands," he replied.

Normally, a person has about five or six records for one lifetime. We were in the Hall of Records, which showed his records for all the life-times he had lived. I had expected the number of records to be more than usual, but not in thousands.

There was no way we could heal all those soul fragments, if we took them up one by one. Anyway, we could heal some, which were disturbing him the most.

"Okay, go to the record which activates your urge to drink. Which is the record which pulls you the most? Have you found it?"

"Yes," he replied.

"Okay, now take the file off the shelf and open it. Do you have it in your hands?"

"Yes," he replied.

"Now, look into the record and enter it. Be that child. Accept the first impressions coming to your mind. NOW," I touched him sharply, with my index finger, on his forehead. "Are you there?"

"Yes," he replied.

"What do you see?"

"There is a boy," he replied.

"How old is he?"

"About seven-eight," he replied.

"Where is he?"

"He is standing somewhere. There are old buildings around," he replied.

"How old? Is there a number coming to your mind?"

"Three-four hundred years old, maybe," he replied.

"Okay, how does he look? What is the expression on his face?"

"He is sad," Dev replied, in a compassionate tone.

"Why is he sad? Ask him."

"He is hungry," he replied.

"Why is he hungry?"

"He has not eaten for two days," he replied.

"Where are his parents?"

"His mother is sick," he replied.

"And his father?"

"His father is a drunkard... They are very poor," he said.

"Does he have any brothers or sisters?"

"Two," he replied.

"Okay... How does he plan to get food now?"

"He is thinking of stealing a loaf of bread from a baker's shop. He is looking at it," replied Dev.

This appeared to be the pirate life, where the child had stolen a loaf of bread, and run away, to later become a pirate.

"What else?"

"Nothing...he is just looking at it," he replied.

The soul fragment was stuck at this point where the child had a craving for bread.

"Okay, then you enter the scene as an adult. Take a loaf of bread in your hand and give it to the child."

"Yes," he replied.

"How does he react?"

"He's eating it," replied Dev.

"How is he feeling?"

"He's happy," Dev nodded.

"Is he looking at you?"

"Yes," he replied.

"How is he looking at you?"

"He's suspicious... but he's happy eating," replied Dev.

"Okay, when the loaf is finished, ask him if he wants some more."

"Okay," Dev replied.

"Give him another loaf and buy him anything that he wants from that baker's shop."

"Yes," he nodded.

"What is he doing now?"

"He is eating hungrily," Dev replied.

"Okay, how does he feel?"

"He is happy now," he replied.

"Is there a smile on his face as he looks at you?"

"Yes, he is smiling," replied Dev.

"Okay, then, ask him if he would come for a walk with you?"
"Yes," he replied.
"Has he agreed?"
"He is not replying," he replied.
"Okay, then give him a hug and tell him it makes you very happy to see him eating, and happy. How does he react?"
"He is looking at me in a funny way," he replied.
"Tell him that you are his older self. You are sorry that you left him hungry and starving for so long. Tell him that you'll never do it again."
"Okay," he replied.
"How does he react?"
"He's listening. He is not sure," he replied.
"Okay, tell him that now you are going to ensure that he is never hungry again. You are going to ensure that he always gets good food. How does he react?"
"He's happy," he replied.
"Now, tell him that he needs to grow up to be you, when he is ready. If he has forgiven you, let him give you a hug. What is he doing?"
"He is standing there," he replied.
"Then, go to him and ask him if there is anything else he needs. What does he say?"
"No, he is full. He wants to go for a walk with me," he replied.
"Okay. Hold his hand and take him for a walk. Enter a beautiful garden with him. Are you there?"
"Yes," he replied.
"What is he doing?"
"He's playing around," he replied.
"How does he look?"
"He is happy," replied Dev.
"Okay, then let him play for a while. Let him see that you are happy to see him play."

"Okay," replied Dev.

"When he is done playing and is resting, let me know."

"Yes," he replied, after a pause.

"Okay, then talk to him for some time… Tickle him and play with him, till he starts trusting you. How is he reacting?"

"He is laughing. He wants me to carry him," he replied.

"Okay, then carry him…He is hugging you."

"Okay," he replied, feeling a little odd, since he was carrying a child for the first time.

"Feel comfortable. Let Light fall from above on both of you… Imagine an energy shower coming from top, and cleansing both of you. Let negative energy fall off you as dirty water. Feel both of you becoming lighter, as you allow the energy of the Light to fill you up."

"Yes," he replied.

"See him integrating into you and becoming the whole of you. See him becoming the adult that you are… Both of you are in one body now. Feel his energy as he becomes one with you."

"Yes," replied Dev.

"How are you feeling?"

"Good," replied Dev, nodding his head.

"Okay, Now that you are feeling integrated, be back in the Hall of Doorways."

"Okay," he nodded.

"Are you there?"

"Yes," he replied.

Inner Child Healing is a relatively quick process. We had time to heal one more child. I intuitively felt that it is was better to try healing one more child, now.

"Okay, now that you are there, and are feeling comfortable, we can heal one more child who needs healing. Is that okay with you?"

"Okay," he nodded.

DEV'S SECOND INNER CHILD HEALING

"Good, then keep the file you have back on the shelf. Do you still have it with you in your hands, or is it gone?"

"It is gone," he replied.

"Okay, then go to the next record which is pulling you the most. Pick that up."

"Yes," he replied.

"Now, open the record, and enter it. Be that child. NOW."

"Yes," he replied.

"What do you see?"

"I am in my house," he replied.

"Which house is this? Your present life or past life?"

"This life," he replied.

"How old are you?"

"About six or seven…" he replied unsurely.

"How do you feel?"

"Sad," he replied.

"What happened? Why are you sad?"

"I am sick. I can't go and play outside," he replied.

"Sick?"

"I had fever…They say I am weak. I can't go out," he replied.

"Do you want to go out?"

"Yes," he replied.

"Who says you are weak?"

"My parents… They say I am sick and weak. They don't allow me outside," he said in a sad tone.

"So, what do you do the whole day?"

"I sit in the room. Or play with rabbits, and the mice," he replied remorsefully, "I don't like it in here."

"Why do they say you are weak?"

"Doctors had made a mistake. They gave penicillin injections. Later they found it was a wrong diagnosis," he paused, "my left arm… It is paining." He touched his upper left arm, in pain.

"Was this where the injections were given?"

"Yes… it was very painful," he replied, almost crying like a six-year-old as the memory was triggered…

"Okay, go in the left arm and see. What do you see there? What word comes to your mind, first?"

"Poison," he replied.

"Which colour is it? Which colour comes to your mind first?"

"It's a green…dirty green," he replied, revulsion showing on his face.

"Okay, imagine a vessel in your hand, and collect all the poison in that."

"Okay," he nodded.

"Have you collected it?"

"Yes," he replied.

"All of it?"

"No, there is lots of it. I cannot collect all of it," he replied.

"Okay, throw away what you collected. You can imagine yourself near an ocean and throw it in the ocean."

"Okay…" he paused and continued. "I see a cliff, and there is an ocean below it," he said in an excited tone, as if he was thrilled to see the cliff.

"Okay, have you thrown the poison in the ocean?"

"Yes," he replied.

"Okay, collect once more, and throw that."

"Okay," he replied half-heartedly.

"Have you thrown it?"

"Yes… there are lots… It's all over the place…" he flinched as his arm was paining still.

"Okay, then rise above your body, and be in the Light."

"Yes," he replied.

"Okay, ask the Light how you can get rid of this poison which is there in your body? What is the first answer coming to your mind?"

"It will go on its own," he replied.

"Okay, how much is there left?"

"There is lots…the arm is paining," he replied, again flinching at the pain.

"Okay, add some white colour in it? How does it feel?'

"It is a little better," he replied, relaxing his arm a little.

"Add some more… Keep adding until your arm feels better. The poison will go on its own."

"Yes," he replied after a pause. "It is okay; now," he nodded, moving his arm to check.

"Okay, now go to that small child, who is feeling sad that he can't go out to play. Go to him as yourself, as his older self."

"Yes," he replied.

"Now, go and make friends with the child. Shake his hand. Tell him that you have come to meet him."

"Yes," he nodded.

"Tell him that you are his older self – you are sorry that you could not meet him all along. How does he react?"

"He's is looking at me angrily," he replied.

"Tell him that you love him, and have now come to play with him. Tell him you have come to take him out to play. How does he react?"

"He is not sure," he replied.

"Tell him that you know he is healthy and strong, and that he can go out and play. The doctors had made a wrong diagnosis. You have spoken to his parents, and assured them that you can take care of him, and that he is going to be a part of you now, and they are fine with it. Ask him whether he will come out to play with you?"

"Yes, he is happy now… He is coming," he replied and nodded.

"When he is out, let him play as much as he wants to. You be there, smiling at him and join him when he wants you to. What is he doing now?"

"He is playing now. He feels strong," he nodded.

"Let him play. When he is satisfied, he will come to you."

"Yes," he replied, after a pause, "he is happy now."

"Is he looking at you with trust?"

"Yes," he replied.

"Okay, request him to forgive you and all those he is angry with. Tell him that you love him, and promise him that you will always care for him now."

"Yes," he replied.

"How does he react?"

"He is holding my hand and looking up at me," he replied.

"Then, carry him and give him a hug. How does he react?"

"He is smiling," he nodded.

"Now, imagine Light pouring over both of you like a shower of water, and imagine all the sadness washing off you both. When you feel lighter, tell me."

"Yes," he replied, after a pause.

"Now, imagine him hugging you and becoming one with you. Imagine him growing up to be you, feeling happy, loved, healthy and strong."

"Yes," he replied.

"How do you feel now?"

"Strong," he replied, and nodded.

"Okay, now that you both are one, feel integrated, healthy and strong."

"Yes," he replied.

"Now, be back in the Hall of Records. Are you there?"

"Yes," he replied.

"Is there any other record which is pulling you now?"

"No," he replied.

"Okay, be out of the Hall of records and I'll wake you up."

"Okay," he replied.

I woke Dev up from his trance.

DEV'S PERSPECTIVE

Dev touched his upper arm, as he got up.

"How does it feel now?"

"It is okay, now," he nodded.

"What had happened when you were six or seven? Were you given penicillin on a wrong diagnosis?"

"Yeah... it was long back. I did not realize it was so painful," he replied, again touching his upper arm.

"Yes... your body has stored it as poison. It will go now... I wish you had cleared it, though..."

Poison stored in his body had come up during the session. It was good that it had come up because otherwise it would have harmed his body and mind more. But, we had not been able to clear it completely. I had no idea how it would go, though I suspected that he would fall sick, get a fever or something for it to leave.

Usually, when a lot of negative energy gets cleared up from within, the person falls sick for a short period before he recovers completely. It is a process of detoxification for the body.

"It will go," he replied confidently.

CONCLUSION OF THE SESSION

The consequences of Inner Child healing in Dev's life were significant for his long-term well-being. Three days after this session, he had an attack of chicken pox. He was surprised when he had the attack because chicken pox usually occurs only once in a lifetime but, this was the second time that he experienced the attack. I suspected that this was the healing method his subconscious mind had created, to throw out all the poison from his body. Dev was a different person after he recovered from his chicken pox. When he came for the next session, the red spear-like energy shape on the top of his head was gone. He also stopped thinking that he was inherently unwell. He started feeling normal and healthy, in spite of his mother's persistent belief that he was sick and could not cope with mental pressure. He no longer believed everything she said. He started trusting his inner voice more, which helped him regain his physical and mental strength.

It was only six months after this session that he almost quit drinking due to a specific incident, which made him realize that drinking and doing dumbbells were causing an increase in his heartbeat. Once he quit drinking and dumbbells, the personality of Maximus and the heartbeat, both came under control. He could also stop his schizophrenia medication with no side-effects. He did restart drinking later but it was controlled and minimized. However, there was no craving. Subsequently, Dev felt far more balanced without painful traumas from within, thereby compelling him to take actions which did not reflect his true spirit.

CHAPTER 24

FUTURE VISIONS

INTERPRETING A RECURRING DREAM

DEV CAME FOR HIS next session after a long break. He had recently recovered from an attack of chicken pox and was generally looking rested.

"How do you feel now?"

"Better," he nodded and continued. "Something weird has been coming up," he said, sounding unsure of himself.

"What?"

"I have been getting dreams. They are recurring dreams," he said in a bewildered tone.

"About what?"

"It's like… I am in the army. I am standing on top of a mountain, and a bullet comes and hits me, and I fall," he said.

"Since when have you been having this dream?"

"About two weeks."

"And it keeps coming?"

"Yes," he nodded.

"What time of night does it come?"

"Around midnight," he replied.

"What is the message you get after the dream is over? How do you feel?"

"That if I join the army, there is a good chance that I would be killed," he said…

"So, your subconscious mind could be warning you not to go in the army?"

"Yeah…It could be. It is the damn corruption there. I won't be party to that…" he contemplated.

"But, maybe you won't be able to stop it, if you are getting killed. How old are you in the dream?"

"Young… I look young. Maybe, a year or so, since I get commissioned," he reflected.

"That young… It is doubtful that you will be able to achieve any purpose of your life if you die so young. If you join the army you may have to overlook the corruption. Otherwise, you may actually get killed."

"I am not going to do that…I am going to the army to fight for justice. I will kill all the enemies of this country," he stated.

"Your subconscious mind does not seem to agree with you. Maybe it is not as simple as you take it to be…If you die again so young, this life is wasted from the perspective of the soul… You were told you reach the salvation point at sixty. If you die so young…Even if it's not a physical death, it may be an emotional death or a death of the soul, your conscience… When you interpret the dream, it is how you feel upon waking up immediately that matters. Did you feel relief or anxiety?"

"I am not sure…" he said doubtfully. His unsure tone and an anxious look indicated that he did not feel relief. I framed the question more specifically.

"Do you feel that you can achieve your purpose of life if you go in the army, at the end of that dream?"

"No…I feel that I will die soon if I go in the army," he said.

"But, is it death after achieving your purpose of life? Do you feel a sense of relief when you get up after the dream?"

"No, I don't…" he shook his head, "but I still want to go. It's just a dream," he replied, though in an unsure tone.

"It is a recurring dream; there is definitely something your subconscious is trying to tell you. We can go to your future and look it up."

"I am not scared of dying," he stated.

"If you die without finishing your purpose of life, you are letting the dark forces win. The soul won't die anyway... but if you die an untimely death, it means that the soul is defeated."

"I won't want that to happen," he said, contemplating.

"If it is coming up, there is a good chance that it is a prediction by your subconscious mind of what is going to happen if you continue on the path on which you are now. You took this path in earlier lives and then, you virtually joined the dark forces."

"I did not... I fought for justice," he stated.

"And killed several innocent souls... The rulers you fought for were corrupt. It can happen again. In the army, you just obey. You don't question."

"The problem is that if I die without killing the enemies... there is no point then in dying. I want to die fighting for my country, not like this... somewhere unknown," he agreed.

"Yes, to check it out... we can see your future. It will be on your Time-Line, as your mind predicts it now. The Time-Line keeps records of our past, present and future. It is like a graph in the mind. The future is an extension of the present. The future is not static as the present is not static. With each choice you make, the future changes. Each of us can have several different futures, depending on each choice we make from moment to moment.

If your mind has shown you a future, it may be recorded that way.

Accept the first impressions coming to your mind. You can see what will happen, if you choose to go in the army. The Time-Line will show you that. If you don't go in the army, your Time-Line will change and that future will change."

"Okay, let's do that then," he nodded.

GOING INTO THE FUTURE THROUGH THE TIMELINE

The Time-Line is an invisible line, which goes through a person's body and mind and connects the person's past, present and future in some sort of a sequence. We had already discovered his Time-Line in an earlier session *(as given in chapter 19 – Satan's Pull)*. I explained the process by which we could test how his life in the army would be in the future, if he got selected.

"You have seen your Time-Line. Now, I will ask you to float above your body, in the clouds, on a line parallel to your Time-Line. Then, I will ask you to float on that Time-Line and stop at the point when you get selected in the army. The mind will make you stop automatically. Then, step down on the Time-Line, on Earth, at that point, and live that event. Next, we would move forward on that same Time-Line to see how your life is in the army – six months later, one year later and one and a half years later. Let's see if something like what you saw in the dream comes up. If it comes up, there are at least eighty percent chances that it will manifest. If you do see something like what you saw in the dream, we can also see the consequences of it manifesting, by moving forward on the line, further up."

"Okay," he nodded.

I took Dev into a semi-trance state and asked him to visualize his Time-Line.

"If I ask your subconscious mind to connect your past, present and future in a line, how would that line look? Accept the first impression coming to your mind."

"Yes," he nodded.

"Is it the same line which you saw earlier?"

"Yes," he nodded.

"From where does it pass? Can you show me with your hand?"

He showed me his Time-Line with his hand. It went horizontally, through the centre of his forehead. The past was behind his forehead and the future was ahead.

"Ok, thank you. Now, rise above your Time-Line. Imagine rising above higher and higher, through the ceiling of this room, higher and higher, into the clouds; keep rising till you see the time-line as a line much below you on Earth."

"Yes," he nodded. His eyeballs were rolled up underneath his closed eye-lids, indicating to me that he was in the clouds.

"Now, imagine a line parallel to your Time-Line, in the clouds."
"Yes," he nodded.
"Be on that line, and keep floating towards the future."
"Yes," he replied.
"You will stop at a point in the future, the point at which you are joining the army as a trainee officer."
"Yes," he nodded.
"Now, Step down in that event, See what you are doing. You have just been recruited, and you have joined the camp. Where is the camp?"
"It's in the mountains," he replied, enthusiasm flowing in his voice.
"What are you doing?"
"We are getting down, from the army trucks. We have just arrived," he replied, nodding his head.
"Okay. How do you feel?"
"At home," he replied still enthusiastically.
"Okay, move forward in time and see yourself a month later. Where do you live?"
"There are barracks. We live in them," he replied.
"What is your schedule? What do you do the whole day?"
"Get up early morning, then go for a drill, breakfast, then rest for a while, then, again exercise," he shrugged.
"How do you feel?"
"Okay," he replied sounding a bit bored.
"Do you notice anything which may interest you?"
"No," he replied.
"Okay, move forward six months down the line. See yourself. What are you doing now?"
"Training," he nodded.
"What happens next?"
"We are training to aim, shooting with a rifle," he replied.
"How do you feel?"
"Good… Okay," he replied, pausing in between.

"Okay, is there anything which catches your attention?"

"No," he replied.

"Okay, move forward one year in time. See yourself as a commissioned officer. Where are you?"

"In the mountains… There is snow all around," he replied.

"Okay, what happens next?"

"I am shot," he said suddenly.

"Where?"

"At the back of my head," he replied in a flat tone, the tone which used to come up when he had seen himself dying in his past lives.

"Okay, do not go ahead. Stop. Move backwards, before you die. What is happening?"

"I am standing there, guarding the post when a bullet comes from somewhere," he replied.

"Before the bullet comes in…What happened? Move backwards in time and see what could have led to that attack."

"I have been called by a senior officer to his office," he focused and replied.

"What happens there?"

"He wants me to allow something to pass through. It is illegal," he replied.

"What do you do?"

"I refuse," he replied.

"Then?"

"I come back to my post," he said, in a decisive tone.

"Then…what happens? What is the next significant event?"

"I am standing on a mountain. It is late evening. A bullet comes and hits at the back of my head. It is bleeding," he said, in the same flat tone.

"Okay, don't cross that… It has not happened yet. Move backwards in time, before the bullet hits you,"

"Yes," he said.

"Now, leave that scene, and imagine yourself in the clouds. From there, be in the Life-between-Life space. Are you there?"

"Yes," he replied.

DEV'S TENTH LIFE BETWEEN LIFE SESSION

"Be in the life-between-life space. Who do you see there?"

"The Old Man is there," he said.

"Okay, ask him whether this attack is possible?"

"*The dark forces would attempt to kill you,*" replied Dev, in the voice of the Old Man.

"Would you be able to survive the attack?"

"*There is a dim chance,*" replied the Old Man.

"What can you do to survive?"

"*Go down the mountain,*" replied the Old Man.

"What does that mean?"

"*If you reach the base of the mountain…there is a chance that you can survive,*" he replied.

"That means that an attempt has been planned. Can the attempt be averted?"

"*There will be several attempts, one after another,*" replied the Old Man.

"When is this attempt planned?"

"*One and a half years, after you join the army,*" replied the Old Man.

"Would he have finished his purpose of life by then?"

"*No, you have to survive their attacks… You have to pass the tests and reach that point where you will get salvation,*" replied the Old Man.

"What if he doesn't?"

"*The fate of the soul has not been decided yet,*" replied the Old Man.

"If he doesn't go in the army, is there a greater chance of survival?"

"*The pull from the dark forces will be less, if you choose a path of your own,*" replied the Old Man.

"So, if he chooses not to go in the army, there is a greater chance that he will be able to achieve his purpose of life?"

"*You have to heal all those souls whose purpose of life you took away… You can go in the path of Maximus or choose your own path,*" replied the Old Man.

"Okay, thank him for those answers. Is there anything else you want to ask?"

"No," replied Dev.

I woke him up from his trance.

CONCLUSION OF THE SESSION

Dev understood after seeing his virtual life in the army that he may not actually enjoy what he thought was an ideal career for him. Through this session, Dev realized that the desire to join the army was very strong within him because of several previous lives, where he had lived and died as a successful warrior. In his present life, he was going in the army because he wanted to experience the same feeling of success… He thought he wanted to save the country from her enemies, but subconsciously, he also doubted his ability to do so.

At a deep soul level, he knew that he was capable of getting carried away by dark thoughts and causing unnecessary destruction. He was aware that if he did not follow the dark forces, there was a nexus of corruption and he might get killed. Thus, his subconscious mind was foretelling his death, a few years after he joined the army. We could not ignore Dev's dream as a fantasy of his mind, because we had cross-checked it by going on his future Time-Line.

The prediction was systematically recorded in his subconscious. Symbolically, the death in the dream may not have meant an actual physical death. It may have meant a death of the principles and values he believed in. Effectively, that would have meant a death of the soul. If he sacrificed his principles, and again became what he had been in his previous lives, he would again not have been able to achieve the purpose of life, as the soul had planned. Thus, it was important for Dev to listen to his subconscious mind and make a choice, which was in harmony with the purpose, his soul wanted to achieve through this life.

The next session confirmed the Old Man's predictions further.

CHAPTER 25

UNDERSTANDING A SOUL'S LIFE-PLAN

DEV WAS BEING FOREWARNED by his subconscious not to go in the army, through recurring dreams. The reason could be that, in his inner mind he did not feel comfortable with the culture of the army. Also, his soul did not want him to join the army and repeat mistakes of his past lives. Dev could not yet believe that the profession he had desired since several years, for which he had fought his parents and which had caused so much turmoil and conflict in his mind, was not what his soul desired.

UNDERSTANDING HOW DEV'S SOUL PLANNED A LIFE

Dev was still frustrated about not going into the army. He was again blaming it on his family, especially his mother. I suggested there must be a reason why the soul did not want to join the army at that point in life.

"This seems to be a life-plan. The choice was yours. The circumstances were such that you almost got pulled into making that choice but the final decision was yours. That is how a life-plan is. Circumstances are created or planned, which lead you to make a particular choice. Then, that choice may lead you to some difficulties, but the intention is that you find the path, which the soul has planned for you."

"Could be," he shrugged heavily.

"We should find that out. We can go and ask the Old Man."

"What is the point now? The chance has gone," he shook his head ruefully.

"At least you will understand why it happened. This issue keeps coming back in your life. If you know your soul planned it, then you will understand that your mother was only a catalyst. She was not to blame. The movie was planned by you. That was her role which she played."

"I don't care about them anymore," he shrugged.

"Okay. Then, we can find out what would happen if you survive that attack in the future."

"Okay," he nodded.

"We will go on your Time-Line and go to the next significant scene after that attack, assuming that you survive the attack."

"Okay," he nodded.

"Then, if we have time, we can go to the Life-between-Life space and ask the Old Man if it was a soul plan that you are unable to join the army when you were seventeen."

"Okay," he nodded.

TIMELINE REVISITED

I again asked Dev to visualize his Time-Line and float up above it as we had done in the previous session.

"Go up in the clouds and move on a Time-Line, which is parallel to your Time-Line on Earth."

"Yes," he affirmed.

"Now, move on the Time-Line towards your future. See yourself having been selected in the army and joining. Be in your training camp."

"Yes," he replied.

"How do you feel?"

"Okay," he replied, unenthusiastically. The charm of being in the army already seemed to have vanished.

"Ok then, be back on your Time-Line in the clouds and keep floating towards the future."

"Yes," he replied, in a more relaxed tone. From his tone of voice and facial expression, it appeared that he was feeling better once out of the army training camp.

"Now, keep floating, and go past the scene when you were attacked after one and a half years of being in the army. Assume that you survived that attack. Float past that event and move to the next significant event installed on the Time Line. Your mind will stop there automatically. When you are there, say yes."

"Yes," he replied, after a pause.

"Step into that event, on Earth. Focus. What is happening? What is the first impression which comes to your mind?"

"We are running down an alley," he replied.

"Who is 'we'?"

"Me and my men," he replied.

"Who are you?"

"I am in uniform. I have two stars," he replied.

"Where are you running?"

"We are chasing some people," he replied, and continued, "there was a shootout."

"Where is this alley?"

"It's a big building. We are chasing some people. We have guns. I'm shouting at my men to move on faster," he replied.

"Who are these people you are chasing?"

"Terrorists, maybe," he replied, in an unsure tone.

"Okay, what happens next?"

"A bullet comes from behind and hits me on the back of my head," he said in a flat tone

"What happens next?"

"We are chasing those guys," he replied, in an unfocussed manner.

"Move backwards in time before the bullet hits you."

"Yes," he replied.

"Now, move forwards in time to the next significant event on your Time-Line."

"Yes," he replied.

"What do you see? What is happening?"

"It is the same. We are chasing those guys. A bullet hits me. We are going down the building...chasing those guys, " he replied.

That was strange. He was not moving forward on his Time-Line. He was stuck on the same point, as if there was nothing ahead to look at.

"Okay, rise above your body and be back on the Time-Line. Connect to the light above your head. Be In Light."

"Yes," he replied.

"Ask the Light, will you survive that attack?"

"*No,*" he replied, in a flat, final tone.

"Ask the Light when this attack could occur after how many years in the army?"

"*About 4-5 years,*" he replied, in a slow, gruff voice. Probably, his Higher Self or his spirit guide was answering his questions in the Light...

"Who are those people you saw yourself chasing?"

"The dark forces," he replied.

"By this time, have you been able to destroy any enemies of the country? Look back. What is the first impression you get?"

"No," he replied.

"Have you achieved your purpose of life?"

There was no answer.

"So, if you die after 4-5 years in the army, your purpose of life is again unaccomplished. Is that wrong? Ask the Light. What is the first word in your mind, the first impression?"

"No," he replied.

It was almost clear that Dev could not accomplish his purpose of life, even if he joined the armed forces. However, Dev was constantly living with the regret that he had missed out on the opportunity of joining the army at seventeen. To move on in life, Dev had to let go. He had to realize that there was no need to feel guilty about making a wrong choice or even blaming his mother. Though, he felt that his choice was conventionally wrong, he needed to realize that his choice had been right, given his soul's purpose of life. We had to ask the Old Man why his circumstances prevented him from joining the army at seventeen, to confirm our interpretation of his future visions…

DEV'S ELEVENTH LIFE BETWEEN LIFE SESSION: UNDERSTANDING THE WORKING OF THE LIFE-PLAN

"Okay, now, you are in the Light. From the light move to the Life-between- Life space. Who do you see there?"

"The Old Man is there," he replied.

"Okay, ask the Old Man why you could not join the NDA when you were seventeen?'

"You were not ready," was the Old man's reply.

"What does he mean by you were not ready?"

"You were mentally unstable," replied the Old Man.

"What does he mean by that?"

"You did not have good judgment," replied the Old man.

"What does that mean?"

"You would not have been able to know between right and wrong. You were too trusting of other people," he explained.

"Does that mean that you could not go in the NDA then because you were not allowed to at the soul level?"

"You would not have been able to follow the other path," replied the Old Man.

"Does the other path mean the path the soul wanted to follow?"

"Yes… You had to learn to be more positive in your approach," he clarified.

"What would have happened had you gone?"

"You would have faced a lot of stress. You could have taken it the wrong way," replied the Old Man.

"Does that mean that he could not join the NDA at seventeen because he was not ready to follow the path the soul wanted him to follow?"

"You needed to be more cheerful, more happy," repeated the Old Man.

"What should he do now so that he can follow the soul's path?"

"*You need to remove the negative energy. You need to get over that and be happier, more positive in approach,*" replied the Old Man.

"Okay, thank the Old Man for that. Is there anything else you want to ask him?"

"No," replied Dev.

"Okay, from what I understand, it seems that the final choice of not joining the NDA at that time was that of your own soul?"

There was no clear answer for that, but there was no clarification that it was not so. It is possible that this revelation was so shocking for Dev that his conscious mind was blocking the precise answers from coming through.

"And now, you need to release all that negative energy, and follow the path the soul wants you to follow, using good judgment. Is that right? Ask?"

"Yes," replied the Old Man.

"Okay, thank the Old Man and I'll wake you up."

DEV'S PERSPECTIVE

Dev was contemplative when he woke up.

"According to the Old Man, it was good you did not join at seventeen. Even if you join now, it is unlikely you would survive the attacks. You saw yourself running in the alley even after the bullet hit you. … But, you had not survived the attack. That means that you had not realized you were dead. As a spirit, you may get stuck on earth, like Maximus again for thousands of years. If you die that way, the soul may not go in the Light at all."

"Yeah…" he agreed, speculating seriously.

"We can look at a different future. You can choose not to go in the army, and then we can see how your Time Line goes."

"I can't back out now. What will my parents say? I fought with them so much because I wanted to go in the army. Now, I cannot choose not to go," he disagreed, worried about what other people would think of him.

"But, you cannot ignore what your soul wants you to do. If you do not pursue what you, soul wants you to do, the soul may decide to die. It'll be a waste of a life."

"But, I have commitments," he replied.

"The soul has too… and it has had them since several lives. Okay, you made a wrong choice. But, it was a learning process. It was needed for you to evolve as a person."

"I understand that, but others don't. What will I tell them?" he stated.

"Okay, let us, at least, change the choice and see the outcome. See how you feel in an alternate profession. Maybe you can imagine how it would be like to be in the police force and see if it helps in achieving your life purpose. You may like it once you see it happening, as much as the army."

"Yeah maybe," he half-agreed.

"If you like the profession, then only do you need to consider changing it. You don't have to choose it, otherwise. Nobody can force you. We can just make a different choice, and see how your career progresses on that. What is the harm in doing that? "

"Okay," he nodded and agreed.

We ended the session at that.

CONCLUSION OF THE SESSION

Thus, in the next session, we moved on to changing his undesirable future. We were hoping that if he made a different choice, he would not face death as seen by him on his Time-Line. He saw himself as a successful officer, though, he could not decipher which profession he was in, except that it was not the army. However, he felt a lot better in that profession than he had when he had seen himself as an army officer, at the virtual level. He realized that it was not necessary to be a soldier to be successful but at the end of the session, he still did not want to back out of the army on the basis of some future visions. He said he would wait for the army entrance results to decide.

CHAPTER 26

MOVING ON

THE NEXT TIME DEV visited me was after two months. He had gone out of town. I had not known that and had been wondering about why he had not called after his army results were declared. Other than the last choice he had to make on whether to join the army or not, Dev was almost healed now. His confusions on why he wanted to join the army so obsessively were no longer there. He no longer spoke about joining the mafia either. He also did not blame his parents for not being able to go in the army, since he realized that it was part of a life-plan. His heartbeat had not raced since quite some time, he was drinking less. He was more at peace with himself, something he had initially desired from therapy. If he could make the final choice by himself, there was no urgent reason for him to seek therapy now. So I was surprised when one day, he suddenly called, saying that he wanted to meet me about something important.

IN A DILEMMA

Dev was smiling confidently when he walked in.

"The army results have come. I have passed," he spoke with glee.

"Congratulations. You have succeeded. I told you that you would, if you focus on the feeling of success.."

"Yeah… now I only have to pass the physical exam, and I can join the army," he nodded with pride.

"Okay," I did not know whether to remind him of his soul needs or not. So there was an awkward pause, before he spoke again.

"There is something I have to tell you," he said, with a worried expression.

"Yes?"

"You have to promise me that you won't tell anyone else," he said intently.

"I won't. In any case, I don't tell anyone, anything about what you tell me, without your permission."

"Okay, It's like .... I don't know how to say it," he paused, as if he was finding it difficult to find the words.

"I don't want to go in the army," he declared, it appeared, with great courage.

"Okay, so?"

"I can't tell this to my parents," he explained.

"Hmm... what do you plan to do now? You can choose not to go?"

"I want to, but something pulls me into it... I can't say no. Being a soldier... I wanted it so badly... but not in this way. I wanted to fight for justice, but if I can't..." He mused. "I will not like it, if I can't take decisions."

"Yes... you won't. These days a soldier is not the same as what it was in your past lives, when the army ruled. Now it is practically the businessman who rules, the one who has the money. Maybe, that is why in your most recent life-plan, as the Don, the original plan was to be a big businessman."

"Yeah... but I cannot back out now," he mused.

"But, do you think it is practical? Can you obey orders blindly? Till now, I have seen you rebelling from anything that has been conventional. Can you stay without asking questions and yet like it?"

"I was thinking I'll learn all about arms and weapons, then leave the army and join the mafia. I'll make a great Don," he grinned.

"I was thinking you had stopped talking about the mafia."

"That was a joke...I know that is not what I really want. That does not give me peace," he spoke with a forlorn look in his eyes.

"But, if you are constantly asked to do what you may not agree with, then, the pull of the dark forces may again become strong. I mean, your focus will always be on the negative aspects of life, and you may again invite excessive stress. The Old Man warned you. It won't be easy. Think and make a choice."

"Yeah! That is true. I don't like that environment," he mused again.

"What is so difficult about deciding not to go? You are afraid you won't get through anything else?"

"Nah... I'll make a success in anything I do," he said confidently.

"Then...?"

"I don't know. A part of me still wants to go," he said ruefully, looking downwards, unable to decide.

"Maybe, you have past life vows and oaths, which need to be removed...We all make decisions in our lives, and some of them are made with high intensity. We make oaths and vows to ourselves. These get stored at the soul level, and once they are stored in the soul level, they get carried over life after life. These prevent you from doing what you need to do in your present life. "

He looked up to focus on what I was saying, almost as if he could connect to it, at a subconscious level.

"If you are deeply in love with someone, and you promise her/him that you would marry her and nobody else... then in another life too, the oath gets carried over because it was declared with such intensity. So, until you find the same soul in the next life, you may not be able to get married. If the same soul is not reborn with you, then you may not get married at all even if you want to. The Oath acts as a blocking program. There are such decisions taken in several aspects of life. They get imprinted on the DNA."

Now, Dev looked at me with a blank, speculative and amused expression. It appeared as if he was not getting the grip of what I was trying to put across. He looked at me as if he was not sure he understood what I was saying. So, I explained further, with other examples:

"If you have belonged to a religious cult, there may be an oath that you will never sell your service for money. It is called a healer's oath. In that case, in another life you cannot earn a normal income from a healing profession because you cannot sell your services due to the oath taken in a past life, which gets recorded on your DNA. So, to be able to make healing a full-time profession, you need to first, release oath that is blocking you. If you don't, you cannot make healing a full-time profession because you would need to earn money from elsewhere. Our core beliefs are challenged in the process of soul evolution."

"Okay," he nodded.

"There may be oaths which prevent you from pursuing any other profession. We need to be able to get over decisions that we took in past lives but are no longer relevant. There is no point in holding on to them in the context of the present life."

"Okay," he nodded.

"Before we go to release your vows, we need to check if you have any spirits of foreign energies in your body. For that, I will ask you to go to a house in the clouds. That house is your own house. It is your body. You need to go inside and check if anybody other than your own energy is there."

"I can't have any spirits. My aura is too strong," he replied.

"There is no harm in checking. It will take a minute. It is a part of the process."

"Okay," he agreed.

DEV'S TWELFTH LIFE BETWEEN LIFE SESSION

I took Dev into the hypnotic trance, allowing the soul energy to take over and gave the command that now, whatever he says in the course of the session would be from the soul level. Then I took him into a deeper state of relaxation.

"Imagine yourself rising above your body in the clouds. Feel yourself flying like a bird."

"Yes," he replied.

"Now, be in a room in the clouds. It is your own energy you are entering into.

Are you there?"

"Yes," he nodded.

"Look around you. Do you see anyone other than you there?"

"No," he replied.

"Okay...Focus on the colour in the room. Which colours do you see? What are the first colours coming to your mind?"

"White," he replied.

"Is there any other colour, any energy there which does not belong to you? Ask it to appear. Do you see any other colour now?"

"There is a little golden colour in a corner," he replied.

"Golden? Okay. How does it feel? Good or bad?"

"Good," he replied.

"Do you think it is a foreign energy? What is the first impression in your mind?"

"No," he replied.

"Then, why is it there? Who is it? Talk to the colour and ask. What is the first answer in your mind?"

"It says it is me... the part which I have forgotten," he replied.

"Okay, why is it in a corner now?"

"You have to become ME," he replied.

"What does that mean?"

"When I achieve my life purpose, I will be that colour," he replied.

"Okay... So it is you. The golden energy indicates an advanced soul. Any other energy? Any person's face coming to your mind right now, living or dead, somebody you may know or unknown?"

"No," he replied.

"Okay, then thank that colour, and start flying in the clouds again."

"Yes," he replied.

"Now, keep flying higher and higher, in the sky, and soon you will be at a tunnel, which is in the sky."

"This tunnel takes you to the Life-between-Life space. You will enter the Great Hall, which is a meeting place for all souls. You may see your soul friends and your spirit guides there, waiting to meet you. Keep flying and when you see a tunnel, say 'Yes,'"

"Yes," he said, after a pause.

"Now, as I count 5 to 0, go down the tunnel. Feel the tunnel as you go in. Feel the walls on both sides of you. Notice the colour of the walls... At 0, you will see a big door. Now, 5...4...3... Feel the tunnel as you go through it...1 and 0. Now! Are you at the door?"

"Yes," he replied.

"Now, open the door and you will be in a Great Hall. As you enter the Great Hall, you will see your friends in heaven, or your spirit guides, or your soul mates. You feel a wave of warmth and welcome wash over you as you enter the Great Hall. You feel at peace, and relaxed as you see your friends waiting to welcome you. Who do you see?"

"The Greek soldier's girlfriend. She is there," he nodded.

"Okay, how is she?"

"She is happy to see me," he nodded.

"Good...Do you see anyone else?"

"The nun is there, also General Ghazni's wife and the German soldier's girlfriend. They are all there," he said, in a relaxed tone.

They were all part of the same soul energy that was Dev's soul mate since several lives.

"Are they saying anything to you?"

"You broke your promise," he replied.

"Which promise? Who is saying that?"

"General Ghazni's wife. He had promised her that he would come back," he replied.

"Okay, is anybody else saying anything?"

"No, but they are all angry...You broke your promise," he said again.

"They are all saying that?"

"Yes," he replied.

"Okay, that is natural... You did break your promise."

"She is waiting for me to come back. After this life, we will be together, forever," he said.

"Who is saying that?"

"The Greek soldier's girlfriend," he replied.

"How do you feel being there, with your soul mate?"

"Good," he nodded.

"Okay, be with her for some time, and when you are done, tell me."

"Yes," he replied after a pause, looking happy.

"Do you see anyone else?"

"My other selves are there," he replied.

"Which other selves?"

"The General Ghazni, the Don, the German soldier, the British army officer..." he replied, focusing.

"How many are there?"

"Nine... and one is in a bottle," he replied.

"In a bottle?"

"It is not in any form. It is just red energy. It's in a blue bottle. It has been kept there," he replied.

"Why?"

"It is too strong and too impatient... It is the part which has been kept in hell," he replied.

"How do you feel about that energy?"

"Good," he replied.

"Okay, why is it in hell then?"

"It is not in hell. It has just been kept there, so that he cannot mix with other beings. In hell, the frequency around is too low. Since this soul is of a very high frequency, it cannot communicate with anyone from there," he elaborated.

"Okay...... Now, if you are ready and comfortable, we will go to the Energy Vortex."

"Okay," he replied.

RELEASING PAST-LIFE DECISIONS, VOWS AND OATHS

"Okay, Move further down the Great Hall, and you will come across an Energy Vortex. It may appear like a beam of bright light or a huge tower of revolving energy. It is like a huge vacuum-cleaner which sucks out negative energy from your aura, which you decide to release. Do you see it?"

"Yes," he replied in his flat tone.

"Okay, go and stand under it. Feel the energy of the huge generator of power touching you."

"Yes," he replied, in a matter of fact voice.

"Okay, now, let the energy scan you. There may be symbols of the vows and oaths you have taken in past lives. See objects or symbols coming out which are blocking you. All your vows and oaths, which you have taken in your lives as a soldier, will come up or you may just find negative energy leaving your body. What is being sucked out?"

"A rifle," he replied, looking a bit startled that he had oaths which looked like symbols from his war lives, in his body...

Dev often spoke of the need to carry a gun in his daily life. He felt it was a must for personal protection. It is a common thought pattern but, not a usual practice in India. In his case, it could be coming because of this rifle stuck in his aura.

"Okay say, 'If I ever took a decision that I would always carry a rifle, I now break it. I delete that decision as unnecessary now for my moving on, as a soul. I let this desire go... so that I achieve my purpose of this life in the highest and best way.' See the rifle being sucked out of your body, as if an energy beam is sucking it out, into the Light, and let it disintegrate. See energy circuits around it like wires connecting the rifle to you. Cut the wires. Let the empty space be filled with white light or see any positive symbols coming in its place. Has it gone?"

"Yes," he replied.

"Okay, now let the laser energy scan your aura once more, and see if there is any other decision. Do you see anything else?"

"There is a suicidal grenade," he replied.

"Okay, that is the reason for you wanting to get killed in war. Release that decision, as it is pulling you towards death without accomplishing your purpose of life. It is no longer needed by your soul. Say, 'I hereby CANCEL any decision I took, to carry a suicidal grenade, and release it into the white light of the universe.' See the decision being sucked out by a vacuum cleaner of energy which carries it out of our body and you are now free from it. See wires around it being cut and being sucked out of your body. See white light filling the holes left behind in your body. Feel golden. Has it gone?"

"Yes, it has gone," he replied.

"Okay, now let God's definition of moving towards your purpose of life come into your life. Feel peace."

"Yes. It has come," he replied.

"What is the colour of the energy which has come in?"

"Pink and gold," he replied.

"Good…now let the energy again scan your aura, and see if there is any other symbol which is blocking your progress as a soul?"

"An armour," he said, in a surprised tone.

"Okay, that must be from your earlier lives… as the Greek soldier Maximus… This was driving you to be a soldier. It is no longer needed in present times. Disconnect from that life. See the armour being sucked in the light. Delete the need to carry armour. Cut the wires around it, and fill the space with positive energy."

"Yes, it has gone," he replied.

"Okay, what else is there?"

"A shield," he replied.

"There are many symbols binding you to the warrior life… Release this too, in the white light. See it being sucked out, and let a peaceful light come in its place."

"Yes," he replied.

"What else is there?"

"A helmet," he replied.

"Okay, release that too... All decisions which bind you to only one profession are being released now. See it being sucked out into the white light. Cut the wires around it. Let it burst and disappear. Let a positive ball of light come in its place, maybe, like a golden crown."

"Yes," he replied.

"Okay... do you see anything else?"

"No," he replied.

"Ask the energy to scan your aura, and release any decision which blocks your energies in your present life, and prevents you from being what you are meant to be."

"There is a dagger... It is to kill my father," he said.

"Okay, from the Greek soldier's life... Release that and with it all feelings of revenge. That life is no longer there now, and you do not need the dagger anymore. It is over. Release the dagger. See it breaking up and being sucked out by a vacuum cleaner. Cut the wires around it and fill the space up with positive light."

"Yes," he replied.

"See your parents in front of you and forgive them. Do you see your parents in front of you?"

"Yes," he replied, a little reluctant about forgiving them.

"Release all this negative energy harming you like poison in your body. Allow the positive energies from the Light to come in its place. See the dagger being sucked out into the white light."

"Yes... It is gone," he replied in calm, firm tone.

"And, have you forgiven your parents?"

"Yes," he replied, almost with a sigh, but feeling freer and at peace with himself.

"Okay, let them go too."

"Yes," he replied.

"Now, ask the energy to scan your aura again, and see if there is anything else, which is blocking you from achieving your purpose in this life?"

"An Afghan dagger," he replied.

"What does that symbolize? What are the first words coming to our mind?"

"Revenge," he replied.

"Okay, that must be from the Afghan life… It again drives you to take revenge, and makes you angrier than is necessary…Release that, as it is making you do things, which you may not otherwise want to do. Say – I hereby CANCEL all decisions to take revenge, for now and all time… and let positive energies come in its place."

"Yes… it is gone," he replied.

"Good… what else is there?"

"A heart. It is bleeding, red," he replied, looking a bit confused.

"A heart? What does it symbolize? What are the first words coming to your mind?"

"Fear …Failure," he replied.

"Okay, that is the fear of Maximus…That life is over, and those conditions no longer apply. You have been succeeding in all your lives since. So that fear does not hold true anymore. Release that fear because it is preventing you from succeeding, as a soul… See it being sucked out of your body, and allow positive energies from the Light come in its place. The energy of a new wisdom will fill you up that is aligned with God's thinking. Take this positive energy in like a white paper of God's writing. You will now understand what God means by success. Feel the energies of success filling you up."

God defines success as a rise in the soul's vibrational frequency to a higher positive dimension. Success for the soul is that which leads to increased positivity; while success in human terms can lead to increased negativity if the choices made are imitative. Usually, in therapy when we ask clients to release vows and we do not know what the soul desires exactly, we ask the energy of God's definition to fill in.

"Yes, it is gone… the heart has turned blue," he replied.

"Okay… Good. Is there anything else? Ask the energy to scan

your body and see if anything else is blocking you from progressing as a soul?"

"No," he replied.

"Okay... ..Now, let Light come from above, and fill all the holes created in your body, from wherever those symbols were removed. Feel yourself filling with light and feel whole and relaxed. Look down at your body and when all the holes are filled up, tell me."

"Yes," he replied, after a short pause.

"Okay, now step out of the vortex and be in the Great Hall. Walk down the Great Hall, and you will see another tunnel, pulling you towards another life which you have lived but was not accessible to you till now because of all these symbols. You go into the life where you were all that you desire to be; in which you were achieving your life purpose. Step into the tunnel. Are you there?"

"Yes," he replied.

"Now, as I count down from 5 to 1, you will move backwards in time to another life, where you were all that you want to be. 5...3...1. Now! Step into that body, and feel yourself; realize who you truly are. How does it feel to be in this body?"

"Good," he nodded.

VIEWING ONE MORE PAST LIFE

"What are you wearing? How do you look?"

"I am bald, very fair... wearing some kind of a robe," he replied.

"Which country do you think it is?"

"Egypt...It's very old," he said.

"Where do you live? How is his life?"

"He is very rich... wealthy. It's good," he nodded.

"What do you do for a living?"

"I am a spiritual preacher... there are several people seeking my advice," he replied.

"Okay and you are very wealthy from that?"

"Yes," he replied.

"Okay, move to the next significant event in that life. What is he doing now?"

"It's the same... he is surrounded by people. He is using sign language," he said, in a bewildered tone, after some focusing.

"Sign language... Why? He does not speak?"

"He cannot talk," he replied, with an expression of relief, as understanding dawned.

"Why?"

"Something happened," he replied.

"What happened?"

"It was long back," he replied and continued, "he does not want to look into that."

"If it is relevant now, for your healing, you can move back into that scene right now."

"No," he stated in a firm voice.

"Okay... how is the feeling in his body?"

"Good," he repeated.

"Can you be more specific? Does he feel successful?"

"Yes," he replied, in a strongly affirmative tone.

"Okay, good... Now, be in that body and feel the positive feelings. Feel the success in every part of you."

"Yes," he replied.

"Now, rise above that body and carry the positive feelings with you as you rise above that body. When you are above that life, in the clouds, tell me."

"Yes," he nodded.

"Now, with those positive energies, step into your present life at a future moment in time, when you are all that you were in that life."

"Yes," he replied.

"Where are you now? What are you doing?"

"I am going into an office," he replied.

"What are you wearing?"

"A suit," he replied, a look of pride on his face.

IN SEARCH OF HAPPINESS

"How do you feel?"

"Good," he nodded.

"Why do you feel good? What have you done to feel good right then?"

"I have received a reward of appreciation," he replied.

"For what?"

"For coming up with some good schemes in finance," he replied.

"Where do you work?"

"In some international organization," he replied and paused, "looks like the WHO or the World Bank."

"And what do you work as?"

"As a finance executive," he nodded.

"And do you like what you do?"

"Yes... I am good at my job," he nodded.

"And do you feel you are achieving your life purpose?"

"Yes," he replied.

"Okay, then be with those feelings of success. Feel them in every cell of your body, and feel good as you feel them."

"Yes," he replied, affirmatively.

"Now, rise above that body and enter your present body. Feel the positive feelings filling up, in every part of you."

"Yes," he replied.

"Now all your circumstances and attitudes would be adjusted, so that you create the feeling shown to you today at the appropriate time, as planned, in your life. From now onwards, you are that person and you live with those positive feelings."

"Yes," he nodded in affirmation. Taking in the suggestion of living with those positive feelings.

"Okay, good...now, I will wake you up from 1 to 5. Feel the positivity once again, and now as I count 1, 2, 3; at 3, I request all the mental, ethereal, astral, emotional and spiritual bodies of Dev to integrate with his physical body, lying here in Delhi in October, 2006. 1, 2, 3... NOW! Feel integrated. And now, as I count 1 to 5, wake up feeling refreshed and relaxed, that you have integrated you true self back in you, and are now making only that choice which leads you towards achieving your life purpose. .. 1, 2, 3, 4, and 5. Eyes Open! Wide awake."

DEV'S PERSPECTIVE

Dev woke up from the trance, feeling a bit surprised, but relaxed.

"There were several symbols," I said.

"Yeah!" He nodded.

"You saw yourself as a spiritual teacher in that life. It must have been very different from being a warrior. How did it feel to be there?"

"Good, he was wealthy," Dev observed.

"And successful. You have taken in those energies, it will come to you."

"Yeah…it will," he nodded with confidence.

"Now, it will be easier for you to make a choice. Did you like the other profession which was shown to you?"

"Yes… That was good," he reflected.

"Okay, you can take your time to make the choice now. All the best! We do need to do more inner child healing with you, but we can do that when you are ready for it. Come back again if something worries you."

"Yes," he nodded, looking relaxed.

We ended the session at that.

CONCLUSION OF DEV'S THERAPY

After this session, Dev's inclination to join the army almost disappeared. He chose not to go to the army. Instead, he decided to join a management program. His parents were disappointed since they had reconciled with the army and repeatedly suggested that he could try for the army again next year. However, he was clear that he no longer wanted to join the army. He gave the state entrance tests for management studies. He is now pursuing a career in financial management.

Once, Dev found that his focus on revenge and failure was preventing him from pursuing the road to happiness, he reflected on his past mental anguish and said, *"Heaven and hell are both on this Earth. It is your choice, where you choose to live."*

AFTERWORD

That Dev's therapy sessions got over did not mean that he was completely free of problems for all times to come. He had successfully resolved one situation of life, which was causing him constant conflict. His burning ambition to be strong by beating and killing all those he disagreed with eventually subsided. He decided to be peaceful as he realized that his thought process was negative and a carry-over from the violent past lives. He had a habit of seeking enemies as his livelihood had come from fighting as a soldier in some lives and a criminal in others. The only life where he felt wealthy and successful was when he saw himself as a spiritual guru who was peaceful in his disposition.

Dev's thought process changed from negative to positive at a subconscious level by his own accord. On viewing his past lives, he had found that pursuing power by being negative was a futile means of gaining happiness. Thus, his need for violence abated. The spirit of the Greek soldier was sent away. Hence, he could stop his medications for schizophrenia. His journey of life continued to pose challenges but he could now deal with conflicts in a wiser way. He is definitely better prepared now to cope with the contradictions, soul conflicts and tests life brings in the course of evolution.

For any queries, you can contact the author at:
Dr SHIVASWATI (@ Dr Swati R Shiva)
RMP (A.M.)
Certified Clinical Hypnotherapist, Past Life Regression Therapist, Life between Life therapist, Master NLP Practitioner, Time Line Therapist, Spirit Release Therapist, Reiki Master, Advanced Pranik Healer, DNA2 Theta Healer, Behaviour Analyst
134, Sahyog apartments, Mayur Vihar 1, Delhi 91, INDIA
E mail – rswaati@yahoo.com

ACKNOWLEDGEMENTS

The following workshops contributed to developing and explaining the integrated healing technique used in this book.

HYPNOTHERAPY

1. An introduction to hypnotherapy conducted by Dr Yogesh Choudhary, California Hypnosis Institute, California (Endorsed and accepted by American Hypnosis association), November 3-6, 2005

2. Advanced Hypnotic Techniques and modalities conducted by Dr Sunny Satin, California Hypnosis Institute, California (Endorsed and accepted by American Hypnosis association), November 23 - 28, 2005

3. Diploma in Clinical Hypnotherapy conducted by Dr Sunny Satin, California , Hypnosis Institute, California (Endorsed and accepted by American Hypnosis association), December 23 – 31, 2005

4. Certified Practitioner of Hypnotherapy conducted by NLP-HYPNOTHERAPY CENTRE, INDIA (Approved by American Board of Hypnotherapy), February 15-17, 2008

NEURO-LINGUISTIC PROGRAMMING

5. Certified Basic Practitioner of Neuron-Linguistic Programming conducted by Dr Somesh Chadda, (The Growth Network , Delhi), February 7-15, 2006

6. Certified Master Practitioner of Neuro-Linguistic Programming conducted by Dr Somesh Chadda, (The Growth Network, Delhi), 2007

REIKI

7. Reiki Levels 1, Reiki level 2, by Sujatha Murali, Muscat, 2005, 16 hrs.

8. Master Reiki Healer A - conducted by Sujatha Murali (Sai Sumanglam Healing Centre, Muscat), 2005, 16 September 2005, 8 hrs.

9. Reiki Master Certification by Lucy Baker, Australia, Member IAART, USA, 2006, 8 hrs.

PRANIK HEALING

10. Pranik Healing Levels 1, 2, 3; Advanced Pranik Healing taught by Dr Rachna, New Delhi, March 10-15, 2006 ,

SPIRIT RELEASE

11. Talking to the Subconscious and Spirit Release conducted by Dr Sunny Satin, California Hypnosis Institute, California (Endorsed and accepted by American Hypnosis association), December 1-3, 2006
12. Advanced workshop on Attachment and Entity Release conducted by Dr Hans Tendam, TASSO INSTITUTE, Netherlands, October 23, 24, 2007
13. Workshop on removing curses, spells and black magic conducted by Dr Hans Tendam, TASSO INSTITUTE, Netherlands, November 29, 2008

PAST LIFE REGRESSION THERAPY

14. Workshop on Past Life therapy conducted by Dr Sunny Satin, California Hypnosis Institute, California (Endorsed and accepted by American Hypnosis association), 2006, August 29,30, 2006
15. Level 3 Regression Therapy conducted by Maggi Van Steveren, IAART Training, USA, March 5-7,2006,
16. Current Life Regression on Physical Traumas conducted by the TASSO INSTITUTE & THE HYPNOTHERAPY SCHOOL OF INDIA, March 2008
17. 2nd World Congress on Regression and Past Life Therapy, New Delhi, India, March 7-11, 2006

TIME LINE THERAPY

18. Workshops on releasing stuck emotions conducted by Dr Somesh Chadda, Jan.27, 2006
19. Workshop on Time Line Therapy, conducted by Dr Somesh Chadda, The Growth Network, New Delhi, April 25, 26, 2006

LIFE BETWEEN LIFE THERAPY

20. Workshop on chakra cleansing, releasing oaths and vows from past lives in the Energy Vortex, conducted by Lucy Baker, October 15-17, Australia, 2006
21. Moving into 2012- Karma cleansing regression therapy for raising consciousness; conducted by the Institute of Thought (World congress on Regression Therapy), March 11-13, New Delhi, 2006
22. Workshop on LIFE START – BIRTH AND PRENATAL TRAUMAS, conducted by Dr Hans Tendam, the Hypnotherapy School of India and the TASSO Institute, Netherlands, 2008
23. Workshop on LIFE-PLANNING AND PREPARATION, conducted by Dr Hans Tendam, the Hypnotherapy School of India and the TASSO Institute, Netherlands, March 2008
24. Workshop on CORE ISSUE TRANSFORMATION, conducted by Dr Hans Tendam, the Hypnotherapy School of India and the TASSO Institute, Netherlands, March 2008

THETA HEALING

25. Workshop on DNA 1 & 2-Theta Healing Techniques, conducted by Hitoumi Akamatsu, from Vianne Stibal's Institute 'Natures Path,' April, 2007

26. Workshop on Advanced DNA 2 Theta Healing Techniques and Processes, conducted by Hitoumi Akamatsu, from Vianne Stibal's Institute 'Natures Path,' April 2007

QUANTUM HYPNOTHERAPY

27. Workshop on Quantum Hypnotherapy conducted by Dr Ashok Jain, USA, January 18, 2007

CRANEO - SACRAL BALANCING

28. Workshop on Craneo-Sacral Balancing, level 1, conducted by Dr Sandeep Bhasin, New Delhi, February, 2007

KAYA KALPA COURSE

29. Basic Workshop on Kaya Kalp Course, December 27, 2006

BEHAVIOUR ANALYSIS

30. 16 weeks of Online course on Learning to Learn, training in Applied Behavior Analysis, conducted by Behavior Analysts, Inc. California, USA., 2005

31. 16 weeks online training on Understanding and Changing Problem Behavior conducted by Behavior Analysts, Inc. California, USA., 2005